FROM AZTEC TO HIGH TECH

Creating the North American Landscape

Gregory Conniff
Bonnie Loyd
Edward K. Muller
David Schuyler
CONSULTING EDITORS

George F. Thompson
SERIES FOUNDER AND DIRECTOR

Published in cooperation with the Center for
American Places, Santa Fe, New Mexico, and
Harrisonburg, Virginia

FROM AZTEC TO HIGH TECH

*Architecture and Landscape across
the Mexico–United States Border*

Lawrence A. Herzog

The Johns Hopkins University Press

BALTIMORE AND LONDON

© 1999 THE JOHNS HOPKINS UNIVERSITY PRESS
All rights reserved. Published 1999
Printed in the United States of America on acid-free paper

Johns Hopkins Paperbacks edition, 2001
9 8 7 6 5 4 3 2 1

The Johns Hopkins University Press
2715 North Charles Street
Baltimore, Maryland 21218-4363
www.press.jhu.edu

Library of Congress Cataloging-in-Publication Data will be found at
the end of this book.
A catalog record for this book is available from the British Library.

ISBN 0-8018-6643-X (pbk.)

All photographs and maps are by the author except as otherwise indicated.

To Vivienne and Adin

CONTENTS

PREFACE

Two decades have passed since my first visit to the Mexican-American border-lands. What I saw in those initial glimpses from the hills of El Paso across the border to Ciudad Juarez—a vivid clash of landscapes on either side of the boundary line—remains etched in my memory. It is an impression that has been reinforced in the sixteen years I've lived along the California-Mexico border. The boundary is a meeting place, and it is becoming the living space of a transnational community. But visually, it is a collision of two cultures with different ways of constructing a built environment. *Contrast* is the driving force of Mexico's relationship with the United States, and it has become the defining feature of the place—the borderlands—that perhaps best expresses the emergence of a new era in U.S.-Mexican relations.

In this age of global technology, distances between nations are growing smaller. The boundary separating Mexico from the United States can no longer divide two neighboring societies. An era of heightened cultural and economic integration is upon us. Mexico and the United States are discovering that they share a common economic and geographic life space. Several of Mexico's largest and fastest-growing cities—Tijuana, Mexicali, Ciudad Juarez—lie strategically close to the United States. A growing chorus of writers, journalists, critics, and politicians now regularly speak of the future of North America, with Mexico, Canada, and the United States joined as a single economic community. In social science circles "cultural integration" is being debated. In the popular media, critics north of the border worry about Mexico's urban ills—poverty, pollution, and drug smuggling—spilling into the United States, while critics to the south lament the inevitable cultural penetration of Mexico from the north.

During the negotiations leading to the North American Free Trade Agreement (NAFTA), I was surprised that virtually no one north of the border mentioned one seemingly obvious advantage of the NAFTA: the chance for some of Mexico's rich design and architectural traditions (both formal and vernacular) to rub off on the United States, as neighbors become more intimate trading partners. The United States and Mexico share a two-thousand-mile border and two centuries of mostly contentious history. Notwithstanding the goodwill rituals acted out among border politicians, cultural practices on either side have remained relatively separate. In the realm of architecture and landscape, the subject of this book, these differences are so notable they have frequently been sorted into clichés: the seedy border town's main street and the chaotic, half-built slums in Mexico; the glittery affluence of shopping malls and neatly manicured tract housing in the United States. Adobe walls, tar paper, and concrete block south of the border; glass and steel and wood frame, stuccoed suburbia to the north. The corner store and open-air market to the south, the mega-shopping center to the north.

But the scene is changing. The poor Mexican shantytown reappears north of the border in the form of Texas *colonias* and California urban migrant camps. U.S.-style shopping malls are bursting onto the landscape of northern Mexico. In the borderlands, our integration takes on a new form. We are headed directly into a new kind of collision—a collision of architecture and landscape. Our future is assigned an acronym—NAFTA—but what will it look like?

To speak of architecture and landscape today is to enter a world that is being second-guessed among North American proponents of technology and cyberspace. Only a short time ago, urbanists north and south of the border lamented the destruction of urban space by the automobile. Now we are being swept into cyberspace. One wonders whether space and landscape will continue to matter.

An advantage of North America's proximity to Mexico is that it might shake us out of cyberspace, and bring us back to the daily experience of urban place and space. Mexico is a nation of city builders dating back some three thousand years. There is much about Mexico's architecture and landscape that evokes a sense of grand purpose. The writer Octavio Paz has spoken of Mexico's withdrawal into the past, its eternal search for true meaning. It is Mexico's built environment, its architecture and built landscapes, that often reflects this longing for a connection to some ancient, sacred place and to its higher meaning.

If the spirit of place is lagging in America, one way to recapture it is by redirecting America's attention to the cultural diversity of its cities and regions. Here, on the Mexico-U.S. border, places like Tucson, San Antonio, El Paso, Albuquerque, Santa Fe, San Diego, and Los Angeles possess rich cultural heritages. Mexico is a primary ingredient in the built environment of each of these places. The borderlands, therefore, offer an opportunity to use landscape diversity—contrast—as a way of exciting interest in the daily experience of place.

The connection between place and Mexican identity along the border also offers an alternative to the ethnic balkanization that is occurring in U.S. cities. Enclaves of "identity groups" (African Americans, Mexican Americans, American Indians, Asian Americans, and Anglos) have staked out their turf in many cities, and even in academia. One even sees a separation between different subgroups of Latinos: recent immigrants, long-term Chicanos, different national groups (Guatemalans, Salvadorans, etc.). Yet all inhabitants of a region like the southwest United States should recognize that they share the regional landscape. Certainly all Latino people share the regional cultural heritage of indigenous, colonial, and neocolonial forces that preceded the modern period of urban development.

A decade and a half spent prowling the landscapes of the Mexico-U.S. borderlands suggests that this is not merely a frontier between two nations; it is the cutting edge of a larger phenomenon of cultural mixing and global blending that is taking place worldwide. The Mexico-U.S. border is a living experiment in the transcultural shaping of urban landscapes, a process that could spread over much of our planet in the next century.

This book is, in part, an odyssey.[1] To understand how Mexico's built environment is mixing with that of the United States, I begin by exploring some basic elements of the Mexican urban landscape. In chapter 2, the reader is taken to the interior of Mexico to review the ways in which history has shaped the Mexican built environment. The three main layers of time—indigenous, colonial, and modern—have imposed various influences on the urban landscape one finds in Mexico. Chapter 2 paints history with a broad brush stroke. It is by no means a comprehensive history, nor does it pretend to identify all the intricate details that go into Mexican design.

From the interior of Mexico, the journey shifts north. In chapter 3, I turn attention to the making of northern Mexico's built environment. I use the case of one border town in particular—Tijuana—as an example of the changes that led to the creation of the now almost folkloric genre of Mexican cities—the "border" cities. For those readers from other corners of the borderlands, the choice of the Californias may disappoint. There are certainly many subregional variations within the borderlands, from the south and west Texas boundary zones to New Mexico, Arizona, and the Californias. Yet, in my work and travel along this corridor, I find that the themes emphasized here—globalization, amid the contrast between Mexican and U.S. landscapes—tend to be consistent. I trust that the reader will find, in reviewing the history of Tijuana's changing cultural landscape, similarities when reflecting on other Mexican border towns. No single case study is ever perfect, but in Tijuana we find a border city that is closest to the largest concentration of population and wealth—southern California—and is directly influenced by the forces of NAFTA and globalization, which are beginning to permeate all Mexican border towns. The Californias offer the most intense case of a process that is transforming the larger Mexico-U.S. borderlands.

In chapter 4, the story shifts north of the border to the southwestern United States, where I review the making of architecture and landscape in this region of North America. Again, I ask the reader's indulgence as my examples draw heavily from the southern California region of the borderlands. I do not claim that the neighborhoods and *barrios* of southern California reflect *all* the unique cultural landscape attributes on the northern side of the borderlands. Yet one finds here the largest total Latino population of the U.S. borderlands, and a representative cross-section of the many forms of emerging Latino cultural expression in the built environment north of the border.

Chapters 5 and 6 embrace the subject of "cultural integration." Chapter 5 focuses on two big concerns underlying the process of integration—tourism development and the changing commercial landscape. Chapter 6 looks at the perceptions and attitudes of one group of actors directly responsible for creating the formal elements in the built landscape—professional architects on both sides of the border. It summarizes a series of interviews carried out in the United States and Mexico seeking to record the spontaneous thoughts, feelings, concerns, and goals of architects working in the two cultures that share the border built environment. Few studies consider the designers as part of what makes places significant. Along the border, the voices of architects offer a probing glimpse into the souls of two cultures that will increasingly need to better understand each other.

Contrast has been the driving force of the borderlands and will continue to be so. At its best, contrast reflects a healthy tension between north and south. There is evidence that ideas about the cultural landscape are filtering across the border in both directions. Cyberspace is crossing the border. Mexicans rightfully want their share of new technologies in the postmodern era. The danger of a rampant "placelessness" surging south across the border should not be ignored.

The journey of architecture and landscape embedded in the changing Mexico-U.S. relationship is just beginning. NAFTA is part of a process of negotiation and the setting up of rules—of trade, labor, and protection of the physical environment. It is hoped that this book will add the question of the cultural landscape to the agenda of North American integration.[2]

ACKNOWLEDGMENTS

I want to acknowledge all those who helped make this book happen. I am grateful to San Diego State University for its support of this project, especially for a 1992 research grant that provided a semester of full-time leave devoted to the initial research for this book. My good friend and intellectual colleague, Arq. Jorge Ozorno, has been instrumental in the evolution of my understanding of architecture as part of the urban landscape. Jorge has been an invaluable companion in numerous field visits and in ongoing exchanges about the meaning of Mexican urban landscapes. In Baja California, a number of people have been helpful in making documents and studies available: Arq. Antonio Padilla, from the Instituto de Investigaciones Históricas, Tijuana, is prominent on the list. I am grateful to all the architects I met and interviewed on both sides of the border: Jaime Venguer, Eugenio Velásquez, Rodolfo Argote, Luis Licéaga, Guillermo Barrenechea, Manuel Rosen, Jorge Ozorno, Rob Quigley, Mark Steele, Joseph Martinez, Ken Kellogg, and Alfredo Larín. Richard Rodriguez and Sandy Close at Pacific News Service in San Francisco are thanked for encouraging me to stretch the boundaries of my writing and thinking about the Mexican border.

A number of scholars assisted in the production of the final manuscript. They include Vivienne Bennett, Nico Calavita, M. Jana Pereau, Leslie Sklair, Raul Villa, and Anibal Yanez. I appreciate the comments of the two anonymous reviewers at the Johns Hopkins University Press. Finally, I am very grateful for the key role of George F. Thompson, fellow landscape scholar, president of the Center for American Places and my editor at Johns Hopkins University Press. George did a masterful job in seeing this project to completion. The input of other staff at the Center for American Places, in particular Carol Mishler, is also appreciated. Thanks also to Tom Farrington in the Photo Lab and members of the Cartography Lab at San Diego State University for assistance in producing the final illustrations. I shot most of the images presented in the book, but I am grateful to those who contributed photographs (their names are mentioned in captions), especially Jorge Ozorno and Raul Villa.

Though she doesn't realize it, my mother, Bernice Herzog, a painter, inspired my interest in exploring the visual text of cities. And equally, though my father,

Arthur Herzog, might hardly imagine it, his steady craftsmanship around our childhood home no doubt ignited my interest in architecture. My wife, Vivienne Bennett, has been a rock of support, as companion, editor, and audience for my impromptu lectures on the urban landscape. Finally, to my four-year-old son, Adin, you helped keep it all in perspective. And thank you for not pushing the delete button on the computer.

FROM AZTEC TO HIGH TECH

ONE

Introduction

Landscapes of the Transcultural City

Poor Mexico, so far from God, so close to the
United States.

It is the 1990s, and Mexico and the United States have begun a journey toward an era of closer ties, spurred on by the North American Free Trade Agreement (NAFTA). One can only wonder what North America will be like when these two very different cultures begin to merge.

Along the boundary where Mexico and California meet, the *Tonight Show* was playing one evening across television screens on both sides of the border. Jay Leno, reminiscing about his early stand-up comedy days, tells a guest, "One night I was bombing in Vegas; it was so bad I found myself telling jokes about . . . *architecture*." In the Mexican homes, this joke meets blank stares. The Mexicans wonder: Why would anyone poke fun at the sacred art of Aztec and Mayan ceremonial cities?

This book explores the emerging collision of Mexican and U.S. cultures through the lens of the "built environment." One of the most basic forms of cultural expression in any society can be found in the built environment—cities and their physical landscapes. The focus of this volume, in particular, is on Mexico's "urbanism"—culture expressed in the form of architecture and landscape—and how it has mixed with the urbanism of the United States at the points of cultural contact, the northern Mexican and southwestern United States borderlands, especially the California-Mexico region.

Transnational forces are dramatically altering late-twentieth-century cities. Globalization is theorized to be a change in social and economic relations,[1] but its impact on the built environment is not sufficiently understood. A basic premise of this book is that the Mexico-U.S. border region represents a laboratory where one can begin to understand how global processes (transnational manufacturing, free trade, immigration, etc.) transform urban and regional landscapes. The Mexico-U.S. border region offers to help students of architecture and landscape begin to unravel the complex nature of transcultural urbanization. Traditional border townscapes, from Prohibition-era casinos and cantinas to plazas and parks, are being eclipsed by the forces of late-twentieth-century urban development. A new cast of international actors—real estate companies, banks, investors, tourism entrepreneurs, manufacturing firms, and national governments—is prepared to reinvent the border. As we enter the era of NAFTA, a new kind of landscape must be contended with: the transcultural urban landscape.

The Crisis of Urban Space and Place in North America

A compelling feature of Mexican urbanism lies in its deep-rootedness to design traditions from the indigenous and Spanish colonial periods. Mexico's urbanism encompasses more than three thousand years of townscape building. The prospect of incorporating some of these traditions into the United States within the area of territorial overlap—the U.S.-Mexico borderlands—is intriguing. It would offer a way of counteracting the late-twentieth-century trend toward the homogenization of cultural landscapes north of the international border. This book is concerned with the way cultural landscapes from Mexico are becoming integrated with those in the United States. A discussion of this kind must begin by noting that in North America there is a crisis of urban space and place.

Gertrude Stein's oft-quoted comment about Oakland, California—"When you get there, there is no there there"—is a telling reminder of the growing loss of identity that many cities in North America have experienced in the twentieth century. Two decades ago, scholars began to lament that mass communications, big business, and powerful central authorities were transforming North America into a state of "placelessness," a "weakening of the identity of places to the point where they not only look alike, but feel alike and offer the same bland possibilities for experience."[2] Cities inherently possess a "sense of place," and in meaningful places it can elicit biological responses in the five human senses.[3] The experience of place can be a very powerful moment in a city dweller's daily experience. For example, as one writer notes,[4] walking through a unique space like Times Square in New York City can be invigorating: one smells the street vendor's food and can almost taste it, one hears the cacophony of honk-

FIG. 1.1 A distinguishing feature of Mexican urbanism continues to be the presence of Spanish Colonial design elements: the interior courtyard of a building in the historic core of Guadalajara.

ing horns, one feels the mist in the air if it has just rained, one sees the lights of the theater district coming on if it is dusk. People become emotionally attached to unique places, landscapes, and districts in cities; their emotional well-being is often connected to a specific place.[5] Place attachment can be a political tool. Interest groups in cities can use their collective memory of urban landscapes as a form of organizing.[6]

Few observers would disagree, however, that late-twentieth-century North American cities consist mainly of shattered, divided, and fragmented space. The city is becoming a mass of scattered fragments and social groups searching for a center, if not for an identity. The organization of space has shifted toward the anarchic. Spontaneous public spaces are disappearing. There are no clear centers or clear edges. Cities melt into other cities. Advanced technologies reduce urban images to simulation. The urban landscape is becoming ephemeral.

Under these conditions, unique places and districts are giving way to homogenized spaces that have little meaning for inhabitants. The contemporary metropolis is the home of city dwellers whose principal state of mind, as they move through urban space, can be likened to a form of psychological "cruise control." In this state, which has been termed *ordinary perception,* urban resi-

FIG. 1.2 High-tech icon of global corporate control over the urban landscape in the United States: the glass towers of the St. Bonaventure Hotel, downtown Los Angeles.

dents tend to move about without taking in their surroundings; they are locked in a nonspatial stream of consciousness, worrying about work or family or paying the bills. To make cities more exciting places to live, it will be necessary to jolt city dwellers out of their numbness to the experience of place, and into a different psychological state, *simultaneous perception,* where one actually notices the urban landscape.[7]

But this will not be easily accomplished. There are powerful economic incentives at work in the transformation of the North American landscape. Urban places have become increasingly commodified. Urban space is controlled by a constellation of economic and political interests—a "growth machine"—including local governments, chambers of commerce, civic associations, merchant associations, corporate boards, newspapers, developers, and architects. These interests are more concerned with maximizing profit than they are in preserving unique places and landscapes.[8] Over time, cities are beginning to reflect the accumulation of corporate control of the landscape. Global corporations may have greater incentive to homogenize consumption (of products or of urban space) than they do to promote the preservation of unique urban places. In fact, it may be in the interest of companies to promote uniform landscapes as part of a more global strategy to encourage uniform consumer behavior, the ultimate marketing weapon of the global age.[9]

The architecture profession has contributed to this process. Many architects become so involved in their own buildings, they lose touch with the question of the larger city. As a result, buildings are designed and placed in locations that are completely at odds with the surrounding environment. This may have the unintended effect of causing people to lose touch with the visual landscape. Regarding one of California's most popular works of architecture, the Hearst complex at San Simeon along the northern California shore, one architecture critic has written: "Despite his architect Julia Morgan's skill and the beautiful landscaping, we remain unconvinced. What is this Italian villa doing in the California coastal range?"[10] Glossy architectural magazines tend to reinforce this kind of thinking. The same commentator goes on to say, "It is thanks to magazine illustrations that we come to perceive buildings as isolated, self-contained objects, as if they were sculpture or automobiles."[11]

As late-twentieth-century North American cities become increasingly fragmented and dispersed, traditional landscapes and unique neighborhoods are pushed aside, replaced by simulated spaces—theme shopping districts, festival marketplaces, and high-tech zones, or, in the words of one recent book, "variations on a theme park."[12] At the same time, residents are responding to the perception that cities are more dangerous and are moving out of public spaces into the private isolation of gated communities or exclusive high-rise complexes.[13] Urban space and place are often trivialized by national and international culture. The visual city becomes an imprint of an ensemble of power relations. In the midst of corporate and high-level battles for real estate and development, the city's vibrant districts and unique places are sacrificed to the market. Place and landscape are virtually lost in the shuffle.[14]

Architecture and Landscape

We are left to wonder about the twenty-first century. Will urban space matter? Will architecture matter? Among those who believe that space matters, growing numbers of people also believe that the *quality* of space matters. What is at stake is the preservation of distinct urban landscapes. The term *landscape*, of course, speaks to a field of study that has been the domain of cultural and urban geographers, architects, historians, and urbanists during the twentieth century. It embraces the visual landscapes of cities and regions and the complex forces underlying their creation and transformation.[15] *Landscape* is an all-encompassing term that focuses on the everyday qualities of the built environment: houses, roads, stores, etc. "Ordinary landscapes" are seen as ubiquitous, inclusive expressions of everyday culture.[16]

The distinction between vernacular (popular) landscapes and formal works of architecture has been made in some circles. For example, this subject was raised in a 1975 debate over the meaning of New York City's public landscape, a polemic that eventually aired on the op-ed pages of the *New York Times*.[17] Herbert Gans, an urban sociologist, argued that New York City government, through the Landmarks Preservation Commission, was limiting the public significance of New York's historic landscape to monumental "signature" buildings. He went on to describe these buildings as "elite," noting that, in the meantime, the landmarks commission was permitting popular architecture to disappear. Ada Louise Huxtable, architecture critic for the *New York Times,* defended the landmarks commission, claiming that monumental buildings designed by great architects are essential to a city's public culture. Gans later countered by declaring that ordinary buildings should be a part of public history: "When preservation becomes a public act, supported with public funds, it must attend to everyone's past." [18]

There may be a middle ground between these two extremes. Both formal architecture and vernacular landscape share a concern with the built environment. In some ways they complement each other. Architects respond to cultural values, styles, and trends, and the demands of the environment. Their work is often an expression of the prevailing ideas and concerns of the time, filtered through individual creative processes. Architects are important to the landscape when, in the best of cases, their artistry creates an emotional response. In the words of one scholar, "The built environment, like language, has the power to define and refine sensibility. It can sharpen and enlarge consciousness. Without architecture, feelings about space must remain diffuse and fleeting." [19]

It is, of course, also true that architects work under abstract rules and personal whim, and that they tend to favor designs that will make their buildings stand out. Yet there have certainly been moments in history when the two kinds of landscapes (formal and informal) overlapped. For example, medieval cathedrals were designed by master architects but produced and adapted by local craftsmen.[20] In the Spanish colonial period, from the sixteenth to the eighteenth centuries, royal architects designed cathedrals, palaces, and town squares; but thousands of miles away, across oceans and in new lands, the builders of Latin American cities adapted the plans to local needs. The well-known maxim of the colonists was "*obedezco, pero no cumplo*" (I obey, but I do not comply). Formal architecture and popular design meet.

Certainly, in the nineteenth and twentieth centuries, the massive growth and densification in cities have tended to fuse formal and informal landscapes into a single mass. "Buildings, whether architect designed, hand-made, or mass produced, are the most obvious human artifacts in urban landscapes."[21] A recent book on Mexico City argues that its urban form consists of both formal architecture (signature buildings in the historic downtown) and vernacular landscapes (squatter housing in poor, suburban neighborhoods). The author states that "if we look at a city's architecture, we may discover both past philosophies and rationales for urban development . . . Buildings carry messages. We need to know much more about the rationality, and about the authors of those messages."[22] Architecture is an expression of culture through its messages about ideology and aesthetics; it also expresses social constructions—modernization, repression, and populism.[23] A recent book on the geography of cities calls for a blending of the traditions of urban geography, architecture, and landscape. The author explains, early in the book, where urban social science fell short in his education: "We studied housing, but not houses, retailing, but not department stores, quaternary functions, but not skyscrapers.[24] All this leads to the conclusion that architecture and vernacular landscape are not always mutually exclusive; they are part of the larger cultural landscape of modern cities. That is the approach followed in this book.

Transcultural Urban Landscapes: The Mexico-U.S. Border Region

The impending crisis of place and space in the North American landscape serves as a backdrop for the consideration of landscape and culture posed in this book. The proximity of Mexico to the United States offers the possibility that Mexico's rich traditions of urban design and landscape might be incorporated north of the border. Equally, it is possible that the trends and processes of landscape formation north of the border will diffuse south into Mexico. In an era of increasing cultural integration between Mexico and the United States, it is time to address that integration in the realm of architecture and landscape. The vast territory of the Mexico-U.S. border region offers an ideal testing ground for doing so.

The United States–Mexico border region, or *borderlands,* is a loosely defined geographic space that generally refers to an area of historic, cultural, and, more recently, economic and functional overlap across the two-thousand-mile international political boundary. While some observers tend to think of the border as only a thin layer of territory on either side of the immediate political boundary, created in 1848, today it is more appropriate to speak of the larger border region. This region is commonly accepted to include the four states on the U.S. side—

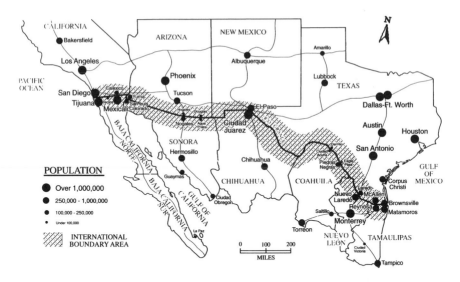

FIG. 1.3 Map of the U.S.-Mexico border region.

California, Arizona, New Mexico, and Texas—and the six Mexican states—Baja California, Sonora, Chihuahua, Coahuila, Nuevo Leon, and Tamaulipas (see Figure 1.3).

There has been a tendency to speak of the border zone, the immediate strip of land a few miles on either side of the boundary, as a unique place with a separate vernacular culture.[25] That was true for most of the twentieth century. But now, the cultural landscapes of the immediate border zone are diffusing to the larger region, so it is more appropriate today to view the border zone as a vast regional entity extending to the edges of the border states, and even beyond. The immediate border zone may still be the "nerve center of *frontera* culture,"[26] but the process of cultural exchange and the transformation of cultural landscapes are spreading to the larger region, and beyond that, to the two nations.

The four U.S. and six Mexican states that meet at the border house between 60 and 70 million inhabitants (depending upon census estimates). Ten million people of Mexican descent live north of the border. Combined with some 20 million Mexicans who live in the Mexican border states, a total of nearly 30 million Mexican people—Mexican nationals, Mexican immigrants living in the United States, and U.S. citizens of Mexican descent—populate the southwestern U.S.–Mexican borderlands.

The border itself is fading as a dividing line between U.S. and Mexican society. NAFTA will merely formalize a process that has been in progress for more than thirty years. Urban life straddles the boundary in defiance of the 1848 Treaty of Guadalupe Hidalgo, which originally created the border. An estimated quarter million workers legally commute from Mexico across the border into the United States to work each day. Tens of thousands of Americans regularly shop on the Mexican side of the border each month. Thousands of children live in Mexico but legally attend school in the United States. Many families live on both sides or do business on both sides. Whereas writers have spoken of border cities as "twins," [27] the reality is that the "twin cities" are gradually blending into single transcultural spaces, where an Iberian and Latin culture grounded in memory and tradition confronts an Anglo, postindustrial, "high-tech" culture, whose cities are increasingly defined by the freeway, the fax machine, and the suburb.

In the traditional boundary zone, there has been a lengthy history of unique place making, encompassing the period between the late nineteenth century and the post–World War II era. During this time, a set of unique *frontera* town-scapes unfolded, most notably on the Mexican side of the border, highlighted by racetracks, cantinas, casinos, traditional plazas and downtown commercial structures, railroad bridges, border gates, and regional house types.[28]

But these traditional border landscapes are facing a period of dramatic alteration as the effects of cultural integration are accelerated by transnational processes like free trade, manufacturing, communication, travel, migration, real estate, and banking. The most visible imprint of transnational integration is, of course, manifest in the realm of economic development. Perhaps the single-most dramatic transformation of the border region has occurred with the "twin plant" (*maquiladora*) program, created through the Border Industrialization Program (BIP). Begun in the mid-1960s, the BIP brought foreign (mainly U.S.) manufacturing firms' assembly plants to Mexican border cities where, by U.S.-Mexico agreement, they could take advantage of cheap Mexican labor and a relaxation of all import-export duties except for the "value added" to their assembled products shipped back into the United States.[29] Since the 1960s, the BIP has brought more than two thousand plants to the border region, employed nearly three-quarter million workers, and, in the 1990s, injected over three billion dollars a year in foreign exchange into the Mexican economy. Moreover, the multiplier effects of this industry have affected commerce, industry, and service sectors on both sides of the border. The result is that this economic boom has impacted both the built environment and the way people think about it. Studies of the transformation of border towns during the 1980s clearly identified the *maquiladora* industry as an important influence on the changing structure of cities.[30]

In a larger sense, the global economy itself has come home to roost in the border region. Border cities were once seen as sleepy towns marginal to the countries abutting the boundary; yet, by the end of the twentieth century, the region

FIG. 1.4 Megacities along the U.S.-Mexico border: the Tijuana metropolitan region as seen from the San Ysidro border crossing in southern San Diego (Aerial Fotobank, Inc.).

housed several cities with more than a million inhabitants, and it had become an important secondary region of production and exchange within the world economy.[31] It is, thus, hardly surprising to note that the global economy is transforming the border region, not only through assembly plants but also through the immense commercial development and infrastructure expansion accompanying free trade. The border region is experiencing an economic transformation and a social and political one as well: "As the long and stealthy fingers of the past reach into the immediate present, the international border dissolves and reconstitutes itself at the levels of economy, polity and culture."[32] One must then ask, What will these changes mean for the built environment?

We can speculate about high-tech, transnational industrial parks for assembling North American goods, modern shopping malls, suburban residential subdivisions, tourism complexes, high-rise office buildings, and new transport infrastructure such as airports, freeways, ports, bus stations, and mass-transit lines. No longer can Mexican border towns be viewed merely as products of an isolated, localized culture. These hybrid settlements are showing greater vulnerability to the influence of the United States.[33]

Mexican Culture and the North American Urban Landscape

Another premise of this book is that in the study of urban landscapes, *culture* (in this case, Mexican culture), matters. Cultures impose unique systems of beliefs on buildings and streets, on the use of public space, and on the larger design of the city.[34] Urban experience and urban culture are both embedded in the built environment, in streets, buildings, public spaces, and public art. One is struck by the vast differences in visual landscapes of cities across cultures. At the micro scale, one notes the contrasts in residential landscapes between national cultures. For example, it has been observed that U.S. houses often have picture windows that look out at the city and what lies beyond, while traditional Asian homes have no picture windows, and rooms look inward toward a courtyard, with only the "overarching sky" apparent. These building styles manifest different outlooks on life and home in the two cultures.[35] So powerful is the impact of culture on cities that numerous books and studies have been devoted to understanding the cultural meanings of such matters as privacy, crowding, housing and building styles, or public space.[36]

Mexican culture has slowly and steadily asserted itself in the American urban landscape, particularly in the Southwest. America has always been a society in which immigrant cultures shaped cities. Los Angeles is the latest in a long line of cities transformed by immigrants. There are so many people of Mexican descent in Los Angeles that it is commonly referred to as the "third largest Mexican city in the world."

What will a greater presence of Mexican culture in the United States mean for our cities? A good answer to this question can be found in architecture and in the urban landscape, especially in the region of the United States where Mexico's presence is strongest: the Southwest, which is, in effect, where the two

FIG. 1.5 Mexican culture asserts itself on the urban landscape north of the border: signature campanile tower in 1994 renovation project for Pershing Square, Los Angeles, designed by Mexican architect Ricardo Legorreta.

societies are functionally juxtaposed. Arguably, the most intense zone of cultural overlap lies in southern California, where the largest Latino population in the United States resides near the most rapidly growing part of northern Mexico. Here Latino and Anglo cultures mix and leave their imprint on the landscape.

The presence of Mexico—its culture and people—in the United States has steadily grown over the last three decades. Yet too much of what has been written and said about Mexico and about America's southern borders has come in the form of "Mexico bashing," whether on the question of illegal immigrants or drug smuggling or environmental pollution. Aside from the economic benefits of greater U.S. integration with Mexico, Americans forget that their southern neighbor possesses a rich cultural patrimony; if some of that has pervaded our southern borders, so much the better!

During the second half of the twentieth century, the United States steered a path away from its two-century-old Eurocentric orientation. It has increasingly become a nation whose future tilts in two directions: west, toward the Pacific Rim, and south, toward Mexico and Latin America. These changes have been fueled by demographics and by economics. By the 1990s, Latinos and Asians represented the two fastest-growing immigrant populations in the nation. At the same time, global economic trends began pushing the United States into a trade bloc with Mexico and Latin America. Mexico, with its more than 80 million inhabitants, is a crucial trade partner for the United States. Its giant immigrant population of more than 10 million is a new market within the United States.

The shift within the United States away from Eurocentrism is echoed in our nation's changing internal geography. For several decades, the socioeconomic landscape of America has gradually been restructured. The nation's center of gravity, measured in terms of population, economic activity, and political power, has steadily shifted from the Northeast toward the South and West. Stories about the rise of the "sun belt" and "southern rim" of the United States came rushing out of publishing houses in the 1970s and 1980s, as demographers, social scientists, journalists, and writers sought to chronicle the emergence of powerful new sun-belt states, California, Texas, Florida, where traditional industry was relocating, along with population and new economic activities (high tech, services, real estate, leisure industries).[37] As the bigger sun-belt states grew, their importance in the national political landscape was elevated, and arguably, each of the three largest sun-belt states, all with significant Latino populations, played an important role in the national elections throughout the 1980s and early 1990s.

Some of the optimism of the 1980s growth phase was softened in the sun belt by the decline of the Texas oil economy in the late 1980s and early 1990s, followed by the recession, which hit particularly hard in California. Yet, the larger structural shifts of geography, economy, demography, and political power within the United States are here to stay. The South and the West have become integral parts of the national trust. The future of the United States will be significantly influenced by how the nation connects with the South and West. And central to America's hemispheric future are the escalating ties with Mexico.

The above leads to the obvious conclusion that Mexican and Latino culture will increasingly occupy a more important place in American life, especially, but not exclusively, in the southwestern part of the country. Mexico historically controlled the lands of the southwestern United States, until they were lost through war and the Treaty of Guadalupe Hidalgo of 1848. For nearly a century, the memory of Mexico was erased in the fervor of Anglo-based settlement and modernization. After the Second World War, Mexico gradually reestablished a presence in the southwestern United States, and in the last three decades that presence has been accelerating. Whereas earlier in this century, Mexico was viewed by a vast majority of Americans as an exotic, very foreign nation of vague indigenous and Spanish colonial heritage, such images are fading. In the 1990s, "assembled in Mexico" is becoming as familiar a household term as "made in Hong Kong" was some thirty years ago. Mexico is a crucial U.S. trade partner. In film, art, music, and literature, among other forms of U.S. popular culture, Mexico's contributions steadily grow. From Linda Ronstadt, Frida Kahlo, and Edward James Olmos to Televisa and Mexican cinema, Mexico is a growing presence not only in America's economy but also in its culture. Architecture and landscape—the kind of things that late-night television pokes fun at—might eventually be the most potent, though underestimated, element of all in the process of Mexico–U.S. cultural integration.

"Aztec"

The Mexican Urban Landscape

The feeling of solitude, which is a nostalgic longing for the
body from which we were cast out, is a longing for a place.
—OCTAVIO PAZ

The complex mosaic that defines the Mexican urban landscape must
be unraveled from the nation's center: the heartland of indigenous settlement
and Spanish colonization in the south, on the central plateau that sits between
two great mountain chains. To understand Mexican cities and their architecture, one must begin here. More than three decades ago, Octavio Paz, one
of Mexico's greatest twentieth-century writers and a spokesman for modern
Mexican culture, voiced the essential dilemmas of a rapidly modernizing Meso-
american society. Paz's "dialectic of solitude"[1] alluded to the idea of Mexican
withdrawal, behind masks or into ritual. It conjured up images of a culture eter-
nally locked in search of its past, in a quest that began as an ancient search for
a sacred place. This search remains embedded in a pre-Columbian landscape of
monumental cities: sprawling ceremonial centers with great avenues lined with
stone palaces and truncated Aztec or Mayan pyramids.

Mexican urban design is embodied in Paz's dialectic of solitude. Mexico is
a nation of great architectural achievement, both past and present, professional
and vernacular. There are few countries in the world with a more distinguished
tradition of urban design and architecture. Here one finds some of the greatest
urban public works in the world—parks, boulevards, plazas, museums, stadi-

ums, theaters, and monuments. Yet here one also encounters some of the most severe planning problems in late-twentieth-century global cities, from housing shortages and inadequate public services, to transportation gridlock and air pollution.

Mexican cities and their design have only recently begun to attract the attention of a wider audience in North America. It was not until the 1950s that Americans even noticed that modern cities south of the border were developing original designs and landscapes independent of the United States and Europe, which in Western circles were considered the mainstream for the fields of architecture and urban design. When the Museum of Modern Art in New York City put together a major exhibit on Latin American architecture and published a book in the mid-1950s,[2] it was the first recognition north of the border of the emergence of important modern urban design and architecture ideas in Latin America. This ignited greater interest in the historic underpinnings of Latin American architecture, particularly from the indigenous period.[3]

Mexican cities, according to one observer,[4] have been shaped by four elements: destiny, design, time, and memory. Destiny is a product of individuals; design has been shaped by government regulation. Both destiny and design were modified through time and preserved by memory. In truly great cities, architecturally speaking, a balance between these elements would be achieved.[5] Mexico's most important city and national capital, Mexico City, has only achieved this balance in three moments: during the sixteenth-century late Aztec period, during the late eighteenth and early nineteenth centuries, and from 1925 to 1955.[6]

In Tenochtitlan—the Aztec city, over whose ruins the current Mexico City superstructure was built—the combination of *chinampas* (human-made islands), palatial structures, and platforms sought to create architectural harmony in the midst of a socially imbalanced society. Tenochtitlan was also an ecologically planned city: Aztec builders used causeways and *chinampas* to integrate human settlement into the lake ecology of the Mexico City basin. During the late Spanish colonial period (late eighteenth and early nineteenth centuries), the royal city builders once again aimed to build a coherent landscape through a diversity of plazas and public spaces and a hierarchy of neighborhoods at a human scale. But the colonial builders chose to dehydrate the lakes in the urban basin, which has had dire consequence for geological stability in the modern period. During the period 1925–55, Mexico City enjoyed its last phase of successful design. The metropolitan structure was still set up on a livable scale, its bus and trolley lines functioned efficiently, and it remained a walkable city. The architecture combined the well-preserved styles of the colonial era with early-twentieth-century imported techniques such as art deco or Californian colonial revival. But after the mid-1950s, the equilibrium between destiny and design was broken, and the coherence of Mexico City's design fell apart. Automobiles facilitated massive decentralization and spatial fragmentation. "We are fatally modernized," laments one architect.[7]

Mexico City

To know Mexico, one must know Mexico City. To understand Mexico's architecture, one must pass through Mexico City. Regional purists may bristle at the idea, but, in the end, the destiny of Mexico and, certainly, the hand of government regulation flow from the center, from Mexico City. Mexico is one of the most centralized nations in the hemisphere. Mexico City is the seat of national economic, political, and cultural power. Nearly a third of the country's population is concentrated in the Federal District and the surrounding urbanized region of the Valley of Mexico. Here lies the main apparatus of national government: the president, his cabinet, the congress, the headquarters of the powerful Institutional Revolutionary Party (PRI), which has controlled government for more than a half century, and a large percentage of the nation's public bureaucracy. Private wealth is also concentrated in the Mexico City region: more than half of all private investment is estimated to be located in the Federal District; more than three-quarters of the nation's banks have their headquarters in Mexico City; and almost half of all industrial production occurs in the Federal District and immediate vicinity. Estimates also suggest that some 45 percent of all high-level corporate executives and management leaders reside in Mexico City, while 90 percent of the nation's investment in research and development locates in the national capital.[8]

Urbanists call this primacy. If all roads in the Roman Empire led to Rome, in Mexico they lead to Mexico City. Not only do most of Mexico's powerful banks, manufacturers, and politicians locate here, so does much of the nation's artistic and creative energy. Imagine the United States with New York, Los Angeles, Chicago, San Francisco, Boston, and Washington, D.C., all rolled into one; that is more or less the kind of urban nation Mexico is.

Since the sixteenth century, Mexico City has dictated how other Mexican cities would be built. As Spain colonized and developed Mexico, the Spanish royal family used Mexico City as the capital of its new empire and as the center from which all other settlements received their instructions. The Laws of the Indies, written in the late sixteenth century, established rules for government and life in colonial Mexico. Detailed "Royal Ordinances for the Laying Out of New Towns" were established. The location, size, and design of colonial cities were carefully managed from the central office of the viceroy in Mexico City. This pattern of centralized control has remained embedded in Mexican culture

FIG. 2.1 Aerial view of Mexico City metropolitan area.

for six centuries. Many design and architectural trends produced in Mexico City are exported to other parts of the country. Mexico City sets the standards for the rest of the nation. Thus, any attempt to read and understand Mexico's urban landscapes must scrutinize the national capital.

As Mexico achieved greater importance in the minds of North Americans and the rest of the world in the last decade, some writers have turned their attention toward Mexico City, one of the largest and most important globalizing metropolitan regions on the planet.[9] Observers agree that this repository for great indigenous, colonial, and modern design is also plagued with management problems. Nearly 20 million people today are crowded into a giant basin surrounded by volcanic mountains some 7,500 feet above sea level. The metropolis can barely service its large population, while the ecological balance seriously erodes. Some thirty-five thousand factories and over 3 million automobiles produce 6 million tons of contaminants in the air each year. Car emissions—hydrocarbons and nitrous oxides—become toxic when they mix with sunlight, and as a result, Mexico City faces one of the worst urban smog levels in the world.[10]

But the crisis in Mexico City is not merely ecological. The pace of population growth combined with severe economic problems lasting more than a decade have converted much of the city into a planner's nightmare. The rectangular streets of the old colonial grid are no match for the thousands of vehicles that traverse them each day. *Embotellamientos* (bottlenecks) create hours of gridlock not only in the downtown commercial districts but also on the *periférico* (freeway) and other roads that ring the metropolis. Most residents, particularly those of limited economic means, are forced to travel on public buses. The subway system, begun two decades ago and still not completed, cannot accommodate the millions who need to use it. Those who can afford to, drive a car. Government attempts to regulate vehicular usage have not been successful. Millions of urban dwellers continue to crowd the city streets in cars, buses, taxis, and jitneys.

Transportation is but one of many services the government is unable to deliver adequately in the metropolis. Water, garbage collection, and health care are not readily available to large numbers of the urban poor, who occupy the shantytowns and squatter settlements of the metropolis. These people live in what bureaucrats might call "substandard housing" or what the Mexican government terms "irregular settlements." Stated simply, millions of Mexico City inhabitants, many from the poorest rural zones of Mexico, live in cardboard or scrap-metal shacks, with plastic sheets for windows and doors, dirt floors, and no running water. Even when they improve their lots with cinder-block walls, these neighborhoods still lack electrical hookups, piped water, sewage control, drainage facilities, and sanitation, not to mention adequate schools, nutrition, and health care. Such shortages have led many of the urban poor in Mexico City and other parts of the nation to create political movements such as CONAMUP, the National Coordinator for Urban Popular Movements.[11] These movements have already gained their superheroes; Superbarrio, for example, is a caped, masked leader who uses the media to portray the problems of the poor.

If all of this was not enough to interrupt Mexico City's architecture and design, the contemporary metropolis is further threatened by the condition of the land itself, upon which twenty million inhabitants and their built city are situated. The terrain is geologically unstable: it consists largely of loose sediment from the dried-up lake bed that the metropolis now occupies. Buildings are periodically subject to intense vibrations and oscillation exacerbated by an unstable subsurface that is easily agitated by even distant earthquake tremors. In 1985, an earthquake located off the Pacific coast caused such massive oscillations in the Mexico City basin that a tragic catastrophe resulted. Many buildings were destroyed in the center-city area, and roads, communications, and other facilities were shut down. Hundreds lost their lives, and thousands were displaced from homes and jobs.

Following the earthquake, Mexicans organized an impressive voluntary

FIG. 2.2 Landscapes of social protest: Urban popular movements in Mexico City use streets and other public spaces to air demands aimed at the government regarding housing conditions, neighborhood services, and wages.

cleanup and rebuilding effort. The triumphant response to this natural disaster led many to believe that Mexican cities can survive any challenge. Despite the magnitude of serious problems, Mexico City is still the nation's showcase for urban design and architecture, and most Mexicans want to live there. It is, after all, where the three moments of Mexico's architecture—pre-Columbian, colonial, and modern—overlap in a mosaic that is chaotic and majestic, perplexing and seductive. To understand this complex place is to consider how its past blends with the present.

Indigenous Memory

In Mexico, architectural memory begins in a rich heritage of pre-Columbian city builders. Beneath the dense jungles of the Yucatan peninsula or on windswept plateaus of central Mexico, the pre-Columbian landscape of Mexico has been gradually unearthed in the last centuries. In the ruins of previous ceremonial sites and settlements, from the pre-Aztec city of Teotihuacan to the Mayan ruins at Palenque, Uxmal, or Chichen Itza, archaeologists, architectural historians, and others have been able to piece together the basic elements of the indigenous built environment. From the existing evidence, we are able to make a number of suggestions about indigenous architecture and urban landscape.

One obvious feature of pre-Columbian building was its monumental scale, which one French geographer calls *giganticism*.[12] The massive pyramids and temples of Teotihuacan or Chichen Itza tower over the avenues and plazas below them. Walking among these ruins one feels small and insignificant, dwarfed by the scale and presence of these gargantuan structures. The indigenous societies that built them were theocratic; the buildings were designed to maintain existing social hierarchies, to keep the priests and their warriors in power. One interpretation of these landscapes is that the architecture was designed to instill fear and obedience in the masses. Not only were the pyramidal structures massive and tall, but their sheer walls also gave even greater illusion of heights, and this furthered the sense of power of these buildings, which we cannot forget were comparable in scale to the great pyramids of Egypt or to the massive walls of Roman cities.

Unlike twentieth-century skyscrapers, the massive scale of temples, palaces, walled courtyards, and pyramids of the Maya, the Aztecs, or the Toltecs did

FIG. 2.3 Monumentalism in the pre-Columbian ceremonial city: El Castillo (The Castle), tallest structure in the Mayan city of Chichen Itza. Note the massive proportion of the base and steep sloping staircase, both of which add to the feeling of monumentality.

not have apparent economic or technical functions but rather were mainly cere-monial. The main indigenous cities were ceremonial in nature; the more im-pressive the architecture (i.e., the buildings that stand today), the more likely it is that buildings were never inhabited, except possibly by a small elite corps of priests. The true residential centers of the pre-Columbian era lie scattered around the ceremonial cities—low-lying, low-density settlements of adobe walls and thatched roofs far outside the monumental ceremonial cities. In that sense, pre-Columbian ceremonial centers were largely artificial.[13]

In speaking about Mayan architecture, for example, one scholar has com-mented: "The paradox of Mayan interior space lies in the fact that it is always weaker than the material mass enveloping it. The buildings resemble hollow monoliths, far removed from the delicate shells and vast interior spaces pro-duced by the Romans.[14] In other words, in most Mayan ceremonial cities, based on observation of the design of palaces, temples, and other structures, there is the sense that buildings were largely not fit for regular habitation. Absent are windows, light, good air for ventilation, or fireplaces for heat. It is generally damp inside these buildings, and badly lit, particularly in the innermost rooms.

Drawing conclusions about these cities on the basis of twentieth-century Western ideas about residence and taste, however, could be terribly misleading. Our notions of what constitute adequate living space and residential amenities in the late twentieth century may be inappropriate to understanding the nature of a Mayan or Toltec city. Perhaps the point of the indigenous city was not residen-tial comfort in the present life but spiritual continuity with lives and realms yet to come. The fact that in the heyday of Mayan settlements, for example, popu-lations as high as 250,000 were dispersed around the core ceremonial cities, in modest homes made of clay with straw roofs, does not necessarily lessen the importance of these centers as examples of urban design. In fact, one could ar-gue that even in the twentieth century, in many nations, the old city centers are merely "ceremonial," while the residential spaces lie sprawled on the outskirts.

However we may judge the larger significance of the indigenous built envi-ronment, we cannot forget that some of the design techniques from this era were innovative and technically important. The uses of various design elements—plat-forms, stairs, pedestals, walls—to create architectural rhythm and a harmony of space have been noted by many pre-Columbian architectural scholars.[15] Many have also been impressed with such construction techniques as the manufacture of sun-baked adobe, the hauling, shaping, and sculpting of stone, the use of mor-tar as adhesive, terracing, mural painting, and mosaic decoration. Still others have commented on the successful accomplishments in the designs of court-yards and plazas. Scholars claim that since Mayan cities were highlighted by the absence of a street circulation system, they could be compared to twentieth-

FIG. 2.4 Balance and harmony in Mayan architecture: Platforms, terraces, and tower combine in rhythmic proportion in the celebrated palace (El Palacio) at Palenque.

century garden cities, by virtue of their pedestrian zones with landscaping and open designs.[16]

We struggle in hindsight to interpret pre-Columbian cities because, when examined through the lens of modern science and contemporary ideas about cities, logical explanations of various landscape elements do not always emerge. There are those who will romanticize the great Mayan or Toltec buildings, while others point to the cosmology of frequent violence. In the end, one cannot help but return to the great beauty and delicacy of their design. The platforms and terraced palaces and temples often follow the contour of surrounding mountains and landscape features. Staircases and observation towers are found to lie in perfect spatial symmetry. Builders utilized skillful craftsmanship to enhance shadows and the play of light, and to create surprise and contrast. Dark, hidden interior spaces contrast with open facades exposed to the hot sun. Light is diffused through windows and archways, across walls, down staircases, and around columns. The exteriors of buildings were covered with finely crafted sculptures, or stuccoed and painted with bright colors. This, too, may be a Western interpretation of this architecture.

Yet, as Octavio Paz employs the term, precolonial architecture is immersed in a *dialectic*. Each building may be a contradiction in terms. Structures reflect an uneasiness with the forces of nature at one moment; in the next instant the spaces generate a sense of harmony and a coming together of built elements in organic space. There is a deafening silence in Mayan or Toltec ruins, a sense that these structures were not built for mere everyday living, for markets, public intercourse, or home life; rather, they were built perhaps to house some journey to a higher consciousness, to some other place. Stand in the middle of the ball court of Chichen Itza. The silence is uncanny. Sounds, voices, laughter are muted by the echoes that forty-foot walls create. It is as if the spaces are too powerful, too otherworldly to permit everyday sound.

If these cities were built for spiritual reasons, to connect with a nonmaterial world, they also reflect the indigenous belief in the spiritual power and meaning to be found in the natural order. Mayan or Toltec architecture is anchored in nature. There is a smooth rhythm between building and landscape, between building and ecology. Witness the ease with which the white limestone temples and truncated pyramids of Palenque intersect with the lush green jungle-covered mountains around them, or the way pyramids at Teotihuacan blend in with the surrounding flat, arid brown landscape. Unlike, say, the Parthenon, which sits on the Acropolis of Athens, set off from the landscape, as if on a pedestal to be worshiped apart from nature, Mexico's indigenous cities were built *in* nature. Like the ancient Greeks, they used local materials, such as limestone or stucco, to further connect them to nature. The main public spaces, such as plazas, courtyards, or quadrangles, were outdoors, constantly linking inhabitants with the sun and the elements. Open space was fundamental to pre-Columbian societies, not only in Mexico but throughout South America as well. Open spaces embraced nature, light, and sunshine. The sun and the heavenly skies are always part of indigenous architecture: pyramids and palaces point toward the sky; stairs lead toward the heavens; observation decks, platforms, and observatories show how these societies built toward the skies.

But these buildings were controlled by an elite society. The design of pre-Columbian cities often segregated social classes. The cities tended to have concentric social organizations, with the elite occupying the ceremonial central core and vicinity, while the workers and the poor lived progressively farther from the city center. These conditions remind us again that great indigenous architecture emerged within a society dominated by vast social inequality.

As if to remind us of this today, the Indian in contemporary Mexico lives under the worst possible conditions: Indians are a conquered people, living on the edge of modern Mexican society, kept down, exploited, alienated, and mostly poor. They usually live well separated from the great cities their ancestors built, cities that today are managed by wealthy, Europeanized, and Westernized Mexican tourism entrepreneurs with connections to the cosmopolitan urban elite. Like many nations, Mexico is a patchwork of contradictions and irony: Mexicans celebrate their Indian heritage—in museums and art galleries, on murals, and in paintings and literature, while, just outside the museums, the real Mexican cityscape is one of Indian poverty and deprivation. A *New York Times* correspondent put it this way: "The modern Mexico that has unearthed its Indian roots and elevated Indians to a symbol of nationhood has little room for the Indians of today." [17]

This too, then, is another form of the silence of Mexican architecture: the silence of fear, of poverty, of inequality, of a past not adequately reconciled with the present or the future. Here is the loss of urban memory. Modern Mexico celebrates its great indigenous architecture, celebrates the ancient walls, the great open spaces, the color and texture of stone. But modern Mexico puts the ancestors of those builders in little dusty cardboard shantytowns, or in cinder-block workers' suburbs. Sadly, even the Indian people themselves, when given the opportunity to design their own buildings, choose to imitate the wealthy, who themselves may imitate North Americans (who often are imitating something they saw somewhere else); "caricatures of caricatures" is what Octavio Paz calls it. [18]

Colonial Memory

If the architecture of the pre-Columbian period was monumental, filled with contradiction, but supremely well crafted, so were the landscapes of the colonial period. The Spanish conquerors ruthlessly destroyed Indian artifacts and sculpture; where they could, they tried to dismantle entire settlements. In a few short years they erased important layers of the indigenous landscape of Mexico. What they didn't wipe away, they built over. Colonial Mexico City was largely constructed on top of or alongside the remains of the great Aztec capital of Tenochtitlan. Ironically, this pattern had actually characterized Meso-american Indian urban design too, where pyramids or temples from one period were superimposed over structures of an earlier era.

In colonial Mexico, churches were often built above Indian temples—another twist of fate—in which the Spanish sought to impose their Catholic beliefs upon the Indians. They chastised the Indians for their pagan beliefs but then built Christian houses of worship on the sacred spaces of the conquered Indian cultures. In the end, the transition from an indigenous to Spanish colonial–built landscape in Mexico was abrupt. The Spanish were not sentimental. Thus, they insisted on creating a European townscape, taking every opportunity to sever

FIG. 2.5 Europeanization of the Meso-american landscape: Metropolitan Cathedral, Mexico City. The master plan for Mexican cities, designed by the royal family in Spain, called for the building of massive cathedrals in the ornate Baroque style of the era.

any potential ties between European-Spanish colonial design and indigenous architecture.[19] However, the indigenous influence hardly disappeared; it has re-surfaced significantly in the twentieth century.

For Spain, like any conquering nation, architecture was a way to proclaim the territorial superiority of the ruling powers over those to be governed and sub-jugated. The town was the main tool of settlement and conquest and, therefore, the main element of this expression. The town had to serve as the administrative organ of a government thousands of miles away. It administered the acquisition of material wealth from the land (through mining or agriculture). It maintained the hierarchy of power, solidifying the Spanish king's position at the top. The town was the instrument of the Spanish monarch's power. The town proclaimed the ultimate importance of the mother country—Spain. Colonial Mexico was not to be permitted autonomy; it was subordinate to the all-important mon-archy across the Atlantic Ocean on the Iberian peninsula. The town was also the mechanism by which Mexico could subjugate its Indian population, recruit them as workers, and convert them to the Christian faith.

To fulfill all these functions and roles, the colonial town had to have a very specific kind of architecture. In 1573, King Philip of Spain had written his *Royal*

Ordinances for the Laying Out of New Towns, detailed instructions on the design of all colonial cities. Here was the blueprint for an architecture of control and subjugation. Every town was to have a gridiron design with a central square, around which would be arrayed the main buildings of the city.[20] The central plaza would be the focal point of towns, and all main roads would lead into it. The two seats of local power rested here: church and government buildings. They would be the most impressive structures in the city; their architecture was intended to win the respect and admiration of all townspeople. Just as the Spanish colonial empire was highly centralized, so were Spanish colonial towns. The king wanted the town to deliver a message: that all his subjects would yield to central authorities. In the towns these authorities were appointed by and responsible to another hierarchy of officials under the king's dominion.

The colonial towns were not without their charms. The memory of Mexico City's colonial era is flooded with romantic images: of ornate palaces and buildings made of *tezontle,* a beautiful reddish volcanic stone, of fountains and balconies, cupola-domed monasteries with Talavera tiles, winding cobblestone streets and narrow alleyways, and high-walled mansions with magenta bougainvillea cascading down over them. Most of these landscapes were created in the period 1500–1800 at the height of the spread of the Spanish colonial empire through Mexico and Central and South America. The Spanish, in turn, drew their inspiration from Greek and Roman town planning, which also emphasized the grid design and the central square.

The churches, town halls, arsenals, hospitals, customs houses, and private mansions that filled the landscapes of colonial Mexican cities were designed by royal officials sent from Spain. The building styles followed the fashions of the Iberian peninsula, which had been strongly influenced by neighboring regions: mosques and palaces of Moorish North Africa, Romanesque churches and monasteries in Italy and France, and later Gothic cathedrals in France and Germany. In southern Spain, the architecture of Sevilla, Córdoba, and Granada was clearly influenced by the Moors. One element of mosque architecture would filter to Mexico: the colorful *mudéjar* tile style. But, while southern Spain may have been influenced by the Moors, the weightless, mystical elegance of Islamic mosque architecture never really reached Mexico. The Spanish colonial architecture of Mexican cities tends to be heavy and somber.[21]

The first wave of stone monasteries built in Mexico would draw from the massive Romanesque cathedrals of France and Italy that flourished before 1200. Mexico's first monasteries, built in the sixteenth century, were really more Gothic than Romanesque, with their rib-vaulted ceilings, high windows, and buttresses. They occasionally mixed in Moorish influence. The monasteries were medieval, in the sense that they were self-contained living spaces, with kitchens,

FIG. 2.6 The courtyard, whose origins can be traced to Islamic influence in Spain, was a common element in the colonial Mexican built environment.

workshops, libraries, and apartments. This may have served the purpose of providing a fortress in a hostile new environment, but one can imagine that the Spanish king had no intention of creating autonomous communities apart from the influence of his town halls. By the end of the sixteenth century, the cathedral became less of a monastery and more a single building attached to the larger urban fabric.

This was a time in which Baroque architecture began to triumph. Baroque was sumptuous and decorative, a way in which the urban landscape could again celebrate the European over the American, and at the same time reject the smooth, rectangular lines of pre-Colombian builders. Baroque architecture had had a particularly strong run in Spain. The talented metal craftsmen discovered that they could use their talents for ornamenting and sculpting the exteriors of churches. The most well known was José de Churriguera, born in Madrid in 1665. His work became known as "Churrigueresque"; and the sumptuous portals of churches, hospitals, and palaces with their twisted columns and other decorations influenced generations of builders. In Mexico, skilled workers employed the Churrigueresque and Plateresque (from the *platero* or silver work craftsmen) design techniques, particularly for secular buildings—the so-called

Plateresque palaces—like the National Palace on the main square in Mexico City or Cortes's Palace in Cuernavaca, outside of Mexico City.

Baroque also was quickly incorporated into the design of some of Mexico's great cathedrals built in the seventeenth century, including the cathedral of Morelia, considered Mexico's finest example of pure Plateresque, and the Cathedral of Mexico City, a mixture of Baroque and classic (Gothic and Romanesque), completed in 1667 but rebuilt and finished in 1797. Baroque was the ideal architecture for colonial Mexico because it spoke of the triumph of the aristocracy, which could express joy over increasing wealth through the everyday urban landscape. It also emphasized the power of the state (government) and of the church. In the realm of private elite life, Mexico City, from 1600 to 1750, was the capital of secular Baroque architecture, a city of sumptuous public buildings, government palaces, state museums, and viceregal mansions. Many of these elegant stone structures with ornate facades were made of two local materials: the reddish volcanic stone *tezontle* or a grayish-white limestone called *chiluca*. Writers of the period referred to Mexico City as the "City of Palaces."

While the elite were erecting monuments to their wealth and power in the cities of colonial Mexico, the working citizens and indigenous cultures lived

FIG. 2.7 Lavishly decorated facades typified the Baroque architecture of the Spanish colonial city in Mexico: Metropolitan Tabernacle, Mexico City.

FIG. 2.8 The nineteenth-century neoclassical landscape: National Palace, Mexico City.

amidst a simple landscape. On the outskirts of the cities, in small villages, the principal native Indian building was the home, a simple, rectangular structure, of mud or adobe walls, thatched roofs for the poor, Spanish tile for the more urbanized. The villages re-created the designs of the larger cities, with central plazas, church to one side, fountain in the middle. Often the plaza served as a marketplace. The working and professional classes lived in rectangular brick or stone or adobe houses with interior patios, balconies, and wrought-iron railings over upper-story windows, and pitched or flat roofs (depending on the climate) with Spanish tiles.

Townscapes changed little during the first half of the nineteenth century in Mexico. The first moment of transition arrived during the French occupation of Mexico in the 1860s. The emperor Maximilian brought a new set of urban design ideas to Mexico. Drawing from the midcentury Parisian redevelopment plan of Baron Haussmann, Maximilian administered the building of a broad new diagonal avenue—Paseo de la Reforma. This elegant boulevard, said to be inspired by Paris's Champs Élysées, ran four kilometers, from the downtown National Palace to the lush Chapultepec park where the Austrian ruler lived in the Chapultepec Castle. Along the Reforma, double rows of eucalyptus trees were planted, gas lamps installed, and the first mule-drawn streetcars introduced.[22] This development was the catalyst for a new phase of growth from downtown Mexico City to the west, a direction that would define the city's structure for the next half century.[23] Maximilian also permanently altered the landscape of Mexico City and other Mexican cities by ordering trees and flowers to be planted in all public squares.

By the 1880s, the elite were moving to new wealthy neighborhoods along the Paseo de la Reforma. A vast array of modern infrastructure soon began to appear: tramways, paved streets, and European-style traffic circles. It was the age of Europe, and Mexico copied everything European, including art and architecture. Mexico City went from being the city of palaces to the city of marble statues and marble mansions. For the affluent, there were mid-Victorian houses or Second Empire homes with gilded chandeliers, plush furniture, and marble fireplaces. Meanwhile the downtown center was being abandoned by the elite and began converting itself into a commercial and financial district. The poor were being pushed into overcrowded tenements on the edges of the business district, or to the newly forming *colonias* (shantytowns) on the periphery in the south and east.

Architecture and Urban Landscape in the Twentieth Century

It is not without irony that as the twentieth century began, in Mexico's national capital and most important urban place—Mexico City—the nation inaugurated the largest urban infrastructure project in its history: the $16 million drainage of the Mexico City basin. The project, engineered by a British firm, consisted of thirty miles of canals and six miles of tunnels, aimed at removing the excess waters that annually flooded the metropolis that President Porfirio Díaz wanted to convert into the showcase of his national program for modernization. Flooding was endemic to Mexico City's ecoscape, and following the destruction of Tenochtitlan, the former Aztec imperial city, in the early 1600s, Spanish colonial engineers constructed a massive drainage tunnel and canal system. Now the arrival of the twentieth century ushered in a grand new water infrastructure scheme, only this one would portend problems to face the metropolis later in the century: By draining the basin, ostensibly for modernization and expansion, Mexico City would unwittingly sow the seeds for its evolution as the most geologically unstable land base underneath what would become one of the world's largest late-twentieth-century metropolises.

But a modern, sophisticated Mexico City was the goal of President Díaz, who was determined to transform the landscape of the nation's capital into one reminiscent of Paris or London, two cities (and cultures) greatly admired by the early-twentieth-century Mexican bourgeoisie. Díaz's Mexico City would be the symbolic and functional nucleus of a nation of "order and progress." Díaz ruled Mexico dictatorially from 1876 to 1911. During his reign, Mexico's economy

FIG. 2.9 A pompous, overstuffed European architecture highlighted the building of Mexican cities during the era of Porfirio Díaz: Palacio de Bellas Artes (Palace of Fine Arts), Mexico City.

began to boom: foreign investment was encouraged, 12,000 miles of railroad lines were built, new ports were developed, agriculture and mining expanded, while new industries were set up. The country plunged into an industrial revolution, created a profitable agricultural export economy, and achieved stable credit ratings internationally.[24]

In Mexico City, Díaz crafted a micro-space in which to foster his dream of a developed Mexico. The truth was that only a small minority of Mexicans—landowners, bankers, industrialists, and those close to Díaz—enjoyed prosperity, while the larger population of rural peasants or urban workers lived an impoverished existence. But for the privileged classes, Mexico City at the turn of the century was a landscape of opulence: French-style mansions, Baroque opera houses and theaters, multistoried office buildings built of reinforced concrete and iron, tree-lined boulevards with statues, electric streetlights, and tram cars. Even Mexico City's former reputation as a crime-ridden city had been calmed by the president's modernized police force.

It was also the age of science and technology: electricity, railroads, and high-rise buildings. European positivism, the belief in a scientific and secular spirit, was popular among the upper classes of Mexico City during the *Porfiriato*. President Díaz's followers called themselves *científicos* (scientists), believing that the economic pie had to be enlarged through massive development before it could be sliced up for the poor.[25]

The architecture of Mexico City at the turn of the century was sumptuous. With the new revenues being generated, there was money to hire top architects to build palatial residences or stylish public monuments and buildings. Most of this turn-of-the-century architecture was not dominated by the memory of colonial Spain or indigenous Mexico, but of modernizing Europe. Spain was seen as a country in decline; England, France, and Germany were admired, and this was translated onto the landscape of the city. With its statues, broad sidewalks, and elegant landscaping, President Díaz converted the Paseo de la Reforma into a Latin version of a Parisian boulevard. Meanwhile elegant French designs showed up in mansions with garrets and steep, sloping mansard roofs. Art noveau designs began to creep into the housing styles of elite families living in neighborhoods off the Reforma. President Díaz had enacted a decree in 1877 that called for the placement of a series of political statues of Mexican heroes along the Paseo de la Reforma. Classical designs were used to build structures such as the Independence monument, the monument to Juárez, and the Columbus Statue.[26] Díaz's conviction about the importance of public monuments in the urban landscape started a tradition that has become permanent in Mexico: public monuments in the twentieth-century landscape.[27]

Most striking were the neoromantic and neo-Gothic designs incorporated into monumental public buildings of the early twentieth century. Two of the best examples were the Central Post Office and the Palacio de Bellas Artes (Palace of Fine Arts), designed by Italian architect Adamo Boari. Cast-iron technology from Europe and the United States allowed for new building designs. Italian marble, European granite, bronzes, and stained glass could now be imported. The Palace of Fine Arts, as impressive a piece of neoclassical architecture as you can find in Mexico City, epitomized the dilemma of Mexico City's landscape at the turn of the century. Unquestionably, the Palace of Fine Arts was a beautiful building. But it was also a symbol of the pompously European atmosphere that gripped the city, and there were those who thought Mexico had had enough of this "overstuffed Europeanism," and that it was time to move forward with an architecture that was more Mexican. The Palace of Fine Arts would be seen by some as "an architectural miscarriage of an ambitious and arrogant dictator."[28]

It can thus be commented that the Mexican Revolution which brought dramatic social change and political transformation to the nation was also a revolution in urban landscape, and in architecture. By the 1920s, as the dust cleared from the revolutionary period of 1910–20, the new builders and those behind art and architectural movements were prepared to deliver a new landscape, liberated

FIG. 2.10 Revolutionary landscapes and muralism: scenes from ancient Mexico in mural by Diego Rivera, National Palace, Mexico City.

from the confines of the European academy that had so dominated Mexico City and other Mexican cities at the turn of the century. The first transformation was brought on by the appointment of José Vasconcelos as secretary of education under President Obregon. Vasconcelos supported a campaign to create political murals on the walls of Mexico City's public buildings. Three of Mexico's great artists of the period joined in the movement—Diego Rivera, David Siquieros, and José Clemente Orozco. The muralists didn't merely paint innocent murals on buildings. Their public art was evocative and powerful social commentary; it appealed to the new revolutionary consciousness of Mexico's workers and re-vealed the artists' sympathies with emerging socialist politics of the 1920s and 1930s.[29] The muralists placed the ideals and realities of Mexico and its revolu-tion on the walls of the city for all to see.

This was also a period during which the government subsidized the design of public monuments—such as the monuments to Cuauhtemoc and to Indepen-dence—to expand nationalistic feeling and give the government another anchor of control over the urban landscape. The evolution of the Mexican cityscape of this period has been compared to Soviet monument building in large cities of the 1920s, where public art was seen by the state as a way of enhancing its ob-jectives of building nationalist sentiment and revolutionary fervor.[30] It was quite a transformation from the 1890s and early 1900s when the buildings spoke only of European aristocracy.

In the meantime, there was also a dramatic revolution of building structure and building style beginning around 1930. Mexican architects were strongly influenced by the Swiss-French architect Le Corbusier, who is considered one of the patriarchs of modern architecture. Le Corbusier espoused an architecture of pure form and simple, clean geometries using primary shapes: spheres, cubes, rectangles, cylinders. He believed simple lines and rectangular designs could lead toward cities designed to meet the social demands of rapid urbanization and industrialization. He envisioned decentralized cities with radial bands of specialized commercial, industrial, and residential use and laid out his idea of sprawling, large-scale, "machine age" cities in his well-known book *La Ville Radieuse* (The Radiant City).

Le Corbusier's ideas appealed to the builders of a rapidly expanding Mexico City, as well as other cities. Architecture needed to be redirected toward the social needs of Mexican society, it was thought. Hospitals, schools, office buildings, and public housing projects were needed to accommodate Mexico's work-

FIG. 2.11 Building Le Corbusier's "machine age" city in Mexico: functionalist, high-rise tower block—public housing at Tlatelolco, Mexico City.

ers. Reinforced concrete and other new technological advances would facilitate this kind of building, and Le Corbusier's ideas provided a larger vision within which to place this new wave of civic architecture. Postrevolutionary Mexico had now found an architecture that expressed the mood of the moment: the need to reject the bourgeois architecture of the previous era as too ornate and aristocratic. Mexico had had a social revolution, and now it was searching for a new architectural expression of the revolutionary spirit: simple, concrete boxes with murals on their walls. An architecture for the masses. A civic architecture that would be clear, efficient, and modern. The giant public housing project at Tlatelolco is perhaps one of the important examples of this kind of architecture in Mexico City, as is the monstrous University City complex. The Mexicans called this architectural school "functionalism." [31]

While functionalism was taking hold in Mexico City's public architecture, the wealthy would escape the growing congestion of the downtown, moving to the western and southern outskirts of the city to old colonial neighborhoods such as Lomas de Chaptulepec, Coyoacan, and San Angel. There they built luxurious but eclectic homes in styles ranging from English Tudor to French colonial or California Mission Revival.

After 1950, the momentum of several decades of functionalist architecture began to slow down. Artists who called themselves constructivists believed that painting and sculpture would merge with architecture. But in Mexico, attempts in this direction were wildly uneven. In Mexico City, for example, experiments where pre-Columbian motifs mixed with modern architecture were attempted in the grand design of the new University City complex, a sprawling mixed-use project of university, residential, and commercial development to the south of the downtown. The central administration building and library designs combined modern construction with indigenous ornamentation. The main library, designed by Juan O'Gorman, is a boxy structure bathed in colorful mosaic tile, a design that ran against the original plan which called for a pyramid-shaped building. The resulting boxlike UNAM library was out of sync, in the words of one observer: "The contradiction between the pure stereometric forms of architecture and the rhythmic, chromatic violence of the candid anecdotes bursts wide open." [32]

The 1960s saw in Mexico City an explosion of a new wave of architecture that might be seen as an extension of functionalism. It was an architecture suited to Mexico City's emergence as a city connected with the global, industrializing world system. It consisted of sleek glass skyscrapers, or tall reinforced concrete modern office buildings. "Internationalism," which had exploded in Europe and in the United States, did not quite take off as quickly in Mexico. At first, Mexico City resisted the new wave of "glass curtain" skyscrapers. It did not wish to

FIG. 2.12 Merging Corbusian functionalism with pre-Columbian art: the mosaic-tiled library at the University of Mexico (UNAM), Mexico City.

be transformed into a midtown Manhattan. But gradually the advantages of industrialized materials—concrete, steel, glass—over local ones (stone, adobe, marble) began to take hold. Large corporate developers soon replaced the traditional small-scale builders, and the *maestro de obra* (craftsman) would disappear.

The question of how Mexican cities incorporated memory into the modern design era is worth considering. Many prominent architects, including Pedro Ramírez Vázquez, Teodoro González de León, and Ricardo Legorreta, claim that their modern designs borrow from the cultural landscapes of Mexico's indigenous period. They cite such elements as monumental scale, the use of light and shadow, color, texture, the use of concrete platforms, patios, and open

FIG. 2.13 Blending the indigenous into the modern: stone, raised platforms, and patios as themes in a contemporary edifice, INFONAVIT building, Mexico City.

space, trapezoidal and pyramid shapes, walls, and landscaping. Modern build-ers don't necessarily try to re-create the style of indigenous buildings in their actual form but rather to test indigenous motifs in a modern context. González de León's designs use exposed concrete to give the look of stone, raised con-crete platforms and staircases connecting outdoor patios on different levels, and open spaces that allow the sunlight to stream through the building site, cre-ating different patterns of light and shadow at different times of the day and in different seasons of the year. In his architectural biography, Ramírez Vázquez compares the elements of the design of the modern Museum of Anthropology building in Chapultepec Park with those in the indigenous landscape. A stair-case to a Mayan pyramid is likened to the steps leading to the raised entrance of the museum. The symbolic decoration around a doorway is paralleled by a simi-lar motif in the museum's door entrance. The massive wall from the ball court at Chichen Itza looks hauntingly similar to the wall on the outside of the mu-seum, both in its scale and the texture of the stone, as well as the way the stone is decorated. Open plazas in an enclosed space in Mayan or Toltec cities are not unlike the open plaza surrounded by walls in the center of the museum.[33]

After 1970, Mexico City's landscape becomes a patchwork quilt of function-alism, internationalism, and toltecism: in a sense, a reflection of the debates raging in Mexico over the ways to transform the modern landscape—debates between traditionalists, who would preserve neocolonial building styles, and internationalists, who saw an elegance and efficiency in sleek glass skyscrapers. Two distinct kinds of designs have recently been identified in modern Mexico City: large-scale, sleek, international-style buildings, like banks and office complexes, icons of modernity and global capitalism that would fit anywhere, and buildings that make a statement, such as museums (Ramírez Vázquez's Museum of Anthropology, for example), universities, stadiums, hotels, and monuments.[34]

In other parts of the city one sees massive walls and pyramidal forms. The Towers of Luis Barragán and Mathías Goerritz, built near the entrance to the suburban Satellite City, have been described as "an experiment that sang in symbolist poetry."[35] Ironically, these symbolic, elegant towers of urban sculpture sat at the entrance to a very U.S.-style, bland suburban residential development, one of Mexico City's early waves of North American–style suburban residences. Of course, one must acknowledge that the most striking architecture of Mexico City's "suburbs" is the *colonia,* a spontaneous expression of the poor in the form of makeshift shantytowns built of scrap wood or metal. The dominant landscape of these "suburbs" is one of treeless plains or isolated hillside shacks on the edges of the metropolitan area. As more and more people abandon the overcrowded tenements in the center of the city, the population of the suburban *colonias* will increase.

Prominent in the contemporary landscape of Mexico City is the modern architecture of Ricardo Legorreta, who injected indigenous and colonial themes into international-style designs. Legorreta's buildings, like the Hotel Camino Real, on the edge of Chapultepec Park, use techniques of popular construction in a very elegant and enticing way: courtyards, fountains, stairs, ceramic tiles, and shocking colors. Legorreta's designs capture the condition of Mexican cityscapes in the late twentieth century: the struggle between the visual impact of the past and the design imperatives of industrialization and internationalism.

By the early 1990s, the Mexican urban landscape had begun to take on a new tone. Whereas U.S. cities evolved from a modernist to a postmodernist landscape north of the border, this has not happened in Mexico. Mexico has resisted postmodernism as a design philosophy. Where postmodernism reflects the eclectic past north of the border in a completely playful and ironic way, south of the border memory is taken more seriously. What some call the "new architecture" of the 1980s and 1990s in Mexico is a kind of thoughtful search for a way to resolve the age-old dialectic of past and future. The new designs are not only emerging in Mexico City but also in Monterrey, Guadalajara, and Puebla— even in the far-flung cities of the northern border. The dialectic of the city is spreading. Mexicans are questioning what *city* should mean, even while most

FIG. 2.14 Urban sculpture: the Towers of Luis Barragán and Mathías Goerritz, Satellite City, Mexico City (J. Ozorno).

continue to expand their population. In the northern industrial city of Monterrey, which shows signs of modernity and global capitalism, there has been an attempt to modify internationalism with more traditional Mexican notions of plaza, as illustrated in the downtown "Macro-plaza" surrounded by the very modern Teatro de la Ciudad, with its clear indigenous vocabulary.

The "new architecture" is finding many expressions in Mexico City; it is inspired by the earlier organic architecture of Luis Barragán, who was the first to reject massive, impersonal edifices of the modernist international mold. Barra-

FIG. 2.15 Where does the craftsmanship of the new architects fit into Mexico's urban future? Home of architect Abraham Zabludovsky.

gán designed meditative structures with blank walls, painted in bright colors, simple cement block partitions through which the light could pass, austere patios, gardens, and pools of water. His followers have taken his ideas and unleashed them in the real city of hotels, office buildings, and government complexes. Teodoro González de León has turned out some very fine examples, including museums and remodeled banks. Ricardo Legorreta's work is rapidly finding a place all over the country, from his Camino Real hotel designs in Mexico City and Ixtapa to his organic desert architectural prototype—the Renault factory in Gómez Palacio, Durango. Agustín Hernández designs startling residential spaces of cylindrical, triangular, prismatic form, or unusual buildings like a meditation center in Cuernavaca, Mexico, which seeks to translate the notion of spiritualism and meditation into spatial form.[36]

In urban Mexico of the 1990s, there remains a feeling of unfulfilled destiny, a sense that the search for a place, a design for living has not been completed. If this search lies behind the designers and people who occupy the built environment, it must also be said that these buildings must confront an increasingly chaotic and confused larger context. Where do the new architects fit in? How can the individual achievements of Legorreta, González de León, Ramírez Vázquez, and others be reconciled against the message of struggle embedded in the scrap-metal-and-plywood shantytowns that blanket the outskirts of Mexico City?

How does this architecture reconcile with the realities of increasing urban densities, overcrowding, and air pollution? Are Mexico's urban landscapes, like those in the United States, only to be observed from the freeways of the future? To what extent will Mexico's changing urban landscape be influenced by the United States in the next century? As we shall see in the next two chapters, much of that influence is already measurable along the frontier joining the two nations.

THREE

The Journey North

A History of Mexican Architecture on the California Border

Any city worth being a city has a historical patrimony, one its
residents can see and touch.　　　　　—LUIS TAMES

More than one thousand miles separate the heartland of Mexico
from its northern border with the United States. Like wave after wave of immigrants who followed the trail north, Mexico's architecture and strands of
her urbanist landscape also journeyed north. But the formation of towns along
Mexico's northern border did not exclusively evolve around the elements of traditional Mexican cities; it was strongly influenced by the colossal neighbor to
the north, the United States. If one follows the course of border town growth in
Mexico, particularly in the period following the Treaty of Guadalupe Hidalgo
(1848), which created the present-day international boundary, it is obvious that
the United States exercised considerable influence on the formation of the regional landscape. Following the 1848 treaty that created the political boundary, most of Mexico's border towns remained isolated from the heartland, and
therefore open to building ties with the United States. Early Anglo-American
influences on the townscapes appeared in the form of wooden (as opposed to
stone) building facades, commercial signage in English, and the utilization of
American regional architectural styles, such as California Mission Revival. But,
following the Mexican Revolution and consolidation of a new political system

(1910–30), a nationalist era began, and Mexico asserted control over her cities, even along the distant northern border. After World War II, the Mexican government crafted formal policies to protect the cultural patrimony both nationally and regionally. Yet by the 1980s, those controls were slipping. The era of the North American Free Trade Agreement once again opened border town landscapes to the influences of the United States. Like the migrant waves that ebbed and flowed north, the visual landscape in the border towns vacillated between complete permeability to the culture north of the border and nationalistic protectionism and isolation from all outside influences.

The Formation of Northern Mexico's Border Cities

The urbanization of Mexico's northern frontier occurred in three relatively distinct waves.[1] The first wave actually preceded the formation of the international political boundary. As early as the seventeenth and eighteenth centuries, Spain's colonization of "New Spain" (Mexico) concentrated in Mexico's central plateau region, but expeditions in search of minerals and other natural wealth dispersed population and settlements in all directions, including the provinces to the north. Missions, *presidios* (forts), and *pueblos* (administrative towns) were all set up in the northern territories, near the present-day international border. The most important northern frontier outpost was established at Paso del Norte (Ciudad Juárez, today) in 1659; others included Matamoros (1700) and Reynosa (1749).

When the present-day Mexico-U.S. border was created, following the Treaty of Guadalupe Hidalgo (1848), the second period of urban border growth unfolded. Most of the settlements organized at this time functioned as military posts or customs checkpoints along the newly formed international boundary. The best-known towns of the period included Tijuana and Nuevo Laredo (both formed in 1848) and Piedras Negras (1849). Several additional "gateways" were formed over the next three decades—Ciudad Acuna (1877), Nogales (1882), and Agua Prieta (1899). A third and final wave of settlements emerged in the early twentieth century. As U.S. capital began to flow south of the border, infrastructure for large-scale agriculture, cattle ranching, and mining led to the formation of new settlements near the frontier. Examples include Mexicali (1903), San Luis Colorado (1917), and Tecate (1918).

Two forces mediated the growth of cities in northern Mexico's border zone: the economic development of the neighboring southwestern United States in the late nineteenth and early twentieth centuries, and the evolution of a geographic strategy of migration which utilized the border zone as a means to enter the United States. Northern Mexico discovered the economic potential of trade with the United States as early as the 1860s when, during the Civil War, various commodities (cotton, munitions, etc.) were exchanged between Monterrey entrepreneurs and the U.S. Confederate states, whose coastal shipping lanes were under blockade by the Union navy. Over the next three decades, foreign capital assisted Mexico in building a railroad connection between the center (Mexico City) and the northern border. In the 1880s, rail lines were completed between Mexico City and two border points—Laredo and El Paso. During the era of President Porfirio Díaz (1876–1910) foreign investment was championed as part of a program of economic growth for Mexico; the northern border region benefited, as the mining, oil, and agriculture sectors expanded.

The second half of the nineteenth century was a period of expansion for the southwestern U.S. economy, most notably in the areas of agriculture, mining, railroads, manufacturing, and defense. The emergence of important new population growth nodes in the late nineteenth and early twentieth centuries, in places like Phoenix, Albuquerque, and El Paso is evidence of the Southwest's enormous transformation in this era.[2] These growing population centers would later become markets for the service economy of northern Mexico's border towns.

Mexican immigration was strongly tied to southwestern U.S. economic development in the period of the late nineteenth and early twentieth centuries. During that period, one of the most important elements of Mexico's border urbanism took shape: the emergence of the border towns as Mexican labor migration deployment areas, as well as enclaves for return migrants. One scholar has called this the "springboard-receptacle" function.[3] It is significant that the border towns became, in this period of economic growth, the staging centers for labor migration, since we will see that much of their twentieth-century character builds upon this early legacy of cross-border dependency.[4] Border towns became entangled with the shifting fate of the U.S. economy. Although Mexicans had largely been untouched by the first U.S. immigration quotas of 1917, during the 1930s, they were hit hard by the Depression and subsequent changes in U.S. federal policy. Nearly one-half million Mexican migrants were deported from the United States back to Mexico; many flooded into the border towns, which were already suffering from the loss of U.S. consumer spending.

The era of the Bracero Program (1942–64) did more to solidify the role of border towns in the larger migration process than any previous period. When the United States and Mexico established the Emergency Farm Labor Program, or Bracero Program, in 1942, it formalized and accelerated a cross-border labor supply system that had been building over some five decades. More than 4.6 million labor contracts were issued between 1942 and 1964. During the twenty-two-year period, several million Mexicans permanently settled in the United States, and hundreds of thousands in Mexican border towns. Perhaps more significantly, the Bracero Program institutionalized illegal or undocumented Mexican immigration. As U.S. growers began to hire Mexican workers without papers, the Mexicans learned that work in the United States could be found outside the formalities of contract-labor. Illegal crossings thus began to increase.[5] The era of undocumented Mexican immigration had begun. Border cities, from 1960 on, became way stations from which migrants would plan their journeys into the United States. Illegal immigration creates jobs along the border for smugglers and other service providers. In some border towns, like Tijuana and Ciudad Juárez, entire neighborhoods have been built by people who originally were immigrants to the United States.

As early as 1885, under President Porfirio Díaz, the *zona libre* (free-zone) program was set up to allow duty-free movement of goods into a corridor twelve miles wide along the northern frontier. This program (1885–1905) gave Mexican merchants along the border a competitive edge over their northern neighbors in pricing imported goods. The border cities established themselves as distribution points for imported retail goods (and later for commercial services) for consumers in the United States. The first of many cross-border functional ties was in place. Although the free-zone program was abolished in 1905, under severe pressure from U.S. merchant associations, an economic strategy for Mexico — tapping the U.S. consumer market — had been put in place and would resurface throughout the twentieth century. By the 1930s, a limited version of the free-zone program was once again constructed. In the 1990s, this process has reached its logical summit: the North American Free Trade Agreement (NAFTA) will allow Mexico previously unheard-of access to the lucrative U.S. consumer market.

During the middle of the twentieth century, as the population of cities north of the border (San Antonio, El Paso, Dallas, Houston, Phoenix, Tucson, Albuquerque, San Diego, Los Angeles, etc.) increased, the Mexican government recognized that transboundary commerce would be essential to the economic survival of the northern borderlands. By the 1960s, ex-*braceros* were being repatriated back to Mexico, and many ended up unemployed in the border towns. In 1961, the Mexican government introduced PRONAF, the Programa Nacional Fronterizo (National Border Program), designed to invigorate the economy of border towns through expansion of agriculture and industry, as well as physical renovation and beautification. The Mexican government rightly surmised that consumers spend more when the physical setting is pleasing to them. The border towns had for too long been stereotyped as honky-tonk, ramshackle centers of corruption, prostitution, and vice.[6] To change that, most of the large cities were subject to massive cleanup campaigns, especially in the tourist zones.

During the 1970s, commercial development policies concentrated on retaining income within Mexico and building spaces for retail consumers, particularly shopping malls. To achieve the former, the *artículos ganchos* (hook items) program was enacted. The hook item strategy revolved around duty-free import of consumer goods within the original "free zones" of the border. These goods would then be sold to Mexicans as a way of keeping expenditures within Mexico. Even if many of these products were bought wholesale in the United States, retail spending (and thus Mexican income) would remain within Mexico. Meanwhile, Mexican and U.S. capital was recruited for the building of shopping centers and regional malls. The program started slowly but picked up considerably during the real estate boom of the 1980s. While peso devaluations in 1982 and in the 1990s have hurt the economy of border towns, NAFTA has the potential to significantly energize the border cities, especially in the areas of retail trade and professional services.

One specific form of cross-border consumption that emerged along the border early in this century was tourism. When the U.S. Eighteenth Amendment took effect in 1920 prohibiting the sale of alcohol, U.S. entrepreneurs and Mexican business interests in the northern Mexican border towns soon moved to fill this niche for the consumer market north of the border. As U.S. border region dwellers became more mobile due to advances in mass transit and automobile travel, Mexico's border towns converted themselves into service centers for the consumption of "leisure" activities (gambling, health spas and resorts, alcohol consumption, prostitution, etc.). Much of the early tourism infrastructure—roads, bridges, hotels, restaurants, wine and beer factories, casinos—was built with U.S. capital. The multiplier effects were considerable, particularly in the areas of new housing and neighborhoods for workers. New commercial areas were built; some became legendary "red light districts" or what the Mexican government termed *zonas de tolerancia*.[7]

The most dynamic economic force in late-twentieth-century transborder urban society has been the "twin plant" or *maquiladora* (assembly plant) sector. One plank in the PRONAF border development strategy was to reduce unemployment by promoting industrial growth. In 1965, the Border Industrial Program (BIP) was created. It was built upon the emerging concept of "offshore" production whereby U.S. manufacturers moved the assembly stage of the production process to cheap-labor zones in places like Hong Kong or Taiwan.[8] The BIP strategy assumed American factories might relocate their labor-intensive assembly operations to the Mexican border. The "twin plant" concept was built upon the notion that a U.S. factory on one side of the border would produce the parts for manufacturing an industrial commodity (e.g., a television set), which would then be shipped south to the assembly plant in Mexico. By agreement, no duties would be paid on the finished products shipped out of Mexico, except on the value added to the original parts. Also, all finished products would be distributed to markets outside of Mexico.

The BIP's impact on Mexican border cities was gargantuan in the period 1970–96. In 1970, there were 160 *maquiladoras* in Mexico, employing around twenty thousand workers. About 90 percent of these plants were located in border cities. A quarter century later, there were more than two thousand *maquiladoras* in Mexico, employing about three-quarter million workers, with a value added estimated at roughly three billion dollars. About 85 percent of all assembly plants remain in Mexico's border cities. They have been an important part of the real estate and development boom of the last two decades, manifest in the form of new physical infrastructure (roads, industrial parks, housing projects), multiplier effects on related economic sectors—such as machinery repair, finance, real estate, services, and additional income earned by workers or through rent collected on the leasing of factory space.

By the 1990s, it was no longer accurate to view Mexico's northern border cities as separate from their counterpart "twins"—U.S. settlements north of the border.[9] So entangled are their economies and social networks with these urbanized neighbors to the north that it is appropriate to speak of a "transfrontier metropolis," a single cross-border functional living space within which common daily activity systems (work, shopping, school, and social trips) and environmental features (air basins, watersheds, etc.) are shared by U.S. and Mexican urban dwellers.[10] Examples along the frontier (moving from east to west) include: Matamoros-Brownsville; Reynosa-McAllen; Laredo–Nuevo Laredo; Ciudad Juárez–El Paso; Nogales-Nogales; San Luis Colorado–Yuma; Mexicali-Calexico; and Tijuana–San Diego. The transfrontier metropolis is the result of more than a century of symbiotic connections between "twin cities" straddling the frontier.

Architecture and Cultural Landscapes in Northern Mexico

Given the history described above, it is not surprising that the cultural landscapes found in the northern Mexican border cities reflect the tension between traditional Mexican influences and the forces of modernity, largely drawn from north of the border. In some cases, these forces—traditional and modern, southern and northern—have mixed into a pleasant hybrid landscape that gives greater character to the region. In other cases, the two forces stand in isolation of each other, creating a polarized border cultural landscape: one (the traditional) concentrated largely in the older downtown areas; the other (modern) dispersed through the suburban zones, the newer commercial areas, and redeveloped tourist zones in the old central business district.

The Traditional Landscape

The traditional Mexican border town was influenced by the urbanism of colonial Mexican cities. It took the form of a high-density rectangular street grid, anchored by one or more *plazas* (town squares) at the center. The traditional urban core—still visible today in downtown business districts like Matamoros, Ciudad Juarez, or Reynosa[11]—has extremely narrow streets, modest low-rise structures, and more residents than most American downtowns. The urban core areas of Mexico's border towns are lively, pedestrian places, where a business district for Mexican residents often stands adjacent to the tourist zone for foreigners. Most striking is that these zones are active magnets for townspeople—they have not suffered the decay of central cities north of the border. The high growth rates of Mexican border cities and the continued primacy of the traditional downtown have, of course, meant that the old central city districts needed to accommodate the automobile. The result has been increasing congestion and less and less space to park vehicles.[12]

The border *plaza*—town square—still serves as an important anchor for the downtown,[13] although in a few cities, notably Tijuana, the original town square disappeared. The *plazas* tend to be rectangular and the size of a city block. They are distinguished by their landscaping, a product of the late-nineteenth-century era of romantic, European neoclassical revival, which quickly grew popular in Mexico after it was first introduced over a century ago. Typically *plazas* in northern Mexican border towns have the same infrastructure one finds in interior cities: kiosks, fountains, and monuments to Mexican heroes or other world historic figures. Tecate's Parque Hidalgo is an excellent example of a traditional Mexican *plaza* in a border town. It lies in the geographic center of Tecate, a medium-sized city of some seventy thousand residents lying in a valley at the center of the northern Baja California–California boundary.[14] The *plaza* covers a city block. Paths from the four corners meet at the kiosk in the center. Palm trees and other semitropical vegetation make it a lush, green refuge.

Another traditional component of the border town is the linear tourist commercial strip. Most of the Mexican border towns have them. In some towns like Mexicali, they appear in the form of neocolonial porticos lined with arches.[15] The atmosphere along the main tourism street tends to be festive—signage is colorful, decorative, and appeals to tourist fantasies. There are often flags and decorations along these streets. Bars, cantinas, stores, and restaurants dominate the scene. These tourism corridors tend to be regional creations—they do not exist all over Mexico but were created to accommodate the unique tourism industry that grew at the border in the early twentieth century.

FIG. 3.1 The traditional commercial strip of Mexican border towns: Tijuana in the 1920s (source: author's photo of public poster).

The tourism districts evoke a carnival-like, playful, and highly colorful, if eclectic, landscape. The architecture ranges from art deco, streamline moderne, Spanish colonial, or Mission Revival[16] to international style and postmodern. The dominant land uses are commercial, typically curio shops in bright colors, bars with wild neon signs, and back-alley bazaars or arcades, sometimes sunken below ground level. These designs, contrary to the often-heard stereotype of an urban society out of control, are deliberately made to be artificial—a sort of Disneyland Mexican exotica for tourists. They may stem from the Mexican ability to use caricature and irony as a way of poking fun at themselves, so vividly illustrated by the postrevolutionary muralists. In the end, the tourist districts of Mexico's border cities are quite unpretentiously honky-tonk and carefree. Mexican architects on the border speak openly of *la arquitectura del chiste* (the architecture of the joke) in the tourism zone. Such contrived places have been termed by one landscape scholar "other directed," since they are designed for consumption by outsiders.[17] Few places in the world are so strikingly "other directed" as the tourism zones of Mexican border cities.

Near the tourism zones lies another urban district that remains part of the folklore of the northern border towns: the red-light district, or *zona de tolerancia,* referred to earlier. Originally conceived as spaces for alcohol consumption and prostitution in the 1920s, these districts survived by redefining themselves over time. During the Second World War, they became "leisure" service areas for Americans in the armed forces, with striptease clubs, alcohol, and prostitutes; after 1950, they survived as a curiosity, "museum" exhibits of an era gone by, and functional space for prostitutes. The original place characteristics of these zones—the small nightclubs with exotic signage, neon lighting, hint of sexuality—have been maintained, although the neighborhoods have slid into physical decline and taken on the look of skid row districts in the United States. In some cities, the red-light districts remain as commercial zones appended to the downtown business district; in others, they have been removed from the downtown and relocated to compounds, or "boys' towns," in hidden, isolated locations. Nuevo Laredo's "Boys' Town" is perhaps the most well known.[18]

The formal landscape of Mexican border towns is highlighted by the combinations of Greek Revival, Federalist, or Mission Revival architecture found in the Municipal Palaces (town halls) of major urban centers. The town hall of Reynosa is a stark, Federalist structure, while that in Mexicali is more purposefully neoclassical, with columns and arches. Some formal architecture finds its way into commercial spaces in the form of French and Spanish colonial two-story buildings with upstairs iron balconies, such as those found in Matamoros.

FIG. 3.2 Formal landscapes on the border: the Federalist-style town hall, Tecate.

Perhaps most notable in the formal landscape are the grand resorts designed in the golden age of tourism (1920s). These resort complexes and casinos were designed to maximize glamour amid the exotic age of gambling and alcohol on the Mexican border of the roaring twenties. Many tend to be eclectic combinations of Moorish, Spanish-Mediterranean, Arab, and Italian architectural influences. In Ensenada, the Hotel Casino Riviera, built in 1928 and recently restored, epitomizes this kind of grand fantasylike building.[19]

While Mexico City, the national capital, is notable for its profusion of monumental buildings designed by signature architects,[20] the border townscapes tend to feature a mix of both formal and vernacular landscapes. Popular landscapes in the commercial sector include two-story stucco or wood-frame stores, with creative, individualized storefronts. In the residential spaces, one finds regional folk house types—including the *jacal* (log) structure and adobe block houses.[21] U.S. influence can be seen in the appearance of wood-frame houses or Spanish/Mission Revival stucco homes in the 1910–30 period. Vernacular landscapes also appear in the form of agricultural, industrial, and transport infrastructure. The former include mills, storage houses, irrigation canals, and cotton gins. Industrial structures appear in the form of breweries, wine factories (mainly from the 1920s and 1930s), an occasional oil refinery or steel smelter (Reynosa), or a coal-processing plant (Piedras Negras). The assembly plant (*maquiladora*) program added a new layer of dull warehouse-type factories to the border townscapes; only rarely does one see elegance in the design of the *maquila* plants. Transport infrastructure includes rail yards and rail bridges, as well as border gates and bridges.[22]

The New Landscapes of Economic Integration and NAFTA

Over the last three decades, the traditional landscapes of Mexican border towns have been dramatically transformed. These changes derive from external forces—the changing world economy—which have impacted the border region and redefined the functions and daily life of Mexico's border towns. As a result, the cultural landscape is changing. Aside from considerable new construction under way, most notable is the physical spread of the urbanized areas beyond the limits of the traditional, pedestrian-scale towns. Northern Mexican border towns are slowly shifting into more suburban, highway-oriented urban regions. These changes were not only wrought by the increasing populations arriving at the border; they were also driven by greater use of the automobile for intraurban transit, leading to the decentralization of land uses away from the original downtown. One must acknowledge, also, that the massive growth of border cities has not been channeled vertically in the form of higher density, vertical high-rises but rather horizontally in the form of a vast sprawl of one- and two-story buildings.[23]

One salient theme found in the late-twentieth-century cultural landscape of northern Mexican border cities is its increasing subordination to the urbanism of the United States.[24] Many of the landscape alterations introduced in northern Mexico—freeways, industrial parks, suburban housing subdivisions, condominium developments, shopping malls—typified the post-1950 transformation north of the border. The changes have not completely eclipsed Mexican identity at the border. On the contrary, in the midst of so much outside influence, distinctly Mexican expressions continue to be incorporated into these modern landscapes.

One of the biggest changes in the northern border cities was in the realm of transport infrastructure. Once the Mexican federal government recognized the value of the northern border towns to the national economy (in the areas of trade, tourism, and assembly plants), steps were taken to better equip the northern border for international transit. Since Mexico and the United States signed the NAFTA, this process has accelerated. Mexico's border settlements must somehow find ways to connect with the emerging global economy, principally through greater integration (functional, cultural, economic) with the United States. New airports have been built or improved in the major cities. Freeways and better roads provide increased access from the border to important development zones. New border crossings make U.S.-Mexico exchanges easier.

As mentioned above, the *maquiladora* program has had the single greatest impact on the border towns. Not only has a new layer of industrial parks been built, but their spillover effects in the service economy (finance, real estate, insurance, etc.) also have been a catalyst for the construction of modern glass and concrete office buildings. The new *maquila* parks have tended to follow the prototype designs of U.S. suburban industrial parks.[25] This includes the use of uniform setbacks and lot sizes as well as controlled landscaping. Such designs provide for a system of screening and security as well as ample parking facilities. It has been noted, as well, that the new *maquila* parks—in Juárez, Nogales, Tecate, Mexicali, and Tijuana—are isolated from the main city and resemble fortress compounds not unlike the *haciendas* of centuries past.[26] Unlike U.S. industrial parks, however, *maquila* parks are often located in the midst of poor *colonias*.

Many of the tourism zones have been substantially revitalized. Racetracks have been rebuilt; the old commercial strips have been widened. Buildings in the traditional downtown have been modernized. The Mexican government has ambitious plans for modernizing much of the tourism infrastructure and built environment. In the Lower Rio Grande Valley, the government plans to build a $50

FIG. 3.3 Landscapes of NAFTA: a postmodern office building in
Tijuana's River Zone.

million resort at Lake Amistad.[27] In Baja California, hotel, luxury condominium,
and other tourism projects hug the coastline between Tijuana and Ensenada.

In the meantime, new commercial zones have opened, most oriented toward
automobile access. The first important commercial ribbons appeared in the
1960s and 1970s and were not unlike the commercial strip development in the
United States that had begun a decade earlier. Later, this kind of commercial
development favored the divided boulevard, interrupted by the popular *glorieta*
(traffic circle). The *glorieta* was a borrowed French design idea that appeared in

Mexico during the mid-nineteenth century when Mexico City was redesigned by Napoleon III's appointed leader, Maximilian. The commercial landscape has also been bombarded by the suburban shopping mall, of which there are many in the border towns, as well as in the interior of Mexico, and the mini-mall/convenience center, set back from the street with a parking lot in front.

Perhaps the most conspicuous feature of the visual landscape of modern border towns is the growing sprawl of squatter housing that has spread over their outskirts. Observers have written about the increasing social class polarization of Mexican border cities.[28] Squatter housing assaults the senses of visitors from north of the border. The houses tend to be quite makeshift, especially for new residents, who may live in tents made of cardboard and scrap wood. The most recent squatter homes usually have dirt floors and generally lack glass windows, and even doors. They house people who live far below what Americans call the poverty level. These homes suggest a way of life quite common for the marginal population of Mexican society, an existence that is made necessary by uncertainty—uncertain status in the job market and lack of capital for permanent house construction, leading to the building of shelters with a haphazard collection of recycled materials.

By contrast with the informal settlements, modern residential architecture in Mexican border cities increasingly reflects the influence of the United States. Mass housing projects tend to locate in suburban areas. As in U.S. suburban developments, the streets are paved, and the homes have all utilities and are usually constructed of masonry (brick or stucco). They have been described as "crisp and clean."[29] Popular housing styles range from ranch to European and North American revival. Much of the modern architecture one finds in Mexican border towns of the glass and steel variety appears in the form of office buildings, luxury hotels, and commercial spaces. "Signature" architecture tends to enter the landscape mainly in formal commissions for important public buildings such as museums, customs houses, town halls, state and federal offices, libraries, and so forth.

Danger and Exotica in Mexican Border Townscapes

What is it that makes the cultural landscapes of Mexican border towns unique? Several observations can be made. First, these are, for Mexico, relatively young landscapes that were created largely in the last two centuries. Mexico is a nation with a history of city building that dates back some three thousand or more years. Obviously, the making of the northern border landscape is a relatively recent phenomenon.

At the turn of the century, young Mexican border towns looked like the frontier cities of the American West: dusty, unpaved streets lined with wooden saloons and a few retail stores. Their existence was defined by the simple fact that, while lying geographically near the United States, they were officially outside its borders and could house recreational activities that would otherwise have been forbidden north of the border. The origins of the Mexican border iconography of gambling, prostitution, and alcohol consumption lie in the period 1910–35 but have proved to be difficult to displace.

The forbidden landscape of the border finds its way into both literature and media portraits of the border. An example is found in a 1970 nonfiction book *Poso del Mundo*. Pretending to describe life on the Mexican border, the author makes no secret about his point of view in the rather blatant book title, which means sinkhole of the world. The 1970s Mexican border is likened to one of the lowest moral places on the planet, "a sixteen-hundred-mile pleasure strip measurably oriented to gringos with low libidinal thresholds."[30] Mexican border town architecture is equated with neglect, decay, and "squat buildings and narrow streets, with the requisite number of potholes."[31] Commerce occurs in "plastic-tropical" bars like the Marabu in Nuevo Laredo, "a barn-sized hall with an elevated dance floor bigger than a basketball court and completely encircled by tables. The decor is Mexican Futuristic, which has much in common with Las Vegas Moderne."[32] This will not be the last time Mexican border towns bring to mind Las Vegas, another town that appears as a stage set for libidinal fantasies in the middle of a desert wasteland. One writer stated that "in Tijuana, as in Las Vegas, another city constructed on sand, and almost as old, history is a matter of matchbook covers and cocktail napkins."[33]

Forbidden landscapes along the border often draw upon references to morality. Red-light districts, called boys' towns, or *zonas de tolerancia,* have frequently been used as iconographic representations of Mexican border cities. Abortion clinics, prisons, cantinas, and whorehouses are mentioned. The desperate living environment for older prostitutes is described: "The alternative to retirement is to rent crib space in a *zona*—windowless, doorless, floorless hovels the length of racing stables, partitioned into areas barely large enough to accommodate a *petate,* or cot, a chair, a charcoal burner, and a small bureau. A votive candle burns before the icon of a favored saint, usually the Virgin of Guadalupe, except when a customer is being serviced."[34]

For too long, books like this were the only documented social descriptions of this region. Even when describing the Mexican government's attempts to modernize the border towns, they painted a dreary view of the border: "This—on a minutely limited scale—has been precisely PRONAF's (the Mexican government agency modernizing the border) contribution: Palm Springs–type motels and shopping centers for gringos, which do nothing more for the community than accent its squalor." [35] While these descriptions offered one slice of Mexican border urban life, they did not give a complete picture of the emerging built environment of Mexican border towns in the late twentieth century. The border cannot be reduced to a metaphor for everything evil and corrupt about a society.

For many North Americans, the modern border landscape, in a sense, is an outgrowth of its Roaring Twenties origins. The term *border* seems to connote an edge, not of nations, but of social responsibility. Beyond the border, for some U.S. citizens, lies a world of escape, of fantasy, of retirement from the pressures of home. The border is the gateway to recreation, entrance into a giant resort zone filled with retirement communities, trailer parks, camps, dune buggies, and four-wheel-drive vehicles. The favored buildings are bars, like the well-known Hussong's Cantina, in Ensenada, forty-five miles from the border, which has been romanticized as the Old West gone south of the border, "the Long Branch, the Crystal Palace and the Silver Dollar all rolled into one." The interior of a dimly lit bar is where "the ceilings are all of coffered tin; the large fireplace around which thousands of *mariachis* have played over the years still stands, and the famous long bar and rough-carpeted back bar are still intact." [36]

Such imagined Mexican border landscapes have been slow to disappear. In the nineteenth century, after all, this was a Wild West "frontier," and stories of outlaws, gunfights in border saloons, and other folklore came with the territory. In the first five decades of the twentieth century, the Mexican government concentrated its resources on modernizing the cities of the interior, with the result that the border towns lagged behind in their development. In the meantime, their proximity to the United States and the rapidly expanding railroad and industrial economy of the Southwest meant that American investment would eventually turn its attention south of the border. In the early decades of the twentieth century, Americans who arrived south of the border were interested in a "quick fix," in making money or in entertaining themselves. It should come as no great surprise that a "quick fix" architecture emerged, and that border towns became the first Las Vegases of the Southwest.

It would prove to be a difficult legacy to overcome. Even after President Lázaro Cárdenas dismantled the gambling economy of the border in the 1930s, interest groups turned their attention to other unsavory activities such as smuggling. Meanwhile, the border towns continued to serve as locales for prostitution and drinking, as American soldiers would discover during World War II. After the war, these activities would take a few more decades to dissipate, but their history was now embedded in the city's lore. By the 1960s and 1970s, the border still carried its share of negative images, most notably in the area of drug smuggling, although fortunes had been earned earlier through less sanitized forms of contraband. During the period from 1960 through the 1990s, global networks of

FIG. 3.4 Landscape of danger: Immigrants await the cover of nightfall to sneak into the United States. Levee of the Tía Juana River at San Diego boundary (J. Ozorno).

cocaine, heroin, and marijuana smuggling ran through the U.S.-Mexican border. In one of many published accounts, a smuggler converts a wealthy home in the hills of Tijuana into a fortress command center for his smuggling operations.[37] More recently, it has become clear that some of Mexico's leading narcotics smugglers built a base of operations in the northern border cities. Smuggling, both of people and narcotics, has left its imprint on the border landscape. Fences built of corrugated steel, former landing mats for U.S. military operations in world conflict zones, were built on the San Diego–Baja California border by the U.S. Army Corps of Engineers. These fences announce to the viewer that the border remains a "contested space," a test of wills between the enforcers of the U.S. border patrol and narcotics enforcement, and the Mexican smugglers. Along the fence, ladders have been placed and tunnels dug, suggesting that the smugglers have won the early battle to control border turf. Numerous well-worn foot trails and dirt paths on vacant land attest to the magnitude of daily movement of illegal border crossers. An infrastructure of services—food vendors, professional smugglers, clothing or equipment vendors—can be seen in neighborhoods lying adjacent to the border. Signage and graffiti found along the border wall record in words and images the thoughts of border crossers.

The view of the border as a landscape of danger and intrigue pervades the work of contemporary essayists, journalists, and writers. Not atypical is a work that characterized the Mexico-U.S. boundary as an out-of-control world of wetbacks, drug smugglers, bird smugglers, boozers, wild radio disc jockeys, and macho border patrol officers, a border that is "sleazy and sleepy, dusty and desolate, places where the poor and the criminal mingle," but also "sexy and hypnotic, mysterious and magical, self-reliant and remarkably resilient. It changes pesos into dollars, humans into illegals, innocence into hedonism."[38] Stereotyping continues. Even social scientists have fallen prey to this. In one 1973 book, the author promised to look deeper into border culture and "demonstrate the inaccuracy of the tourist stereotype of the Mexican border city as a center of vice and poverty."[39] Yet that same book ended up devoting two of its most important chapters to the subjects of drug traffic and prison life, both topics that reinforced past thinking about border cities.

It is as if these themes are too enticing to ignore. Photographers, for example, remain fascinated by the old myths and current reinventions of border folklore. One of the best recent collections on the subject[40] follows the journey of immigrants from Mexico's rural small towns to the border, and into the United States Southwest. A metallic border of handcuffs, chain-link fences, and patrol vans is captured in black and white, alongside images of undocumented aliens running through underground tubes or over fences, imprisoned in the trunks of cars, in border patrol vans, lying on the ground with their hands tied behind their backs, or living miserable existences in cardboard shacks or east Los Angeles tenements.

If any medium has exploited these border themes of danger and exotica, it has been the film industry. Most of the border films produced in Mexico—and there have been more than one hundred made[41]—focus on negative themes like crime, immigration, drug trafficking, prostitution, and the border mafia. Some have been likened to Mexican versions of *Rambo*. These films reflect both the view of the border from Mexico City and stereotypes that were exaggerated for the purpose of making money.[42] Films about the border made in the United States have repeated the same themes, albeit within the usual Hollywood formula for filmmaking, with heroes seeking to accomplish a goal, romantic interludes, sex, and violence. *Borderline* and *The Border,* two films made in the 1980s with two of the leading actors on the American screen (Charles Bronson and Jack Nicholson) both exploited the theme of illegal Mexican immigration and the problems of the border patrol. Another film, *Losing It,* portrays American teenagers looking for sex south of the border, reconstructing the old stereotype of Tijuana as a "dirty, sleazy, criminal" town.[43] A more recent film, *El Mariachi,* is set in a Texas border town and reinforces yet again the themes of violence and drug smuggling.

During the 1980s an emerging group of writers and observers began to sketch out a new vision of the border. Some saw it as a third country, neither the United States nor Mexico. "It's a third country with its own identity.... It obeys its own laws and has its own outlaws, its own police officers, and its own policy makers. Its food, its language, its music are its own."[44] Others were both fascinated and confused by the juxtaposition of two cultures at the border. In his search for baseball south of the border, one writer notes upon crossing the boundary that "no amount of posted officialese can smooth the abruptness of this most traversed demarcation between First and Third Worlds, soften the sharp distinction between two ways of being on the planet." He goes on to comment on his first view of Tijuana: "It sprawls down a narrow valley in huge boulevards that replicate the American West's grimy fast food, oil and lube strips—except that here the rotating neon needs translation." [45] In the span of one recent magazine article, another writer likens Tijuana to Calcutta, Cairo, Marrakesh, and Shanghai, some of the more exotic cities on the planet. He writes: "People in Mexico City will tell you, if they have anything to say about Tijuana, that Tijuana is a city without history, a city without architecture, that it is, in fact, an American city." [46]

The Example of Tijuana

It may be simplistic to dismiss Tijuana as just another Americanized city. Certainly, there has been a hemispheric attachment to the idea of the quintessential "border" town—no-man's-land, with turn-of-the-century wooden saloons, gambling halls, taxi driver pimps, and Roaring Twenties Hollywood stars indulging libidos as big as block-long cantinas. The question is, Can Mexican border towns like Tijuana have a history? How much of a Mexican border townscape is simply an invention of U.S. interests that, like the traveling circus or carnival, closes down and moves on when the show is over? Where is Mexico in the landscape of Tijuana?

The irony of Tijuana is that it lies in a country so rich in urban design tradition that, at times, it seems as if the government has placed a higher priority on subsidizing architectural commissions for grand projects (museums, ministries, public monuments) than on solving social problems like housing shortages or unemployment. Mexico cherishes its urban landscapes. Many of Mexico's large cities are built on or near pre-Columbian ruins. Mexico City, of course, is built over the ruins of the Aztec capital, Tenochtitlan. There are subway stations named for buildings and districts that existed before the Spanish arrived. Other Mexican cities, from Merida to Oaxaca to Morelia, lie near ruins of an indigenous past. This not only makes the indigenous past present in modern Mexican urbanism; it has also moved many in high government posts to lobby for architecture that continues to pay homage to the rich pre-Columbian memory. The past calls for more than remembering the physical ruins; it speaks to the way Mexicans build their cities. It lies in the open *plazas,* the massive walls, the stone, the colors.

But geography left Tijuana outside these great twentieth-century debates. From its post on the northwestern edge of Mexico, across the span of great deserts, over the Sea of Cortez, and up the eight hundred miles of peninsular

FIG. 3.5 Remnants of a Roaring Twenties Mediterranean fantasy tourism boom: tiled entrance and patios of the Agua Caliente resort, Tijuana.

wilderness called Baja California, far from the great pre-Columbian sites or the Baroque colonial towns, Tijuana has only come into the debate as the twentieth century comes to a close.

There are "ruins" in Tijuana, but they do not speak of an Aztec or Mayan past. They speak of North America. The "ruins" are the last vestiges of the city's finest architectural moment in its brief hundred-year history: the great resort of Agua Caliente, built in the latter part of the decade of the 1920s. Once an eclectic Spanish-Moorish–styled complex of tiled patios, arched corridors, and red-tile-roofed Mediterranean splendor, there is little left today. A tall, thin tower, a Moorish-looking minaret with colorful mosaic tile, once served as the chimney for the ovens and driers in the complex. On the former grounds of the spa building, all that remains is the arched entranceway with faded mosaic tiles and an outdoor swimming pool that is empty and badly deteriorating. Only mud and brackish standing water lie at the bottom. Green mosaic tiles evoke memories of a lavish past, when Hollywood actresses Rita Hayworth or Jean Harlow came to lie in the sun near a sparkling pool. Today the tiles are covered with graffiti. Once, the finest Italian tile lined the patio around the pool. Created in southern Spanish-Moorish style, the design work was compared with the Alhambra of Spain.[47] Most of it has been ripped out today for parking lots or basketball courts. Schoolchildren scamper on the remaining old tiled benches during their recreation hour. Nearby, boys with T-shirts that say "Chicago Bulls" or "Lakers" run up and down the cement basketball courts in their modified school uniforms.

The Agua Caliente resort was designed in 1926–27 by two San Diego, California, architects, Wayne and Corinne McAllister.[48] It may not be surprising that the resort was destined to be destroyed, no matter how successful its design. Its fate was sealed only a few years after construction had been completed. In 1935, Mexican President Lázaro Cárdenas declared gambling illegal. His administration marked a clear shift in Mexican politics. Here a Mexican president was responsible for closing down the greatest casino complex in North America, whereas a previous president, Abelardo Rodríguez, in 1927, in conjunction with American partners, was the one who had bought the rights to the land and invested in the building of the complex in the first place. But with Cárdenas's decree, casinos would quickly close down along the entire border. The Mexican government expropriated the casino and its ample grounds in 1937. The complex's acreage included the hotel, surrounding bungalows, the casino, and the spa. The whole site was turned over to the Ministry of Public Education, which made the complex into a public high school. The luxury hotel was transformed into general dormitories for students, the giant casino into workshops on carpentry, mechanics, and electronics. The old dog-racing track became a sports field for children's recreation. In 1939, the Instituto Técnico de Agua Caliente was created, the first serious technical high school in the area. Top-notch teachers were recruited from as far away as Spain. Later the complex would expand into two high schools. Tijuana's casino days were over.

In the 1960s and 1970s, fervent nationalists advocated complete demolition of the entire Agua Caliente complex, as a way of erasing what they termed Tijuana's *historia negra* (black history). Administrators of the schools thought it might be best to replace the old buildings with modern ones. According to one native Tijuana architect, "In those days, the thermal baths were still intact; the salons were intact, with their original decor—rugs, curtains, everything. But the complex was lapsing into a state of chaos. Some of the old casino buildings had been converted into classrooms. This was before the fire that destroyed most of the buildings. The director of our school was convinced that the Agua Caliente casino was shameful, and that all the casino buildings should be demolished and replaced with something modern."[49]

"The school was in the hands of nationalists who held the attitude left over from the Cárdenas period, the idea that the Casino should be destroyed, that it was a reminder of an unpleasant piece of Tijuana's history. What we didn't understand in that era was that the buildings weren't at fault for what had taken place in Tijuana's past; they were simply works of art. In an architectural sense, the Casino Agua Caliente had great value. The buildings were designed with conscience, with great attention to detail; they weren't imitations or caricatures. They had artistic and historic merit — they were part of Tijuana's essence — and to have destroyed them was to commit a grave sin against Tijuana architecture." [50]

The ruins are not without their folklore, even as they fall into greater disrepair. Among the celebrities who stayed at the private bungalow colony was a young dancer who became known as *La Faraona*. She was allegedly murdered by an ex-lover, and there are those in Tijuana who claim her ghost can be seen wandering through the bungalows at night today. "In those days, stories and rumors circulated among the students. The salons, with their original tapestries, curtains, and furniture, were protected by security guards. But sometimes, students would play hooky; they would go and hide. There were tunnels underneath the resort complex that supposedly went all the way to the border. Some of us went into the tunnels or the salons. There was talk among us about a dancer, a beautiful woman who had been killed back in the days of the casino, but who would reappear as a ghost. Sometimes, when we skipped school, to prove that we were brave, we had to sneak into the main salon where it was very dark, and suddenly, we'd go running out screaming, 'the ballerina, the ballerina.' We never saw her." [51]

Today, a gymnasium sits on the site of the former Salón de Oro, which was mostly destroyed in a fire in the 1970s. In the corner of the building, there is what looks like it may have been the vault: foot-thick masonry walls and the remains of a solid but worn steel door. Outside, on a patio, are crumbling walls with rounded columns. Most of the ruins are nearly gone, and even though they were designed and built by U.S. interests, some Tijuana historians bemoan the disappearance of this complex.

"We have a tendency to try to save our past in photographs," says a Tijuana historian. "We save our memories in photographs, in books, instead of actually taking care of the buildings." When he visited the grounds of the Agua Caliente resort, the historian was upset that some old bungalows were being rented to taco vendors, or that a major road was built through the complex grounds. "It's a disgrace," he noted. "Part of the *sanctum sanctorum* of the place, a priceless period in the history of this city turned into taco stands. And hundreds of plants began to die once the road was put in, because of the smog and contamination spewed daily by thousands of vehicles passing through. The thick vegetation of the place was destroyed. Thousands of birds used to gather there, but now you hardly see any." [52]

Agua Caliente, as its name implies, was a natural thermal water bathing site used as early as the 1880s, when a simple two-story wooden hotel was built on the site of the hot springs. Before the 1880s, when a settlement actually appeared in the area of what we today call Tijuana, this was just another small ranching village in the large valley cut by the river that swept from the mountains to the east toward the sea. Americans call that river the Tía Juana river today, and the variation in spelling hints at the identity crisis that has long been suffered by a city with only a wisp of history. Even the origins of the name Tijuana remain unclear. It may have come from several places: from an Indian tribe occupying the region and naming the place "ticuan," after a nearby mountain that they thought looked like a giant tortoise;[53] from another Indian word *teguana,* or "place without food" (because the landscape was so barren); or for a woman from Sonora who lived in the area at the turn of the century and ran a popular nightclub-restaurant, a woman whom everyone called *Tía* (Aunt) Juana.[59]

Whatever the origins of the town's nomenclature, the various explanations convey the early images of this region: flat grazing lands, upon which even the smallest mountain might have made an impact on the daily landscapes of indigenous peoples; or a woman of the turn-of-the-century wild frontier, who ran a saloon-restaurant in the tradition of the period of cattle ranchers whose small adobe or reed mat dwellings, surrounded by corrals of cows, dotted the arid landscape of the early 1900s.

The Emergence of a Border Town Landscape

Tijuana's appearance at the edge of Mexico's northwestern provinces coincided with Mexican president Porfirio Díaz's wishes to open his country to foreign investors and foreign trade. During the last two decades of the nineteenth century, American investors were encouraged to pump their dollars into areas south of the border. The first buildings thrown up in the town were those of a frontier ranching settlement coping with the new responsibility of being a gateway to one of the booming states of the American West—California.

In 1886, while Tijuana was still a ranching village, the first serious building appeared on the landscape, the Customs House (*aduana*). It was a simple adobe one-story structure, with a front porch. The facade consisted mostly of wall and few windows, leaving the impression that it was more of a fort than anything. It evoked the presence of the Mexican government and communicated the new control function of the boundary crossing. Its simple adobe construction looked much like the adobe Spanish-style structures in the original Mexican settlement in San Diego, twelve miles to the north, later called "Old Town." Its lonely, isolated appearance would very quickly be overshadowed by events soon to come.

With the exception of the customs building, the landscape of Tijuana in the last two decades of the nineteenth century was somewhat unexceptional. A reporter from *The Nation* arriving in town in the 1890s found some irony in coming across a restaurant called Delmonico's (at the time a swank steak house in New York City) adjacent to a cigar store named the Last Chance. His observations of the town suggested that "there are more cantinas in Tijuana than buildings, and the only Mexicans here are with ponchos and serapes. I told myself, 'my God, this is a desolate place.'"[55]

As Tijuana's population gradually expanded toward the turn of the century, the town that took shape was very much a carbon copy of dozens of other young western towns in the United States during that period, as well as mining and farming communities in northern Mexico. Buildings were constructed entirely of wood frame, a material not normally associated with Mexican architecture, which tended to favor adobe or stone. Wood-frame construction technology of the period involved building walls with slats of wood, and then raising the sides, front, and back of a building in a one-swoop action. Some of Tijuana's wooden structures were actually built in San Diego, then shipped in pieces across the border. In the 1880s and 1890s, Mexican store owners tried to "Mexicanize" their wooden buildings by hanging colorful *sarapes* (blankets) over the facades, or by rebuilding the roofs Mexican style.[56]

By the early 1890s, Tijuana was a small town with a customs house, post office, a market (the Mexican Bazaar), and a few other buildings housing small restaurants or stores. Photos from the period reveal a dusty, wide main street with a few wooden buildings with simple front porch overhangs that typified western United States settlements of the period. Most of the store names appeared in English. There were very few signature Mexican landscape elements, save the *sarapes* hanging from the odd storefront. With the arrival of the new century, little changed. One observer described Tijuana in the early 1900s as "a score of squalid, poverty-stricken native farmers."[57] Indeed the town was still dominated more by its ranching past than by any sense of an urban future.

The population of Tijuana at the turn of the century was less than three hundred, and the town still consisted of a few cantinas, a school, church, small military outpost, one block of stores (Second Street), and scattered cattle ranches on the outskirts of town. This was a time when the western frontier of North America was expanding, and small towns could easily be victimized by adventurers and thieves. If Tijuana was to bring more population into the region, and safeguard its well-being, apparently it would be necessary to build tourist-oriented enterprises: bars, cantinas, and the like. In the first and second decades of the new century, while Mexico as a nation was in the throes of a social revolution, the town experienced the first phase of its tourism expansion. A small hotel had been built near the Agua Caliente hot springs. Cantinas, bars, and restaurants began to be concentrated in the area of Avenue A, or what is Revolution Avenue today. This popular tourist corridor was lined with wooden one-

FIG. 3.6 Tijuana's early streetscapes were no different than those of other western frontier towns: wood-frame buildings with signs in English line dusty streets in Tijuana, 1907 (Bancroft Library).

and two-story buildings with striped awnings over the front porches and signs in large English letters, such as the Big Curio Store.

Meanwhile, to the west of the commercial zone, hidden behind the emerging tourism street, was a small, more serious and formal Mexican community that had been quietly evolving during this period. Here was an architecture that attempted to re-create the temperate, religious ways of the Mexican workers who lived off the activities of U.S. consumers. The landscape of the Mexican residential side of town consisted of a modest church, small primary school, the customs house, and a few wooden cottages painted white. A small residential enclave was beginning to evolve alongside the entertainment and commercial district. One historian describes the emerging townscape of Tijuana in 1915: "This quiet border town now offered a show that was animated by multicolored curiosity stores, inns, and other businesses that were frequented by tourists who now visited with regularity. It's thought that in these times, the number of inhabitants had reached 900." [58]

The neat separation between well-manicured Mexican residential town and wild, chaotic foreign tourism enclave was interrupted in 1915 when the first big casino in Tijuana was built on the corner of Second Avenue and Constitution, in the midst of where the Mexicans of Tijuana lived. The Casino Tijuana Fair was the first good example of Tijuana posing for America, Tijuana as a world's fair—a landscape for recreation, celebration, and advertising, an architecture of the carnival. The Tijuana Fair was epitomized by its entrance, a grandiose archway between two white towers, a gesture of invitation to pass into the interior. On top of each tower was a giant flag, Mexican on one side, American on the other. The fair coincided with the Panama Canal Exposition in San Diego in 1915; the celebration of the opening of the Panama Canal meant that San Diego's port would become more important; more people and more money would travel through the region, and there would be more attention paid to lands south of the border. The investors in the Tijuana Fair (supported by Colonel Esteban Cantú, the new governor of the Northern District of Baja California) received permission to allow gambling at the fair. It was believed that the fair could attract many of the Americans who came to San Diego to attend the Panama Canal Exhibition in Balboa Park. The fair offered boxing, gambling, cockfights, bullfights, and free barbecues. Besides the gambling casino, there was a nightclub featuring female models brought in from San Francisco.

The Casino Tijuana Fair closed down after only a few years. But Tijuana had gotten a taste of what might be done to attract U.S. dollars from north of the border. Tijuana discovered that its role might be to lure the American consumer to an exotic and foreign country only a short distance away. Ironically the site of the Tijuana Fair would later be converted into the Municipal Palace of the city of Tijuana, a formal, solemn, neocolonial building. But meanwhile, much of the city was to be converted into America's after-dark playground.

Sodom on the U.S. Frontier?

The experiment with the Tijuana Fair and its success in 1915 overlapped with changing social conditions in the United States in the second decade of the twentieth century. The United States was entering a period of moral reform, and the popular consensus was that society had to be cleansed. Boxing, horse racing, gambling, and alcohol consumption would soon be declared illegal. In 1919, the Volstead Act was approved by the U.S. Congress, and the sale of alcoholic beverages became illegal. Prohibition's impact spilled across the United States's southern borders, and nowhere was this felt more quickly than in Tijuana.

Just prior to its transformation, we can picture Tijuana as it was described in 1915: "a number of wooden stores, restaurants, and saloons, mostly one story, with a scattering of wooden bungalows, some neat and whitewashed on the side streets. All streets are dusty and often rutty and, in wet weather, very muddy but wide."[59] This image would shortly be shattered, when in 1915, a new governor, Esteban Cantú, arrived in Baja California's northern territory. Cantú was determined to lay the groundwork for the arrival of moneymaking businesses that were being prohibited north of the border: horse racing, gambling, drinking, prostitution, and drugs. It is easy in retrospect to adopt a moralist voice and criticize Cantú for allowing these vices into this ex–cattle ranching town. But Mexico was in the midst of a revolution that had thrown the nation into chaos. Towns and ranches in northern Mexico had been destroyed in battles between various factions of the revolution. An atmosphere of uncertainty pervaded the landscape. An anarchist movement headed by the Mexican Ricardo Flores Magón was brewing in Los Angeles. It was believed that an invasion of Baja California might provide a platform from which to launch a social revolution in Mexico.[60] In 1911, Flores Magón's Mexican Liberal Party seized Mexicali and Tecate, and a group from the Wobblies (nickname for the Industrial Workers of the World [IWW]), captured Tijuana. Unfortunately, newspaper coverage made the Flores Magón incident appear ridiculous. The siege of Tijuana lasted only a few days. Its leader fled, and others looted the town, including its numerous liquor stores, leaving a river of whiskey to flood the main street.

Mexicans had a name for the adventurers or mercenaries of the early twentieth century. They called them *filibusteros,* or filibusterers. In the aftermath of the attack of the *filibusteros,* and the success of the Tijuana Fair, Tijuana could hardly resist the business gains offered by conversion to an early-twentieth-century Las Vegas or Marrakesh. Tijuana's fate was decided from the national capital, Mexico City. In the second decade of the twentieth century, Mexican leaders in the national capital recognized gambling as a useful source of income along the northern border. The Mexican government wanted to minimize the evils linked to gambling—mainly prostitution and crime—but from their distant offices in the national capital, they did not experience border life firsthand.

One therefore has to take care in pinning the label of "immorality" upon Tijuana. After all, it's not as if Tijuana is the only city whose growth stemmed from the lure of underworld activities—New York, Chicago, San Francisco, Hollywood, and Las Vegas all at one time built up their economies as a result of illegal activities. Even San Diego, considered a relatively conservative town throughout much of its history, had a downtown district called the Stingaree, where crime and vice were probably worse than anything in Tijuana in the early twentieth century.

Between 1909 and 1911, an American businessman, John Spreckels, financed a railroad line connection from Yuma to San Diego, by way of Tecate and Tijuana. The Panama Canal Exposition of 1915 then turned the attention of Californians toward their vast neighbor south of the border. One of the first to jump on the bandwagon was James Coffroth, a boxing promoter from San Francisco, who in 1916 financed the building of Tijuana's first racetrack (Hipódromo), just south of the border crossing at San Ysidro, and east of the river. On the same day that the San Diego–Panama Canal Exhibition drew twenty thousand visitors to Balboa Park in San Diego, ten thousand spectators, including Charlie Chaplin and other Los Angeles celebrities, attended the opening festivities at the Tijuana racetrack. The racetrack quickly became a catalyst for the construction by a number of other North American investors of a separate, high-profile district east of the main town, a place where Hollywood stars, politicians, or sports figures could mingle with millionaires in a new tourist complex that included the racetrack, a huge, lavish, twenty-four-hour cabaret named the Monte Carlo, which one observer called "a great barn of a place," [61] and the restaurant-bar Sunset Inn. The three structures were connected by a railroad station and a covered wooden runway. So striking was this new consortium of the U.S.-style racetrack, gambling emporium, bar-restaurant, and wooden railway station that people began referring to the original part of Tijuana as "old town."

For about a decade and a half, from 1916 until the early 1930s, Tijuana's landscape of dusty streets and whitewashed wooden bungalows would be eclipsed by the arrival of everything prohibited north of the border. In a very short time, a 1920s gambling and drinking mecca arose on the banks of the Tía Juana river. Cabaret owners fleeing California's sudden moral renovation landed south of the border. Ex-boxing and -racetrack promoters soon joined them and formed the core of an American business group that choreographed the design of a gambling mecca. One consortium of former Bakersfield, California, saloon and brothel owners relocated to Tijuana, calling their new common business venture the ABW Corporation (named for the last names of Marvin Allen, Frank Beyer, and Carl Withington). Around the big investments, smaller operations — bars with prostitutes, opium dens, distilleries, wine and beer factories — would quickly appear. Some of these activities became so successful, they generated export activity. For example, the Bódegas de San Valentín winery, established in 1912, began with a capacity to produce 10,000 liters, but by the 1920s, it was producing 650,000 liters of muscatel, white, port, and vermouth.[62] The biggest boost came in 1919, after the U.S. Congress had approved the Volstead Act, prohibiting the sale and consumption of alcoholic beverages in the United States. On July 4, 1920, some 65,000 Americans in more than 1,300 vehicles crossed the border to celebrate Independence Day in Tijuana. Tijuana quickly ran out of gasoline, and many tourists spent the night; an estimated one million dollars was earned by businesses in Tijuana that day. This marked the beginning of a decade-long period of American tourist presence.[63]

Tijuana had everything you would expect of a bawdy Roaring Twenties town: elegant casinos, La Ballena (the whale), promoted as the world's longest bar, wineries, distilleries, and houses of prostitution. Tijuana had its Moulin Rouge, named after the famed Paris establishment. It sported a miniature red mill on its front roof, a lavish interior, and women of all races. The Moulin Rouge was typical of most of Tijuana's landscape of the 1920s: the glittery, lavish, red-light-district look. It was financed, owned, operated, and patronized principally by Americans. They constructed their playground on the edges of southern California, just beyond the reach of America's legal hold on the morality of the era.

If the architecture was temporary, it left long-lasting scars on Tijuana. It created an image of "sin city" that was resurrected by investors in the 1940s (when U.S. soldiers fighting in the Second World War came south of the border for rest and relaxation) and continued to plague Tijuana through the 1960s and 1970s. Tijuana *did,* of course, have a vibrant night life in the 1920s, with prostitutes, bars, and gambling casinos. But the force of this period has often been exaggerated by the U.S. media, leaving Mexicans to lament their city's "black history." We must not forget that Tijuana's expanding economic base, and its role as an evening entertainment center, was created *north* of the border. Much of its bad reputation was also created *north* of the border and exacerbated for years to come by the California press, particularly the Hearst, Spreckels, Otis-Chandler, and Copley newspapers. These papers fostered the notion that Tijuana was one big center of vice and sex, and that "all Mexican women are whores." In fact, 90 percent of all the prostitutes in Tijuana during the 1920s were non-Mexican.[64]

Still the stereotypes would prove amazingly resilient. Even as late as 1968, for example, a tourist guidebook for Americans included a section entitled "For Men Only" that grabbed the reader's attention with racy descriptions of "B-girl bars" in Tijuana's old red-light district, the Zona Norte: "The tables are crowded around a central stage. A ballring trio provides music for a steady stream of shapely dancers, who cha cha around the stage in various stages of undress, and frequently permit the show to be enlivened with what we will euphemistically call audience participation games."[65]

1920s Tijuana was filled with false references to famed exotic resorts from other parts of the world. The Moulin Rouge, mentioned above, was supposed to bring visions of Paris to the dusty landscape of the Mexican border. There was also a Hotel de Paris Cantina, bars called Tivoli or The Savoy. The United States was as much a part of the landscape as Mexico. The signs for "The Blue Fox Cafe" or "The Black Cat" were in large English words, with smaller Spanish words beneath. Images of the Wild West abounded in the signage, too, with names like "Klondike Saloon" or "Last Chance Bar," while Mexico was represented by "The Sonora" or "Bazar Mexicano."

By the late 1920s, Tijuana had become a Hollywood set, front and center on the stage of the northern border at the height of its tourism boom. Relegated to a back lot was the Mexican town, with its church, its school, its military

FIG. 3.7 Palatial concrete Jai Alai building displays Moorish touches, Tijuana.

headquarters, government palace, prim and proper park, two sedate movie theaters, and wooden cottages surrounding a typical Mexican *plaza*. Across the river to the east was the lavish gambling casino of Monte Carlo and its racetrack complex. Appended to the 1920s stage set were a number of scenographic-like buildings. The most important hotel of the era was the Hotel Comercial, a formal, neocolonial-looking structure, while nearby was Hotel Caesar's with its pseudocolonial facade, where famous bullfighters were said to stay. Tijuana had begun to craft itself as a caricature, made up for visitors.

The most monumental building in the old downtown was the Moorish-style Jai Alai Palace (corner of Revolution Avenue and Eighth Street), "palatial concrete rising majestically above the business center of Tijuana." [66] The Jai Alai Palace became the anchor on the south end of Revolution Avenue. Designed by San Diego architect Eugene Hoffman, the festive, Moorish-detailed structure was begun in 1926 but not actually completed and opened until 1945 (the Depression of the 1930s had a way of slowing things down). Its massive concrete walls owe less to the architect than to the fact that, at the time of construction, the owner of the building cut a deal with the government on a massive amount of cement left over from the construction of the Rodriguez Dam on the southeastern outskirts of Tijuana. The extra concrete was purchased at a bargain and used to build the Jai Alai structure.

Anchoring the northern end of Revolution Avenue was a 1929 building, El

FIG. 3.8 Teniente Guerrero Park, one of the traditional anchors of downtown Tijuana, with manicured hedges and well-groomed garden setting.

Banco Internacional (at the corner of Second and Revolution), originally the turn-of-the-century site of one of the town's first commercial establishments, The Big Curio Store. It would become one of the few early Tijuana neoclassical structures to be refurbished in the 1980s, with a handsome black marble base, pilasters and arch windows, finished exterior stone and plaster relief, including decorative cornices, spiral scrolling, and floral design around a large clock.

Several blocks east of Revolution Avenue a small slice of traditional Mexico was created in the 1920s—the Parque Teniente Guerrero—a well-manicured neighborhood park with a central kiosk, street vendors selling hot dogs and corn, and the quintessential wooden Mexican shoeshine stands. The park's creators wanted to honor one of Tijuana's army officers who had helped defend the city from the "filibuster" invaders of 1911.

Just east of downtown, on a hill, the city's first important school was built—the Escuela Álvaro Obregón, named after the Mexican president who was assassinated on the same day in 1930 that the building was inaugurated. The school featured a classical Greco-Roman- or Beaux Arts–inspired formal design, with a series of columns forming the building's facade—the kind often used in libraries, schools, and public buildings north of the border in the 1920s and 1930s. Indeed, the design of the original building in Tijuana was a copy of a school in Yuma, Arizona, with the exception that the Yuma school was of yellow brick and the Tijuana one of red brick.

But, of course, the Agua Caliente complex really dominated the city after 1927. It was the vision of Baron Long, a horse-racing promoter from Los Angeles who also owned the elegant U. S. Grant Hotel in San Diego. Long was among the many investors and builders who in 1920 fell in love with the myth of old Spain and old Mexico and wanted to "revive" their memories in the architecture of the 1920s on both sides of the border. Long told the architects he interviewed for the Agua Caliente project that he wanted it to look like an old mission. He ordered his workers to tear down the old wooden hotel, which had been built on the site of a natural hot springs, called the Tijuana Hot Springs Hotel, where Americans suffering from tuberculosis at the end of the nineteenth century had come to seek the curative powers of the earth's mineral-filled waters. When they were through yanking out the original buildings, all that was left were two sycamore trees standing at the main entrance. Now would come the palatial casino with its Arabian-like baths and swimming pool, a touch of paradise just south of the border. One of the impressive things about Agua Caliente was the natural landscaping, the rows of palm trees and other exotic tropical plants and the bright green lawns, all the work of a Mexican landscape expert, originally from Scotland, who had previously worked on one of the great urban parks in the West: Balboa Park, across the border in San Diego.

This was truly a bicultural architectural achievement. The funding of Agua Caliente was both American and Mexican, although it was presided over by the so-called border barons, Long and another shady businessman named Wirt Bowman. The land itself was owned by a Mexican, the governor of Baja California, Abelardo Rodríguez. The architects were American; the workers came from both sides of the border. The lumber came from a San Diego building supply company, custom tiles and appliances from northern California, and elegant decorative materials (carpets, tapestries, chandeliers, furniture) from Europe.

The complex was actually built in phases. The first phase, including the hotel, spa, and casino, cost three million dollars. The second phase saw the building of an Olympic-sized pool, golf courses, a greyhound track, an Islamic minaret, gardens with tropical birds, clinics, work areas, and an airstrip. The second phase also cost around three million dollars. Later, a new racetrack with a four-million-dollar price tag would be added to the complex. At its peak the hotel had five hundred rooms, while the twenty Spanish bungalows offered four apartments each.

Gambling was the main source of income at Agua Caliente. There were the main casinos, and then there was the Gold Room (Salón de Oro). Only high-stakes gamblers—aristocrats, tycoons, Hollywood stars, and gangsters—made

FIG. 3.9 Replica of the bell tower at Casino Agua Caliente, which, seen and heard by distant approaching vehicles, ushered in the automobile age in the 1920s.

it to the Gold Room. The room was designed to create a mood of gaudy, Old World, dark European opulence: rose brocaded drapes, long mirrors, tapestries, marble floors, a vaulted heavily decorated ceiling, stained glass, five large chandeliers, and Louis XV furniture. Images of Paris and Versailles were injected onto the Mexican frontier landscape. American gold pieces were used to bet, and the betting for the period was astronomical: $10,000 bets on one hand of cards, daily wins and losses of $100,000, and in one case, one person lost $6 million in three years.[67]

Outside, on the edge of the sprawling grounds, was Agua Caliente's great symbolic landmark: a tall bell tower that served as a reference point for automobiles. You could see the white-plaster, several-story-high tower from a distance. The ringing bells were supposed to re-create the sounds of the old missions. The past and the future were brought together here. The bells were there to recapture sounds of the past, but the tower was visually placed to serve the automobile. Tijuana was ushering in the era of the automobile city.

While Tijuana had grown beyond the dusty frontier town of the pre-1920 period, by the middle of the decade of the Roaring Twenties, it had not entirely overcome its image as a kind of Mexican version of a Wild West hick town. American writer Ring Lardner's description of Tijuana in 1926 was acerbic and to the point: "For the benefit of those that has not been there, I will state that Tijuana is a city of about 50 buildings of which 3 ain't saloons."[68] Syndicated columnist O. O. McIntyre visited Paris, Havana, and Tijuana in the late 1920s and, of the latter, wrote: "This town, so extravagantly headlined for wickedness, is a mixture of a street carnival in Circleville, Ohio, and a movie close-up of a western cowtown . . . The town sits in a bowl of sagebrush and cactus dotted hills. It has one big main street lined on either side with open fronted saloons and gambling halls."[69]

Tijuana's casino architecture era was spectacular; it put the Mexican border on the world map. But it was also short-lived. Ironically, just as the Agua Caliente phenomenon was surging, world events brought it to a stunning halt. In 1929, the stock market crashed. The beginning of the Depression in the United States meant that fewer dollars were available for leisurely spending. The wealthy Hollywood set would, at first, continue to come to Tijuana, and business remained strong at Agua Caliente and other casinos in the early years of the Depression. In fact, Tijuana's original racetrack closed down and was replaced by a new one at Agua Caliente (where the racetrack is still located today).

But Tijuana began feeling the effects of the Depression in ways that would forever reshape its built landscape. By the early 1930s, employees at the large casinos had begun to build a new residential area in the hills east of the Tia Juana River. They were part of a workers' movement that wanted to guarantee access for Mexicans in Tijuana to jobs that sometimes were being given to foreigners. They also wanted to establish territorial control over their rights as Mexicans to jobs, housing, and a place to live in Tijuana. The expression of their political will could be found in the new neighborhood they formed east of the river. They called it Colonia Libertad,[70] Freedom Neighborhood. It marks an important moment in the history of Tijuana's urban landscape. Up until then, Tijuana

had gone along with its destiny as a city built in the image of Americans: entertainment center, city of the evening. Tijuana allowed itself to be molded in the
image of a giant carnival; the small village near downtown where the workers
lived was just that—a village, outside the main path of urban life.

Now the citizens were taking back their city. They were lobbying for territorial control, for guaranteed jobs, for their rights as Mexicans. The first families
that started the Colonia Libertad neighborhood began by taking over a cluster of
unoccupied stables from the original Agua Caliente racetrack, which had been
abandoned and rebuilt on higher ground to the south. They were ordered out by
the government but held their ground, saying that their years of hard labor for
the racetrack merited that they be given these lands. They were supported by
other groups in Tijuana, and eventually the government backed off. On the site
of the original racetrack of Tijuana, the first independent community, the new
generation of border Mexicans, was formed.

When massive numbers of Mexicans working in the United States were deported back to Mexico, many sought refuge in Colonia Libertad, hoping to live
close to the border to get back across as soon as the crisis passed.[71] Colonia
Libertad became the first significant migrant community in the city, and it spread
quickly through the hills hugging the international border. It has remained a migrant passageway into the United States and a somewhat transient neighborhood
while, at the same time, increasingly becoming a stable community of middle-
and working-class Tijuana residents. Its one- and two-story, simple wooden or
stucco houses of red, pale blue, and other pastel shades sit on chaotically shaped
lots pointing in all directions, looking out over the valley of Tijuana today, testimony to the chaotic and spontaneous way in which millions of migrants have
reshaped life in the Tijuana metropolis.

The legacy of the 1920s—an entire city built by U.S. dollars on Mexican
soil in the interests of American consumers—can also be found in many of the
older neighborhoods around the original downtown business district. Just east
of Revolution Avenue is an old cluster of buildings surrounding the only downtown park, Parque Teniente Guerrero (Lt. Guerrero Park). Many of the homes
built here are "California style"—one-floor houses built of wood and stucco,
with sloped, red Spanish tile roofs, front porches, gardens, small backyards,
and garages. They are identical to their counterparts in older Mission Revival,
Spanish Colonial Revival, or bungalow-dominated neighborhoods north of the
border in southern California.

Yet another legacy of the 1920s and 1930s lies in the street grid that emerged in
that era in the downtown area. Whereas the original plan of Tijuana had been a
rectangular grid, crossed by major diagonal boulevards, the diagonals had all but
disappeared by the 1930s. Because the main downtown commercial zone had be-

come very crowded during the 1920s, with commercial uses occupying the main streets and residences on the back lots, a series of alleyways (*callejones*) evolved as a way for residents to reach their homes. The alleyways ran parallel to the major street grid and created a second world in the interstices of the major grid. The alleyways offered a kind of lively, intimate residential space within an expanding commercial city, as Tijuana would continue to grow in the next decades.

There were other incipient changes in the fabric of the cityscape. Although Tijuana was physically distant from the national capital and heartland of the nation in Mexico City, the coming of railroads and highways would usher in a new era of closer contact with the national government. The completion, in 1930, of another serious public structure—the Delegación del Gobierno (government delegation) building—symbolized Tijuana's emerging integration into Mexico. Soon, nationalistic President Lázaro Cárdenas's hand would be felt in Tijuana. The repeal of prohibition in the United States in 1933 led to the closing down of bars, distilleries, and wineries. Of one hundred bars, it was said that some sixty were closed by the repeal. When President Cárdenas declared gambling to be illegal in 1935, this effectively brought the operations of the remaining casinos to an end, including the Foreign Club and Agua Caliente (the latter, as mentioned, would become two schools). Speaking of this era one resident who had lived in Tijuana at the time said, "When the gambling ended, Tijuana became as lonely as a cemetery."[72]

But at the same time, the decline of 1935 offered a glimpse into the future. Only one week after the ban on gambling began, the Tijuana Chamber of Commerce reported that tourism on Revolution Avenue had returned to normal, even without the casinos. Boosters of the town saw that American tourists might be lured by the image of Tijuana as a place of gamblers, rebels, bandits, and lost treasures. In short, one could argue that in 1935 the "border town" legend began.

While the casino culture of Tijuana was winding down, a hint of the future emerged. By the early 1930s more retail and tourist commodities were being sold than ever before. Calle Segunda (Second Street) became a booming commercial street during this period, mainly due to the Mexican government's decision to create a legal mechanism to attract capital to the Tijuana region. In 1933, Mexico created the *perímetros libres*, or free perimeters, program, which allowed imports along the border duty-free. So while the manner in which money was earned changed, it was still mostly money from north of the border, and the cityscape reflected that.

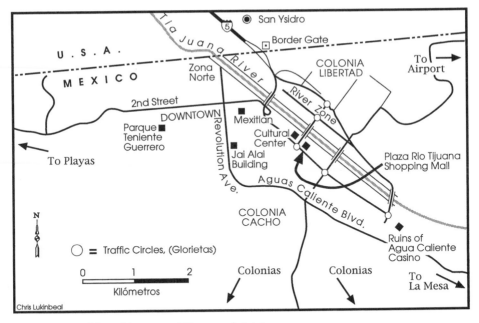

FIG. 3.10 Map of downtown Tijuana and vicinity.

Modern Border Architecture, 1940–1980

By the 1940s, Tijuana had settled into being a small border town of some twenty or thirty thousand inhabitants. The days of grand casinos were past. Cattle grazed on what had been the Agua Caliente golf course. Revolution Avenue more often than not looked like a ghost town, with no bandanas flying and little if any beer flowing in the bars. Most of Tijuana's residents chose not to live along the avenue.

But history would not let the memory of the Roaring Twenties rest in peace. Although a small manufacturing economy was beginning to emerge here, World War II resurrected Tijuana's wild side, bringing waves of U.S. military service personnel through San Diego on their way to the Pacific theater. The soldiers were lured by the legendary glitz of the 1920s and early 1930s as they crossed the border into Tijuana searching for excitement. Tijuana's entrepreneurs, seizing the obvious market opportunity staring them in the face as the great parade of American military personnel headed west via San Diego–Tijuana, quickly adapted to the new market. The city began to reinvent itself for the American GIs. So Tijuana's reincarnation of its 1920s "golden years of tourism" occurred at the height of the century's second great war, being fought on other continents, far away. Tijuana would put itself on the map again; it would be a place that many thousands of American military personnel would remember for the rest of their lives: the place in exotic Mexico they visited on their way to the war.

One place that symbolized Tijuana's 1940s incarnation was what became called the *zona norte*, the modern-day red-light district. Zona Norte would form in the 1950s, as clubs were gradually pushed to the northern end of Revolution Avenue, to clear the way for more family-oriented tourist establishments. What

FIG. 3.11 Sexual border landscapes: reference to the exotic Orient in Zona Norte, Tijuana's red-light district.

the American GIs or aircraft workers probably remember were the dark speakeasies with familiar names like the Chicago Club or Brooklyn Club. The bars
they attended sat mainly in squat two-story buildings in the zone wedged between downtown and the border, where the streets were alive with pedestrians,
vendors standing by their carts, and drug dealers. It was not unlike New York's
Forty-second Street. In fact, so alarmed were San Diego citizens about the *zona
norte* that, in the 1950s, a campaign arose to restrict the entry of U.S. minors
to Tijuana, where San Diegans were convinced over three thousand prostitutes
operated, alongside marijuana peddlers, pornography shows, abortionists, and
bars that sold alcohol to minors.[73]

While American GIs were busy in the *zona norte*, Tijuana was also beginning
to feel the impact of national expansion and modernization. A rail service now
connected Baja California to the state of Sonora to the east, and thus to the
national rail network. The Mexican government had signed a treaty with the
U.S. government in 1942 creating the *bracero* program, which legally permitted
Mexican agricultural workers to fill jobs north of the border. As hundreds of
thousands of Mexican workers traveled north to California and other western
states, they passed through Tijuana. Some would eventually return to settle here.

Over the next several decades, Tijuana's population would begin to grow
at astonishingly high rates—from 4 to 8 percent per year, according to most
reliable estimates—making it one of the fastest-growing cities in the Western
Hemisphere. From 1950 to 1990, its population would increase from 65,000 to
nearly 2 million.[74]

The postwar expansion of Tijuana in the 1950s was typified by some of the
new communities forming on the southern edges of town. One salient example
was a neighborhood called Cacho, where Mexicans proudly began to build a
permanent neighborhood, typically Mexican but also influenced by the United
States. Even today, the neighborhood has retained its pedestrian 1950s feel: the
corner stores, the patios, and porches that once faced the street (but increasingly
lie behind fences and walls), the sidewalks. Later development would unfortunately drive homeowners up into the hills, leaving their older homes in various
states of decline. Still, many of the fine homes were preserved and offer a sample
of 1950s Mexican functionalist modern architecture. The Casa Walícias, a large,
white, dignified structure, was built in 1952 on Aguas Calientes Boulevard; the
rotunda-shaped house belonged to a wealthy Tijuana family of the era and reflected a blend of international design trends of the era: Frank Lloyd Wright's
horizontalism, German Expressionism, Le Corbusier. It has tremendous presence, the kind of building you imagine housing an embassy.

The Cacho neighborhood has elegant street corners (*las esquinas de Cacho*),
where the biggest and most interesting homes were built on the larger lots at

FIG. 3.12 International architectural styles arrived in Tijuana in the 1950s: the Casa Walícias shows evidence of Frank Lloyd Wright's horizontalism and Le Corbusier's simple, white box modernism (J. Ozorno).

street intersections. These houses share a number of attributes: inclined, angular roofs, balconies, porticos, and columns. Some have large bay windows and stone walls. There are Spanish Colonial Revival–style houses, whose designs were copied from prevailing examples in Los Angeles and San Diego. Nearby is the original Plaza de Toros (bullring) of Tijuana, a great steel engineering feat of the late 1940s, painted fire-engine red. Also nearby is a fine church, the Iglesia del Carmen, whose elliptical roof brings to mind the parabolic designs of contemporary Mexico City architect Felix Candela.

In addition to growing toward the hills to the south, the city also extended its settled boundaries to the east in the 1950s to middle-class homes along Agua Caliente Boulevard in a new community called La Mesa. But, as more and more poor Mexicans from the interior arrived in Tijuana, many were also forced to squat on undesirable land outside the city proper. One important settlement occurred in the bed of the Tía Juana River as it passed alongside the downtown. The area was called Cartolándia because many of the shacks were originally built of nothing more than cardboard.[75] Mixed with small family cottages and small manufacturers or artisans was an underworld of smugglers, thieves, drug dealers, pimps, and prostitutes—again, a post–World War II re-creation of the

FIG. 3.13 A 1950s functionalist residence: house on a street corner in Colonia Cacho, Tijuana (J. Ozorno).

1920s legacy of Tijuana, but re-created within the social realities of contemporary urban Mexico: large cities with growing populations of poor migrants from farms who squat on unwanted land in flood-prone riverbeds, or steep sloping hillsides, or on flatlands miles from downtown. They would call them *favelas* on the hills of Rio de Janeiro or *pueblos jovenes* (young towns) in the dusty fields outside of Lima, Peru; in Tijuana, it was Cartolándia—Cardboard Land.

Tijuana's landscape in the modern era has become much more complex. As Mexico expanded its role in the world economy in the 1960s, distant cities like Tijuana begin to become more integrated into Mexican culture—in such areas as art and architecture. As a nation, Mexico was experimenting with rich and varied architectural forms; its cities began to reflect that. Neighborhoods were filled with buildings that emphasized simple functional styles in the form of schools, hospitals, and office buildings. There were also more grandiose designs from international architecture in the form of elegant high-rise glass towers and skyscrapers, or lavish private residences with modern, horizontal forms and generous amounts of masonry and stone. Tijuana, once a town of only wooden buildings, was notable in the post-1960 period for its transition toward the more Mexican style of building with natural stone or industrialized cement. Observers began to notice that Tijuana was more than a dusty border town, and that its landscape was distinctly different from that of San Diego. In Tijuana, one found bold color, bold form, exterior murals, and, frequently, aesthetic surprise. Said one writer: "The stone walls of Tijuana are without a doubt the finest sights to be seen in town."[76] As the 1960s unfolded, more and more new designs began to appear on the Tijuana cityscape: buildings with strange geometries: steep angles, circular and elliptical shapes. The trend continued over the next three decades.

The arrival of modern Mexican architecture on Tijuana's public landscape came in 1965, with the commission of a new public building—the border-crossing facility, or Puerta de Mexico ("door" or port of Mexico), designed by Antonio Bermudez. It has been described as a "capricious border funnel intriguing as a nautilus chamber."[77] As the modern period unfolded, the city's landscape seemed polarized between two extremes: On the one hand, there was no denying the presence of U.S. culture—in everything from the 1930s and 1940s wooden California-style bungalows and small cottages imported into the area west of downtown to shopping mall architecture, strip commercial development, the urban signage (typically in English), or the increasing orientation of the city toward the automobile. On the other hand, there were many emerging Mexican elements woven into the physical and visual experience of Tijuana: from the streets designed on a vastly more pedestrian scale to the existence of the *glorietas* (traffic circles), the public monuments, the bullrings, open plazas, and increasing use of murals on the facades of buildings.

Most of what was or is built in Tijuana comes either from the United States or from deep in Mexico's interior. There is unquestionably something unique about the flavor of border towns like Tijuana. The very fact of being a border town has created a unique culture and history, and these *are* reflected in the built environment. It is also true that the cityscape is still in the process of forming. As one designer told me, "Architecturally speaking, Tijuana is pregnant. We still don't know what the urban landscape is going to look like in the near future."[78] The passing of recent decades has seen the 1920s tourism street scene recast in a new mold: serious, modernist, and international. Concrete highways, shopping malls, and industrial parks arrived. The old Tijuana is nearly extinct, the sex shows in dark Latin speakeasies relegated to a back lot—the *zona norte*—of the downtown.

To find the essence of Tijuana's modern landscape, you must find the *zona del Rio,* the River Zone. Once this was where poor squatters built cardboard shacks, under the old Puente Mexico, the Mexican bridge that had allowed Americans to cross the river to get to the racetrack and gambling casinos in the Roaring Twenties. But in the 1970s the Mexican government decided to reclaim this land by building a concrete channel that would control the floodwaters of the Tía Juana River and free up adjacent lands for the development of a new high-density

FIG. 3.14 Abstract monument anchors a traffic circle in Tijuana's River Zone. The monument symbolizes two cultures—European and indigenous—coming together in Mexico's *mestizo* heritage. Locals refer to it as *la tijera*—the scissors.

downtown. Today the River Zone is the shining triumph of modern technocrats and planners. It is a linear corridor broken only by the *glorietas*. The *glorietas* fling traffic around the streets lined with shopping centers, office building complexes, hotels, and restaurants. The River Zone is high tech. It has international-style glass-box office buildings in the four-to-eight-story mode. It is the quintessential zone of Le Corbusier's "machine age" metropolis, oriented to the car. The decor is for viewing from the car—for example, the tall monuments that anchor each *glorieta* in succession: the high-tech abstract M sculpture (two arms, one white, one brown, cross at the base to symbolize Mexico's "mestizo heritage"), the giant bronze 6½-ton statue of Aztec leader Cuauhtemoc, the statue of Abraham Lincoln. Pedestrians find it difficult to circulate within the River Zone. At the Lincoln *glorieta*, one slice of the new Tijuana comes into focus. Three buildings surround the *glorieta*. On the southeast corner is a sheer wall with a slit for an opening, shaded in blue. It is the facade of a failed discotheque called Heaven and Hell. Across the street on the northeast corner is another discotheque called Baby Rock, which offers the observer a series of large rocks mounted to form walls, giving the feeling of entering some great mountain cave, or some walled citadel, the citadel of Tijuana's new evening life of discos. West across the street on the third important corner lies a restaurant and night club called Guadalajara Grill, a pink, pseudo-colonial building, created mainly to give foreigners some sense of authenticity, even though the architecture is at the same time patently inauthentic, leading one Mexican architect to call it "Mexican post-modern."[79] Here is the Tijuana of high tech, the Tijuana of disco-thec. At the nearby Cultural Center a sign announces that the Rolling Stones are playing in a film.

Most of the contemporary architecture of the 1980s lies in the River Zone. The most striking addition to the cityscape is the Centro Cultural de Tijuana (CECUT) complex, notable for a sandstone-colored spherical element that stands out against an L-shaped companion building. CECUT, like some extraterrestrial orb set gently on the river plain against the chaotic backdrop of overdeveloped hills, was completed in 1982. Townspeople affectionately call it "*la bola*" (the ball). CECUT sits in a great outdoor plaza, and one has the feeling of the earth (the sphere) gently resting in two hands.

Nearby are modern glass office buildings of varied shape and form, some ugly, some ordinary, a few outstanding. The hulking, somewhat dull black crystal box in the center of the River Zone is the ASEMEX (Aseguradora de Mexico, an insurance company) building. Nearby is Bancomer, a miniaturized copy of a Mexico City–based bank (several buildings here are copies of larger Mexico City ones). The Banco Internacional has a three-story-high triangular-shaped glass facade. The architect, Luis Licéaga, who designed the gray Torremól high-rise office structure adjacent to the CECUT building, says he tried to design a modern

FIG. 3.15 A haunting tribute to Mexico's mystical search for meaning in the past: the Cultural Center of Tijuana.

skyscraper using the elements of a traditional colonial church: base, tower, and windows. A great cathedral window in the tower part of the building "turns" to face the street corner it lies on. The tallest modern skyscraper in the River Zone is the Twin Tower of Agua Caliente complex, which houses offices and a hotel.

The River Zone is noteworthy also for its array of new shopping centers. Most well known is the Plaza Río Tijuana, an unpretentious and somewhat conventional U.S.-style outdoor regional shopping mall. Nearby are two shopping centers designed to look like colonial Mexican towns: Plaza Fiesta and Pueblo Amigo, with their lanterns hanging above old wooden doors, second-floor balconies with iron railings, and courtyards with public fountains. Their stucco comes brightly painted in lime greens and pink pastels.

The newest section of Tijuana is the beach community of Playas de Tijuana, which from a distance could be mistaken for an Italian coastal resort, with white-stucco and red-tile-roofed houses cascading down the hills toward the azure Pacific Ocean. Here lies Tijuana's famed bullring-by-the-sea, La Monumental de Playas, a massive structure of exposed concrete built in 1962. Strangely, the designers did not think to pry open the bullring structure, so that the ocean that lies a few blocks away could be seen from inside, not to mention the light at sunset. Where southern California cities tend to be oriented toward the coastline, curiously, Tijuana did not develop its beach area until the 1970s and 1980s. The city's history has been tied to its proximity to the border crossing. Only as the city expanded and needed more flatland for growth did the beach zone capture the attention of developers and the government as an area for urban expansion.

Revolution Avenue was modernized and widened in the early 1980s, paving the way for a wild mix of stores both along the street and in its numerous arcades and interior shopping spaces (*galerías*). At the north end of Revolution, Zona Norte, remains the once legendary red-light district, with its seedy nightclubs and the flophouses that poor Mexican immigrants sometimes stay in for a night or two before heading across the border to find work. Just north of the North Zone is the international boundary, replete with a new metallic wall, completed recently by the U.S. Army Corps of Engineers. The wall is built of recycled landing mats acquired from the U.S. armed forces from various former combat areas around the world. It is a sobering reminder of the relations between Mexico and the United States—a dull gray barrier to the north. Residents of Tijuana are gradually covering its miles of length with murals and graffiti, including one that questions the wall's presence in Tijuana: "*Si él de Berlín cayó, él de Tijuana, porqué no?*" (If the Berlin one came down, why not the one in Tijuana?).

Reflections on Tijuana and the Mexican Border

Tijuana is not unique among Mexican border towns. The basic elements of Tijuana's early evolution—its dependence on U.S. capital, its tourism-oriented landscape, and its red-light district—are replicated in most of the other major border towns. Obviously there are regional variations on the theme of U.S. dependency, but the reality of transfrontier linkages remains consistent. Tijuana, it might be argued, offers a more dramatic example of a process of landscape transformation that is affecting all of Mexico's northern border. Equally, the examples of Tijuana's gradual embrace of more Mexican landscapes—in its public buildings, its formal architecture in the modern era, and, of course, in the ubiquitous squatter phenomenon of recent decades—is also matched in the experience of all Mexican cities along the border. Finally, the 1980s period of global markets and Mexican economic integration with the United States, leading to the 1992 signing of NAFTA, has affected all the Mexican border cities. The border cities cannot remain solely linked to central Mexico. The pressure to become more connected to the transnational economy and culture of North America will grow. The contrast between south and north, between Mexico and the United States—so essential to what makes the border landscape unique—will face new challenges from the transcultural processes of economic integration.

In the 1980s, Mexican border cities began to take control of their destiny. While Mexico's economy sputtered, border cities prospered. *Maquiladoras* (assembly plants) attracted U.S., Japanese, Korean, and other foreign investors.

FIG. 3.16 Landscape of spontaneous urbanism: Migrants build makeshift shacks on the outskirts of Mexican border cities.

The incredible growth of the *maquila* sector invigorated the border construction industry, especially in cities like Tijuana, Ciudad Juárez, and Matamoros. Despite Mexico's economic crisis of the early 1980s, the international assembly plants kept the border economy booming. The resulting landscapes of Tijuana and other border cities reflect this: waves of modern hotels, shopping centers, housing projects, and industrial parks.

"Our *maquiladoras* remind us of the nineteenth-century technology of Eiffel," noted one Mexican architect, who now lives in the interior. "They too arrive in pieces, and then get assembled. I don't think we've taken full advantage of *maquiladora* technology. We could be using assembly techniques to build schools, libraries, health centers, fire stations, all metallic industrial structures. We could be recycling. In Los Angeles, Frank Gehry has shown us that good design can be done with scrap materials." [80]

The assembly plant embodies the architecture of what has come to be called the "global factory." Like every Third World assembly operation, Tijuana and other border towns' *maquilas* are the new shop floor of the age of transnational manufacturing. Once, assembly operations were carried out in factory towns built around the mother companies, in Schenectady or East Lansing or Tokyo. Today, cheap labor has brought the company town to the Third World, to the

Mexican border. Some *maquiladoras* in the border towns are hastily and cheaply built concrete shells, many without windows. The workers (mostly women) can be seen wearing the faded blue uniforms of the global labor force. Even the newer sleek glass structures are impersonal and anonymous. They are not Mexican.

The population of many border cities—Tijuana, Mexicali, Juárez, Matamoros, Nogales—exploded in the 1980s. The only ones who seemed to doubt the fact that it was one of the fastest-growing regions on the continent were Mexican government officials. Their 1990 census grossly undercounted border city populations, due in part to their ignoring the large squatter communities not recognized on government maps. For example, the Mexican government estimated the Tijuana population at below one million in 1990; it was probably 50 percent higher. The city will probably surpass two million inhabitants by the end of the century.

Migrants from southern Mexico continue to move north to the border cities. Here, they build their makeshift shacks; the *colonias* are spreading. In Tijuana, they rise up along mountainous terrain to the east of the city. Theirs is not architecture from the drafting table but from the kitchen table, an architecture of survival. On steep sloping hills, poor migrants from Mexico's interior discovered ways to stabilize the land by constructing terraces of recycled American tires, bought cheaply in large quantities by wholesalers. They've learned the art

FIG. 3.17 *Colonias* sprawl up the mountainside on the eastern edge of Tijuana.

of recycling. The junkyard is a primary commercial establishment in the outer-lying communities of the Mexican border. Makeshift houses begin as a tent of plastic or cardboard. The important thing is to establish tenancy on a parcel of land. Later, as income is found, plastic shacks become small cottages of scrap wood and metal, and these in turn may be rebuilt as small pillbox structures of cement block.

In the early 1990s, while southern California was mired in a recession, Tijuana and other Mexican border cities enjoyed a continued growth surge. In the wealthier sections of Tijuana—like the River Zone—a glitzy city of night-life emerged. Dozens of new discotheques were built, many boasting high-tech glass facades, waterfalls, and lush vegetation. One disco looked like the entrance to a Roman temple. The idea was to appeal to wealthy Mexican teenagers and to young Americans. Both groups may have similar disco fantasies, since they watch the same television programs and listen to the same radio stations. Beyond the discos were the new high-rise glass towers, chic boutiques, and international restaurants, postmodern shopping centers, and elegant condominiums with balconies high above the Tía Juana River. The old city was sliding to the side, the "B-girl bars" and the exotic clubs that used to show French movies had been erased in a building frenzy of factories, condos, and shopping malls draped Corbusian-like around well-landscaped four-lane highways, with neatly spaced traffic circles and stately public art.

What all this implies for border urban landscapes can be summarized by one Mexican's comments on the future of Tijuana: "Right now, cities like Tijuana have to be more concerned about what to do with their vacant land, than about becoming beautiful. In Mexico we are growing so fast that, over the next ten years, we will have to build, in square meters, the equivalent of what we built the last five hundred years since the Conquest."[81]

FOUR

El Otro Lado

In Search of Mexican Landscapes in the Southwestern United States

The average person in southern California doesn't know what Mexican architecture is. It's like putting jack cheese on something and calling it "Mexican food." There's no jack cheese in Mexico. The same thing happens with architecture. Americans create what they call "Mexican" architecture. That's what they like. That's what they get.   —MANUEL ROSEN

Mexico's cultural expression in the built environment does not end at the northern edge of its national territory. It spills across the international boundary with the United States and is deeply embedded in the region sometimes referred to as the "Hispanic southwest." The Southwest was once located entirely within Mexican territory. Its heritage is strongly tied to a Mexican and indigenous past.

But the Southwest has also been dramatically transformed over the last century and a half. Following the Treaty of Guadalupe Hidalgo (1848), which created the present-day U.S.-Mexico international boundary, industrialization and urban growth spread across the mountains and desert landscapes of the Southwest. During the second half of the twentieth century, there has been massive urban growth in the desert valleys of Phoenix, Albuquerque, Tucson, and El Paso, in the lower Rio Grande/south Texas region, in central Texas and along its Gulf coast, and on the California–Baja California border. Along with the huge, sprawling cities have come military installations, railroads, interstate freeways, mining operations, and tourists, feeding out of the cities and into the wilderness areas. This massive deployment of economic infrastructure and modernization has permanently altered the cultural landscape of the Southwest. It is not easy to find, amidst all the new development, evidence of Mexican influence on architecture and place identity in the region. This chapter seeks to explore some of the disappearing slices as well as the new forms of Mexican identity in the southwestern cultural landscape.

The Idea of Regionalism

On the United States' side of the international border with Mexico, the region called the Hispanic southwest—generally the four major border states of Texas, Arizona, New Mexico, and California[1]—is for most observers a recognizable cultural region and place. Its identity springs from a combination of ecological factors (semiarid desert in "basin and range" topography) and cultural ones (indigenous origins of Anasazi/Pueblo, northern Mexican Yaqui and Tarahumara, Apache, and Navajo, followed by Spanish colonization). Despite the strong forces of the region's geography and the dual influences of Indian and Spanish culture, southwestern border regionalism has been difficult to define.[2] In architecture, recognition of the Spanish southwest as a distinct place has been slow to materialize. Mexico is often left entirely out of textbooks on American architecture. Until recently, the Southwest was also regarded as a relatively marginal part of the story of American architecture, with the possible exception of recognition given to the early Pueblo and Anasazi periods.[3] Professionally, there has been a lot of criticism of the way Pueblo architecture has been caricatured and badly reinterpreted in some of the modern Spanish Pueblo-style architecture of the Southwest, particularly in New Mexico. Yet, residents of the Southwest have shown that they are emotionally attached to this architectural style.[4] More recently, possibly due to the NAFTA, there has been a notable surge of national interest in architecture and design in the southwestern region.[5]

Yet architects themselves have been skeptical of this kind of regional design because they fear any association with the commercialism and oversimplification that often goes into mass marketing of "southwestern style" in architecture, interior design, or furniture. Such thinking is revealed in an interview with one of the Southwest's leading architects, Antoine Predock of Albuquerque, New Mexico. When asked about southwestern regionalism, Predock could only name the "laser quality" of light as a regional element influencing his work. He made clear his concerns on the subject: "Discussions about regionalism are suspect; regionalism is not a word that belongs in an architectural lexicon. It is a highly

FIG. 4.1 Contemporary southwestern architecture is oriented toward its desert setting: Nelson Fine Arts Building, Arizona State University, Tempe, Arizona, designed by
Antoine Predock.

negative term, an inappropriate term to characterize architecture and art . . . I
want to dwell in other places. I want to dwell in magical places, places of illumination and mystery. I don't want to be a regionalist. I don't want to be obsessed
with reinterpretation. I want to be more of a flyer than that." [6]

Spain and Urban Design in the Americas

No matter how far a designer "flies," no matter how much one tries to transcend
the region just north of Mexico, there is no getting away from its past. To understand the southwestern region of the United States one must explore the connection between Spanish/Mexican culture and the making of urban landscapes. [7]

To understand how Spanish architecture was transplanted onto the North
American continent, we have to travel back to the sixteenth century. The Spanish
empire had reached its zenith in wealth and power and was busy setting up colonization efforts across the Atlantic Ocean in the Americas. The Spanish royal

family left no stone unturned in deciding how, where, and in what capacity the New World would be settled. The Laws of the Indies were the most detailed administrative guidelines given by any mother country to its wandering colonizers who would settle upon the unknown frontiers of the world across the sea. The imperial system that Spain imposed upon the New World—a rigid set of codes and a top-down administrative hierarchy in which all power emanated from the king and his appointed viceroys—left little room for local improvisation.

This was especially true in the design of towns in the New World. King Philip II laid out detailed plans for the colonies in his 1573 Royal Ordinances for the Laying Out of New Towns. Philip was known to highly value Roman town planning, not surprising since much of Spain had been part of the Roman Empire before it was conquered by the Moors. King Philip was said to have also admired Vitruvius's *Ten Books on Architecture*, along with the block designs of Roman military towns and the gridiron designs of Italian architect Alberti. All this is reflected in the amazingly precise Royal Ordinances of 1573. The new settlers of the Americas were instructed not only on how to select a site for a town (elevation, land fertility, and availability of water were key criteria) but also on where to build the central square, or *plaza,* and how to align the rectangular street system around it (the four principal streets were to lead outward from the center of each side of the rectangular *plaza,* whose four points would be oriented toward the cardinal points of the compass). The *plazas* would be surrounded by buildings with arcades. A town hall and church would locate on or near the main square. Settlers would build uniform structures on plots of land whose proximity to the all-important *plaza* would be determined through a lottery system.

The first detailed European designs in Mexico and parts of the southwestern United States came from a Spanish king who had been fascinated by Roman gridiron towns. Thus, sixteenth- and seventeenth-century Spanish/Mexican colonial towns physically embodied the social and political realities of the era through the physical design of their living spaces.[8] Two forces controlled the lives of those who braved the New World: the Spanish monarchy and the church. The towns revolved around the main squares, and on these squares stood the symbols of authority—the government palace (or town hall), through which the power of the king was communicated, and the church, which constituted the second social force. The wealthiest citizens of Spanish colonial towns lived closest to the center of the town. They did this for practical reasons (it was nearer to the armory and to food supplies, and therefore safer during attacks) but also because it was considered more prestigious to live close to the center of colonial life.

Being one of the richest nations in the world, Spain and the monarchy of the fifteenth and sixteenth centuries were heavily invested in architecture. Strangely, Spain itself had been a melting pot of cultural influences before the 1500s; these were most visible in their variable impact on the built landscape of Spanish towns: Roman aqueducts and bridges, Moorish palaces and mosques, Romanesque churches, and Gothic cathedrals. Yet by the time Spain began contemplating colonies across the Atlantic, it had begun to develop its own architecture styles, notably the ornate Plateresque, and later the baroque Churrigueresque with its twisted columns and decorative palace and church entrances. This newly discovered autonomy of purpose is reflected in the absolute precision of the directions Philip II gave to his colonial town builders in the Americas.

Spain's impact on the design of buildings in Mexico takes form in walled monasteries, decorative Plateresque palaces, and Baroque and Churrigueresque cathedrals.[9] While Spain was busy in the colonial New World constructing gridiron towns built around carefully laid-out public squares, or *zocalos,* it was also erecting uniformly styled buildings that would remain as symbols of this period, and landmark buildings for centuries to come. It is noteworthy that some of the impressive buildings of the early colonial period were built by indentured indigenous people under the instructions of Franciscan, Dominican, or even Jesuit priests. The first great buildings of the era were fortresslike monasteries with thick walls to shield against invasion. The monasteries, like their European predecessors, were towns unto themselves, with apartments, inner patios, and cloisters that served as schools, libraries, hospitals, and living quarters for the friars, and had arcaded courtyards with lush vegetation.

In opposition to these were the sumptuous Plateresque palaces. If the New World priests believed that the hardships of colonization in the harsh frontier territories merited austere religious buildings, the new Spanish colonial aristocracy did not necessarily follow suit. The viceroys, governors, and provincial captains favored elaborate residential buildings, literally palaces, like the great Cortes Palace built in the town of Cuernavaca, on the outskirts of Mexico City. In fact, early in the settlement of Mexico City, the aristocrats were said to be embarrassed by the simple gray cathedral that sat on the main square, or Plaza Mayor. One wealthy resident remarked: "It is deplorable in a city of such renown, whose equal I do not know, with so many wealthy citizens, that there has been erected here for all to behold a church so small, so humble, and so lacking in adornment."[10] Cortes had become one of the richest colonists, and perhaps one of the wealthiest Spanish men in the world at the time,[11] mainly through tributes paid to him by Indian slave farmers, as well as the mines, livestock, and sugar mills he owned. Cortes had previously constructed an elaborate royal palace in the former palace of an Aztec nobleman in Mexico City.

The Legacy of Spain on the New Continent

In 1565, Spain founded the city of St. Augustine, Florida, the first Spanish city in what would become the United States more than two centuries later. St. Augustine epitomizes the traditions of Spain transplanted onto the wild, untamed landscape of the peninsula called Florida. The city was built as a strong base on the east coast of the Americas to protect Spanish treasure ships of the sixteenth century and to launch counterattacks against pirate ships that roamed the Caribbean. The city served the interests of Spanish royal planners. It encapsulated the three functions that the royal family intended for its colonial towns in the Americas: military garrison (*presidio*), civil settlement (*pueblo*), and religious center for conversion of Indians to Christianity (*misión*). The design of the city followed the uniform format that had been decreed by the Spanish king: plaza and gridiron street plan.

Across the continent, in the mountains of present-day New Mexico, in 1609 a group of Franciscan missionaries founded the first important Spanish colonial city in the southwestern United States at Santa Fe. Its early design revealed that in the desert Southwest, the architecture would be austere and rough as fits the desert region, but also quintessentially Spanish. The combination of the vernacular (adobe structures)—built by Indian labor using local materials and tied to local ecological conditions—with Spanish ideas and building methods made for the evolution of a unique regional style of architecture.

One has to remember that the Pueblo (Anasazi) culture produced the most notable layer of permanent townscapes prior to the arrival of the Spanish colonists. The Pueblos built their cities in the midst of a vast, silent, and very spiritual setting, or what one observer termed "the empty soul of the Great American desert."[12] Their buildings epitomize the ecological meaning of *organic*. Many were literally built into canyons and mountainsides, "a labyrinth of communicating cells, a galaxy of circular pits."[13] The great cliff dwellings at Mesa Verde were striking cells of circular and rectangular form built into the cliffs of a mesa in a dramatic, almost theatrical way that a contemporary Western architect would find difficult to re-create.

Like its counterparts of indigenous architecture farther south, Pueblo architecture does not draw its inspiration from the efficiency models of later European cultures. Pueblo buildings were designed to connect humans with higher spiritual forces. The sunken residential spaces and the ceremonial *kiva* speak to the ancient Anasazi belief in a spiritual underworld, and the need for an architecture that connects with it. The open squares in Pueblo towns were not enclosed by walls and buildings, excluding the outer world, as did European squares of the era. The plazas of the Anasazi suggested an intersection of vistas—a bring-

FIG. 4.2 Anasazi/Pueblo adobe terraced landscape: Taos pueblo, New Mexico.

ing together of the surrounding mountain and desert landscapes within a single sacred place in the settlement.[14]

Adobe and sandstone were the primary materials used by Anasazi builders. Adobe, a material composed of sand and clay, was essential to the Pueblo culture, and it has continued to influence the traditional cultural landscapes of the Southwest. It is a central feature of New Mexican, Arizona, and parts of the traditional California architecture. Few ancient buildings remain in the region, however, because of adobe's inherent vulnerability to the elements. Its greatest strength—being organic—is also its biggest weakness. It decomposes too easily when exposed to rain and sun. Too much sand in the mix causes adobe to turn soft and weather poorly; too much clay causes it to crack. No matter how carefully it is maintained, it will eventually return to its organic form—it will melt into the earth. It is therefore a material with a limited life span.

The technique of shaping mud into adobe bricks was brought to the Americas by the Spanish, who had learned it from the Moors. But adobe was a material the Pueblo culture had worked with before, although not in the efficient brick form. The Spanish helped the indigenous cultures perfect the art of adobe con-

FIG. 4.3 Use of adobe in early Spanish colonial settlements: decaying adobe residence in downtown Phoenix, Arizona.

struction, and some of the most inspiring adobe buildings came after the Spanish arrival in the seventeenth century. Learning to work with adobe meant dealing with the problem of water. Moisture inevitably crept in. Water could be drained off the roofs through *canales* (roof gutters), but eventually enough water would get to the roof beams (*vigas*). The buildings that survived longest were those in which the ceiling beams would be replaced periodically.[15] It is interesting also to contrast the design of southwestern roofs with those farther south in Mexico and South America. Whereas in the latter, Spain demanded that decorative domes be built on churches and other important structures, using fired brick, in colonial New Mexico colonists once again adapted to local (indigenous) architecture. The regionally favored flat roof and earthen (adobe) constructions dominated colonial New Mexican townscapes.[16]

The Spanish built an adobe church with ten-foot-thick walls in Acoma, the "city of the sky." At Acoma, the Spanish had encountered blocks of indigenous terraces houses built into the cliffs on a mesa towering above the vast desert. There, presumably inspired by this great sight, they used Indian labor to build probably the largest and finest mission church in New Mexico. The Indians pulled off the seemingly impossible task of bringing supplies (timber, sand, and water) up the steep rock slopes and built a structure that reflected Indian sensibilities in a newly settled Spanish domain. The upper Rio Grande Valley landscape from Albuquerque to Santa Fe and Taos soon became dotted with Spanish-style adobe ranch structures, with their long, low porches, thick white adobe walls, and enclosed courtyards. Taos became the meeting place of cultures, where Pueblo memory meshed with Spanish technique, yielding simple, yet powerful, buildings. The rest of Mexico was moving toward the sumptuous and the Baroque, but in the far reaches of New Spain, in a place they would come to call "New Mexico," the land was a force in itself, and there was memory of a past, of regional indigenous people and a way of life. Spain paused to consider that memory, and its first buildings, its first towns evoke something of the quietly dying Pueblo Indian towns, the cliff dwellers, the mud brick *kivas,* ceremonial spaces, and the silent, awesome presence of the desert. All would soon be forgotten, as the Spanish colonization swept across the southwestern desert landscape.

By the 1840s and 1850s—the time New Mexico achieved independence from Mexico and Spain—a new "territorial" style of architecture emerged in the region. It began to eclipse some of the indigenous and Mexican design elements that had sustained the regional cultural landscape. Interior patios disappeared, adobe was replaced by wood frame or brick construction, buildings began to appear in the form of European revival designs; Greek Revival classical col-

FIG. 4.4 Spanish colonial buildings borrowed ideas from the indigenous structures in the southwestern United States: the church at Taos, New Mexico.

FIG. 4.5 Modernism in the desert: Frank Lloyd Wright's neo-Mayan–inspired Hotel Biltmore, Phoenix, Arizona.

umns were especially powerful icons of the mid- to late nineteenth century. The railroad era (1880–1910) in New Mexico continued the destruction of regional landscapes, with the exception of locally based preservation movements. For example, in Santa Fe in the early 1900s, a renaissance movement crystallized around conservation of the city's historic buildings. The pueblo-revival style of architecture probably traces its origins to the Santa Fe renaissance at the turn of the century. Other cities—Albuquerque, most notably—were more tied to the future and a landscape of growth and change centered on technology and economic expansion.

In neighboring Arizona, similar developments can be observed. Tucson was built in 1782 as a *presidio* (fort) in a more remote region of Spanish colonial settlement. The town plan followed the traditional Spanish grid, although its design incorporated not one, but two large public squares—the Plaza de Armas (main square) and the Plaza Militár (military square). When Arizona became part of the United States, Tucson was transformed by new Anglo settlers. The colonial core was diminished by new growth to the north and east, while architectural styles shifted from adobe to brick and lumber. Front yards began to appear; green lawns were imported from the East Coast. Residents also brought their East Coast tastes in architecture. The latter part of the nineteenth century favored wooden houses in Victorian Gothic design.[17] It is not without irony that in Phoenix, one of the cities experiencing a boom in Queen Anne and other Victorian-style grandiose wood-frame houses in the 1880s and 1890s, the wealthy occupants of the new houses soon began to learn how poorly adapted they were to the regional landscape. During the sweltering summer heat, affluent residents were forced to move their beds onto outdoor porches or to the backyard, since the wooden homes had been heated by the day's heat far beyond a temperature comfortable for sleep. Meanwhile, in their tiny, but cool, adobe boxes, "poor" Mexican and Native American families slept soundly.

The arrival of Anglos in Arizona reached its zenith architecturally in the twentieth century during the height of the modernist movement. Modernists were flawed in their obsession with buildings-as-objects. Modernism tended not to question the relationship between a building and its physical environment. In Arizona, in the Phoenix metropolitan region, the largest in the former cultural zone of the Anasazi, one finds a modern landscape virtually devoid of significant respect for the past. Much of Phoenix consists of wood-frame suburban tract housing, glass-and-concrete commercial buildings, and strip development. Until recently, much of the built landscape divorced itself entirely from the ecology of the region. The result is that cities like Phoenix are completely at odds with their ecological setting. One would hope that local designers begin to address issues such as the provision of shade, management of water in the desert landscape, and preservation of interior courtyards.[18]

In what is now the southern part of the state of Texas, Spain sent its colonists northward from Mexico to settle. San Antonio, Texas, was the first important mission in the province of Texas, built early in the eighteenth century. San Antonio would become known for its Governor's Palace, a long low white building with iron-grilled windows and *canales* (drainage pipes) projecting from the parapet. Perhaps best known to all Americans centuries later was the San Antonio Mission, remembered for its nickname, the Alamo, named after the grove of nearby poplar trees.

Texas represents a somewhat different subregion of the larger Southwest. It is not, in fact, one single, coherent place but an amalgam of cultural subareas, ranging from East Texas, which is more tied to southern U.S. culture, to south and southwest Texas, which are tied strongly to Mexico.[19] Texas did not embrace adobe to the extent that New Mexico and Arizona did. Its indigenous settlements were dominated by either dome-shaped huts, built of wooden poles and thatched grass, or *tipis*, made of animal skins.[20] Mission architecture was also more limited than in New Mexico, Arizona, and California. Most notable in Texas towns and cities were the large Spanish-Mexican ranch homes on one end of the economic spectrum, or small, flat-roofed, cubelike adobe dwellings,

FIG. 4.6 The mission constituted one of the important buildings in the landscape of the Spanish southwest: Mission at San Antonio (*El Alamo*), Texas.

on the other end. The latter are dominant in south Texas cities like El Paso, Brownsville, and Laredo.[21]

Most dominant in the Texas regional landscape by the nineteenth century were images of the western frontier town: a main street lined with stores, saloons, and hotels, all two-story structures built with wood frame or brick, many with porches on both the ground and second floors. Even border towns were cast in this image. Elizabeth Street in Brownsville is a good example. In fact, careful examination of the landscapes of mid-nineteenth-century Brownsville uncovers scant evidence of traditional Mexican landscapes.[22] Similarly, Iturbide Street in Laredo around 1875 gives the same impression. Only a few buildings in town in that period suggest something Mexican. The St. Augustine Church appears as a kind of hybrid of Mission style and Romanesque. The two-story Zapata County courthouse looked like a colonial Mexican structure of adobe and brick with decorative trim around the windows.[23]

The largely wooden townscapes of Texas would also be subject to a transformation during the crucial nineteenth century. As more Anglo settlers from the East Coast arrived, assisted by rail technology, a building boom swept across Texas cities. Its greatest expression came in the form of Greek Revival buildings. A period of Mission Revival lasted from 1895 to 1945, but its impact on Texas was weaker than in other parts of the Southwest.[24] Far more longer lasting than formal Spanish-Mexican landscapes are the vernacular ones, particularly along the border. Cities like El Paso, Laredo, and Brownsville retain a large number of simple one-story adobe or brick residences that are similar to houses located south of the boundary. Yet, even in south Texas's Lower Rio Grande Valley, the most Mexican subregion of Texas, there is no strong Spanish-Mexican identity in the landscape—a flaw that architectural groups believe ought to be addressed in the future.[25] The more pervasive element in the cultural landscape of this region is the boundless array of "mobile homes," trailer parks for winter migrants from the United States and Canada.[26]

California offers perhaps the best illustration of how quickly Spain took control of the southwestern U.S. territory. California, which in the beginning was two territories, upper (*Alta*) California, which covers most of present-day California, and lower (*Baja*) California, in Mexico, was the last of the northern frontier of New Spain to be settled by Spanish missionaries and colonists. Whereas Santa Fe had been settled as early as 1609, the first mission in California wasn't built at San Diego until 1769. California was farther by land from the northern Mexican frontier settlements, and it was the last of the mission territories of colonial New Spain.

FIG. 4.7 The simple wood-frame building with porch, one or two stories in height, dominated the cultural landscape of Texas cities in the nineteenth century.

FIG. 4.8 California missions brought plush gardens and a Mediterranean ambience to the semiarid Pacific coast in the late eighteenth and early nineteenth centuries: the Mission at Santa Barbara.

Once Spain arrived on the scene on the West Coast, it would quickly cover the land with three settlement types: missions, *presidios,* and *pueblos.* A string of twenty-one missions would be built in California from 1769 to 1822. The missions brought more than Christianity to California; they completely transformed the landscape of the California desert frontier. Plush gardens accompanied early mission construction: Spain brought citrus and olive trees, figs, and grapes to create a Mediterranean ambience on a dusty desert landscape. The Indians of California had not built the kind of durable architecture that the Pueblos had; their simple structures were soon replaced with crude Spanish ones.

The missions were not unlike their counterparts in New Mexico or Texas. They were built in the form of quadrangles, with ornamental cloisters and plush interior courtyards, and housed a plethora of activity—schools, workshops, apartments—inside the walls of the mission compound. *Presidios,* too, were enclosed quadrangles with walls three feet thick and twelve to fifteen feet high, many with bastions (towers) in the four corners. The *pueblos* were self-contained farming areas laid out in the classic gridiron pattern.

Just as the mission system had reached its zenith early in the nineteenth century, the course of history would take a series of turns that would, within a span of merely fifty years or so, diminish more than two centuries of Spanish/Mexican influence on the landscape of the U.S. Southwest. In the 1820s, the nations of Spanish America finally achieved their independence from Spain. It happened in Mexico in 1821, some three centuries after Cortes had conquered the region for mother Spain. Only twenty-five years later, the northern provinces of Mexico, including the territory of upper California, were lost to the U.S., following the war and subsequent Treaty of Guadalupe Hidalgo. The U.S.-Mexico boundary was drawn, and thousands of Mexicans living in what had become the United States were forced to change their citizenship. Waves of Anglo settlers flocked into the Southwest—cattlers, miners, farmers, bankers, newspapermen, speculators, and drifters. As they flowed across the deserts and settled into the most promising places, they would come into direct contact and confrontation with the Mexican settlers who had occupied these lands, however sparsely, for centuries. The "Californios," as they would be called, soon saw their land taken away, their wealth lost in a newly forming Anglo economy, and their political power decline, as their numbers were weakened by a growing majority of new Anglo voters. The decline of the Californio, or Mexican, population of the mid-1800s is one of the least told stories of the changing cultural landscape of the nineteenth century in California. As the Californios lapsed into economic and social isolation, the architectural legacies of their era—the missions and the adobe *presidio* towns—would also fall into decay.

The Myth of Spanish-Mexican Heritage in the Modern American Period

> The missions are worth more money, are a greater asset to Southern California, than our oil, our oranges, or even our climate.

To speak of architecture in the southwestern United States in the late nineteenth century is to recognize that this was still a relatively remote frontier, no longer the northern outpost of one nation but now the western outpost of another. New technologies were rapidly arriving and changing the nature of places: railroads, irrigation systems, and mining infrastructure. The scale of settlement was still small, by East Coast standards. But gradually, Anglo populations were overshadowing Mexican ones in most of the important settlement areas. By the 1870s and 1880s, in California, what had once been a territory of small Indian communities and Spanish mission settlements along the coast was gradually being transformed into a booming region of farms, cattle ranches, small industry, ports, and trade.

The memory of Spain and Mexico was rapidly fading. The demise of the Californios unfolded in only a few decades.[27] The Californios had set the tone for culture in California—music, art, language, and architecture were all infused with a good deal of Spanish influence. The Californios lived either on rural *ranchos* built of solid adobe, styled after the Spanish colonial homes and *haciendas* of Mexico, or in adobe mansions in the towns created by the missionaries along California's coast. But the arrival of Anglos in the middle of the nineteenth century meant not only that new economies—railroading, commercial farming, mining, shipping—would populate the southwestern landscape but also that new forms of building would alter it.

The Anglo population brought its "East Coast" ideas about architecture and building to the southwestern desert territories, including California. In the late nineteenth century, a great deal of building was done with wood. Except for ceiling beams and door and window treatments, neither the indigenous populations of the Southwest nor the Spanish colonial and Mexican populations built extensively with wood. So when Anglos began to populate the towns of California and other southwestern regions after 1850, wood-slat commercial and residential buildings began to dominate the new townscapes, and not always with favorable results. As mentioned earlier, in Phoenix, Arizona, in the 1880s, the poorest immigrants from Sonora, Mexico, were living in modest adobe structures that stayed relatively cool in the hot desert heat. Meanwhile, the wealthier new arrivals, just off the train from the East Coast, built giant wooden Queen Anne mansions with high ceilings, towers with cupolas and turrets, and wraparound porches.[28] The rich even tried building double roofs to counteract the summer heat, but the wooden houses remained uncomfortable during the summers.

While the Anglo-European immigrants from the eastern United States began building their wooden cities, the remnants of Spanish colonial building were falling into disarray. Missions had been abandoned and within a few decades were overrun with wild vegetation, while the doors and windows, and even some adobe walls, were all decaying. It is said that Anglos occasionally used the missions for nostalgic picnics, a social event on the ruins of some unknown past.

Anglos arriving in California in the 1890s viewed the adobe structures they associated with Mexicans as not very practical. They had been built with a technology (mud and straw bricks dried in the sun) they considered primitive. This was the 1890s, after all—a time of prosperity and new industrial machinery, milled lumber, nails, and glass. The early Americans looked at the old missions and saw them as primitive and not worthy of imitation.[29] Even one of the foremost experts on the history of California architecture in the nineteenth century dismisses the architectural importance of the missions: "For all of their religious significance and romantic connotations, the Franciscan missions are of only limited importance to a social history of California architecture."[30]

The 1880s marked the beginning of a period of rapid economic growth in California. There was a land boom on, and everywhere there was new railroad construction, new towns, land speculation, and growth. Many speculators, investors, promoters, and wheeler-dealers came from the East Coast and Midwest to join in the boom. A recent study of Los Angeles describes the period of 1880 through 1920 as the first wave of real estate capitalism, a time when a number of Anglo entrepreneurs, notably Henry Gray Otis and Harry Chandler, created Los Angeles as an "eden on a semi-arid southwest Pacific Coast." What was needed was a bit of "myth making and literary invention."[31] Thus would be born the "mission myth."

Charles Fletcher Loomis would carry the flag of the mission myth during its early phase. Born in Ohio, Loomis moved to Los Angeles in 1884 to begin working as an editor at the *Los Angeles Times*. In a few short years, he became enamored of the Spanish past and its architecture. He formed the Association for Preservation of the Missions in 1892 and the Landmark Club in 1895. He believed (see the quote at the beginning of this section) that the mission legacy was fundamental to the growth and future well-being of California. Meanwhile, all around him Anglo wooden housing, particularly Queen Anne and Craftsman styles, was leading the way as boomtowns were constructed.

Loomis's dream to resurrect California's mythical Spanish past was aided by a number of events and circumstances that swirled around him. In 1881 a writer and journalist from the East Coast, Helen Hunt Jackson, after touring the Spanish missions and ranches of California, wrote the novel *Ramona,* about a beautiful half-Indian, half-Mexican girl brought up on a *hacienda* near Los Angeles. The novel painted California's Spanish-Mexican past in the most idyllic way, and as one observer has written, gave southern California "a myth by which to know itself."[32] *Ramona* was one of the biggest-selling novels of its time, and it generated a new nostalgia and excitement about California's "Spanish" past, a past that, in one observer's words, "was more Spanish than Spain itself"[33]—far more romantic in memory than it had been in reality.

But California now had the possibility of an identity, grounded in a mystical, romantic past, and the boom of the 1880s and 1890s was as good a time as any to begin the search for some sort of Mediterranean tradition, particularly when it might also serve the function of enhancing real estate and business interests who were investing heavily in the growth of southern California. Thus, when architect A. Page Brown designed the much heralded Spanish-style California building for the Chicago World's Fair in 1893, many began speaking of a new form of architecture: California Mission Revival. It had four elements: an adobe look, missionlike parapets, bell tower, and arcades. As Mission Revival began to catch on in the 1890s, Charles Loomis continued his criticism of its competitors—wooden houses transplanted from the Midwest to southern California.

Mission Revival fed off the "mission myth" that had been given impetus by Helen Hunt Jackson's *Ramona*. The mission myth portrayed California's Spanish past as graceful, romantic, and idyllic, a land of friars and missions and well-fed ranchers. It made no mention of the larger reality of California's Spanish-Mexican past: the brutality of forced Indian labor, racial tensions between Mexicans and Indians, and later Anglos, or the record of lynchings and hostility toward the Mexicans during the 1850–80 period of early Anglo immigration into the region.[34] Not until as late as 1946 would any writer challenge that characterization with a crisp reconstruction of events that actually took place.[35]

Thus was born Mission Revival architecture, which flourished in California from 1891 to 1915 and was largely an ornamental style used for houses, railroad stations, museums, city halls, and schools. Roundly criticized for being merely decorative, early Mission Revival buildings often seemed trivial and out of context, and many critics have looked back on these buildings and found them to have been repetitive and boring. One observer believed that "Mission Revival failed because it proved impossible to adapt the primitive architecture of a religious order to the commercial and worldly society of the late nineteenth century."[36]

In 1915, the Panama Canal Exposition was held in San Diego, California, to celebrate the completion of the canal (on which construction had begun in 1904) and the new connection between North and South America. San Diego, on the border with Mexico, was a logical place to hold such a fair. For architecture, this would prove to be an interesting moment in southern California. Mission Revival architecture was on the wane, but the organizers of the Panama Canal exposition decided they wanted to design the Balboa Park setting for the exposition with a Spanish/Mediterranean flavor. Just as Mission Revival had gotten its impetus from A. Page Brown's California Building at the Chicago World's Fair in

FIG. 4.9 Mission Revival architecture flourished in California early in the twentieth century: the Christian Science Building, San Diego, designed by Irving Gill (later demolished).

1893, so would a new architectural style—Spanish Colonial Revival—get its first push from the designs of the principal architect for the Panama Canal Exposition—Bertram Grosvenor Goodhue. Goodhue was an architect who had designed buildings in Panama and Cuba and had written about Mexican architecture.

Many were surprised at Goodhue's selection over Irving Gill, whose modern interpretations of Mission Revival had already seen the light of day in southern California. Grosvenor Goodhue was committed to a much more European interpretation of "Spanish" architecture, and his buildings in Balboa Park reflected this "Spanish Colonial" theme. The highlight of the exposition design was the California Building, a cathedral with red-tile roof, stucco walls, arches, ironwork balconies, and ornate portals, thought to embody most of the elements of the so-called Churrigueresque school well represented in churches and government buildings in colonial Spain and Mexico.

Spanish Colonial Revival regenerated the continued search for a Spanish past in southern California's built landscape. Although Mission Revival had lost some of its mystique and attractiveness for consumers, developers, investors, and boosters of growth had not lost *their* enthusiasm for the romanticism of a mythical Spanish-Mexican past. What happened after 1915 seems to be that all pretense of the connection with *Mexico* was cast aside, and the "fantasy" ele-

FIG. 4.10 "Spanish Colonial Revival" reflected the continuing search for a Spanish/Mexican past in southern California: private residence in Los Angeles.

ment was brought center stage. The idea was no longer to re-create the feeling of the missions that had come from Mexico, and that had actually been in California, but rather, the idea was to seek a Mediterranean, European, and, as many would come to call it, Andalusian (a region of southern Spain strongly influenced by the Moors) flavor in building styles. Bertram Grosvenor Goodhue's highly ornate, Churrigueresque buildings started the ball rolling—or kept it rolling, one might say. While the Panama Canal Exposition had originally been planned as a temporary exhibit, the San Diego public became so attached to the buildings that funds were raised to convert many to a permanent status. So it is today that Balboa Park is a built landscape of Andalusian and Spanish Colonial structures.

San Diego (which is discussed in greater detail in the next section) was not the only place touched by the second wave of Spanish-style architecture in southern California. Indeed, many towns became so attached to Spanish-style architecture in the second and third decades of the twentieth century that they put into place zoning legislation that prohibited all forms of building design *other* than Spanish-Mediterranean. The best known examples are the communities of Santa Barbara, Ojai, Palos Verdes, San Clemente, and Rancho Sante Fe. The typical attitude of residents and builders is captured in the statement by the builders of San Clemente, who claimed to envision "happiness and prosperity in Spanish homes on the shores of the sundown sea."[37]

The twentieth-century building of Santa Barbara has been described as the materialization of a Spanish dream city.[38] What is conspicuous in the reading of any history of the building of Santa Barbara is that both the promoters (politicians, businessmen) of its development and the architects hired to design the buildings to fit the desired Spanish fantasy townscape were all primarily of Anglo descent. For example, three of the best-known architects in Santa Barbara were Arthur Page Brown, Francis Wilson, and George Washington Smith. Furthermore, the increasingly Anglo community in Santa Barbara consisted of a large number of citizens who were active defenders of the vague notion of "Hispanic" architecture and culture. They not only made it politically possible to have an entire city of Mediterranean flavor; they also favored Spanish art, landscaping, and other cultural elements. To achieve their goals they formed interest groups and political coalitions, called the Community Arts Association and the Plans and Planting Committee. It may not be entirely fair to say that *all* the impetus for these actions can be ascribed to the powerful builders, investors, and economic interests in southern California, who stood to gain from popularizing the myth of a romantic Spanish past, achieving higher growth rates, and thus increasing land values, and greater profit. It is probably also the case, as illustrated by the incredible sales of Helen Hunt Jackson's book, that many who came to California simply wanted to believe in a rich past. It is also true that California inspired the search for a Spanish-Mexican connection, even if the one that was found had never really existed. The act of searching, and the visual landscapes that that search produced, created a rich outpouring of interest in the notion of Spanish-Mexican culture, at a time when southern Californians were first discovering how intimately connected the land was to a Mexican past. What is perhaps unfortunate is that the details of that past were never sufficiently publicized or understood; this is still largely true in the 1990s. But then, America is a nation with so little history, it tends to have a short memory and does not typically mobilize in ways to enhance its memory.

The Spanish myth held strong in California in the early decades of the twentieth century. If all the developments already described were not enough to sustain the interest of many Californians in Spanish-Mediterranean culture, during the 1920s another popular media event pushed this process further along. Some have called it the "Zorro myth." Based on a novel called *The Mark of Zorro,* a series of films, television programs, radio shows, and comic books began to portray the image of a masked hero called Zorro (*fox,* in Spanish). Zorro defended the poor in a historic, uniquely wealthy fantasyland said to be Spanish California. Such creations illustrate the degree to which the larger Spanish cultural movement had become caricature, exaggeration, and fantasy, amidst what has been described as the "illusion of mountains, seashore, and channel, of Andalusian architecture, polo fields, tennis courts, golf courses, hotels, costumed festivals, and ceremonial pageants." [39]

That is how southern California imagined itself in the early part of this century, and that is why such architecture is found in abundance in much of the region. What is also clear, however, is that no force was sufficient to sustain such illusory, tentative styles of building, when they were not sufficiently based on real events and real people from the region. The Anglos imported their fantasy of Spain and, to a lesser extent, Mexico. When the fantasy worked as a market tool, Spanish-Mediterranean designs would drape the landscapes of towns and cities. If other systems of building came along to displace it, so be it. That was the American way, and southern California became the twentieth century's quintessential example of how places can become homogeneous and devoid of original character and uniqueness, if no effort is made to sustain the meaning of place.

Southern California's twentieth century would prove to be a very fickle one as far as Spanish-Mexican architecture and urban design are concerned. The essence of twentieth-century southern California is that it is the "self-made" place, where people thrive due to self-reliance. The icons of southern California culture became those of the individual—privacy, single-family housing, lush private gardens, and individual mobility within city space (through elaborate freeway superstructures and skyrocketing rates of private automobile ownership). All this defused any collective formation of memory, any collective notion of a past, of architectural tradition. Southern California had lost its connection to the Mexican-Spanish past.

A visiting German architect's book on Los Angeles architecture, which has become a classic, emphasizes the uniqueness of the regional ecology, and of the cultures of freeways, surfers, and Disneyland, but he also has this to say about the past: "For the purpose of the present study, Spanish colonial revival will not be treated as an identifiable or consciously adopted style, but as something which is ever present and can be taken for granted, like the weather." [40] A number of other well-known architects favored Spanish-style architecture for California, including Charles Moore. [41] But Moore also thought that Disneyland, the quintessential make-believe place in southern California, was probably its most characteristic architecture. He wrote that Disneyland had saved the public realm in southern California by providing a far more exciting space than any of the existing downtowns. Yet Disneyland was the ultimate fabrication, a completely made-up ambience, and Moore seems to revel in it by quoting Noel Coward's comment about Los Angeles: "There is always something so delightfully real about what is phony here; and something so phony about what is real." [42] What is real and what is not are intertwined, and one is not sure which is more cherished.

Architecture and Spanish-Mexican Identity on the Border: San Diego, California

In the year 1542, Juan Rodríguez Cabrillo traveled north from the Viceroyalty of Guatemala to explore unknown territory along the Pacific coast. Entering a bay surrounded by hills, he found the harbor was deep and well protected, and he claimed this land for Spain. More Spaniards would return two decades later and build an outpost for ships in the great sailing fleet of the Spanish empire making the Acapulco-Manila run. The outpost was named San Diego de Alcalá.

For nearly two centuries, this distant settlement remained but a small dot on some navigational charts of Spanish sailors. In 1769, the Spanish finally returned, and San Diego de Alcalá became the first of twenty-one missions to be built along the Pacific Coast in present-day California. The intent of the Spanish settlers was twofold: to settle the California territory in the name of the Spanish king and to impose Christianity upon its dwellers through the construction of the missions. Father Junípero Serra was the founder of the first of the Franciscan missions. He named it after the settlement: San Diego de Alcalá.

As best as historians can reconstruct it, the original mission of San Diego de Alcalá was the simplest and least decorative of the twenty-one California missions built between 1769 and 1822. The San Diego mission was completed in 1780, after an earlier effort had been raided and destroyed by local indigenous groups. The 1780 building was constructed about six miles inland. It consisted of three-foot-thick adobe walls, pine roof beams, and windows covered with grilles made of cedar. The structure was quadrangular shaped, typical of mission design. It incorporated the Spanish Colonial design elements of the interior patio and arcades. The facade was notable for its gracefully curved pediment and a bell tower.

The San Diego de Alcalá mission was the first important structure built by Europeans in a region that would eventually become a meeting place of Anglo America and Latin America. Today, the restored mission sits on the slope of a hill on the north side of Mission Valley, a stone's throw from one of the region's busiest freeway interchanges. The mission is easily lost in the visual and audio cacophony of the freeways, shopping centers, condominium complexes, and apartment buildings. It sits like some strange white apparition of San Diego's eighteenth century dwarfed by the techno-modernism of the late twentieth century. It lies just up the freeway from one of the icons of 1960s modernism: the San Diego Qualcomm Stadium, a hulking concrete modernist structure. The restored mission is significant not only for its intricate details as a building but also for the extent to which it has been smothered by the twentieth century,

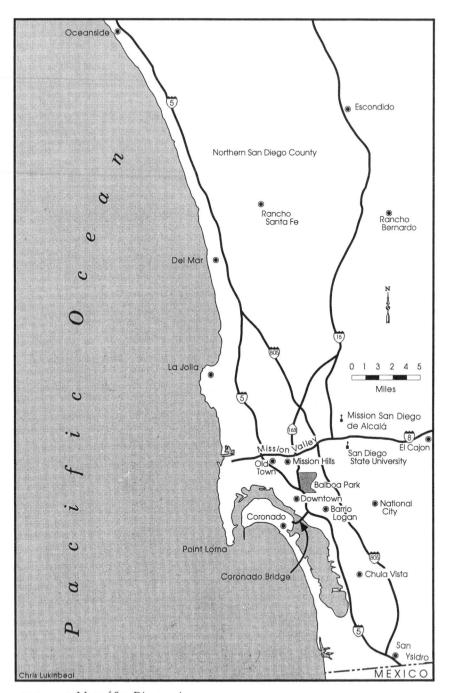

FIG. 4.11 Map of San Diego region.

just as Mexican cultural influence in architecture has been overshadowed by the contemporary freeway metropolis.

San Diego is like the rest of southern California. It names its baseball team the *Padres,* it has Mission Valley and Mission Boulevard and Friar's Road, an island called *Coronado,* a mountain called *Soledad,* a valley called *El Cajón (the box,* in Spanish). But it doesn't embrace its Mexican past. Some of the most beautiful sights in the San Diego region are heavily influenced by Mexican-Spanish design: parks, churches, or residential neighborhoods. Most San Diegans, transplanted Americans from other parts of the continent, do not appear to greatly prize the past. San Diego is a high-tech, freeway, coastal city, oriented toward the future. The past can be bulldozed away by developers or packaged by real estate entrepreneurs.

Old Town is the name that has stayed with the original settlement area of the eighteenth-century Spanish colonists who settled in San Diego. Located near the confluence of the region's two main rivers—the San Diego and Mission Rivers—Old Town nearly disappeared in the mid–twentieth century, only to be rediscovered and converted into a state park and historic preservation area, and one of the major tourist attractions in the San Diego region. It sits tightly wedged against one of San Diego's wealthiest city neighborhoods called, not unsymbolically, Mission Hills. Down in Old Town historic buildings have been refurbished to create a feeling of neighborhood, all reinforced by the restaurants and retail shops that cater to the hordes of tourists that flow through the area. Old Town is notable for its historic buildings preserved from the "Mexican" period (pre-1848) and the "American" period (post-1848). The name Old Town seems to have become a kind of regional phenomenon in the Southwest, where cities like Los Angeles, Tucson, and Albuquerque all have their original Mexican areas preserved as historic landmarks, and utilized for tourism and for retaining commercial vitality near the present-day central business districts.

In San Diego, Mexican period buildings include the Casa de Estudillo, an enclosed adobe structure built by Captain José Maria Estudillo in 1827. The Estudillos were one of the early "Californio" (elite colonial Mexican settlers of Spanish origin) families. There are also the Casa de Machado, built by Juan Manuel Machado in the 1830s, and the Casa de Bandini. The House of Bandini's history is a fitting architectural metaphor for the experience of Spanish-Mexican families and their culture in nineteenth-century California. Juan Bandini built the original single-story adobe house in 1829. The romantic view expressed at the turn of the century that pictured old Spanish mansions with second-floor balconies is largely a myth: structural limitations in the type of adobe buildings created by the Californios tended to limit even the most lavish ranch structures to one story. The Bandini house in its Mexican-Spanish phase was, indeed, one

FIG. 4.12 The overlap between Mexican and Anglo building styles is evident in this two-story version of an original one-story adobe Mexican home: Casa Bandini, Old Town, San Diego.

story. During the transition period from Spanish-Mexican to Anglo control in California during the late 1840s and the 1850s, Bandini was among the Californios who suffered tremendous economic losses. He sold his home to an Anglo, Albert Seeley. Seeley added a second story made of wood to the Bandini home. He then turned the house into the Cosmopolitan Hotel. Today the building is preserved as an important landmark of the period. It houses a Mexican restaurant whose main clients are Anglo tourists.

Old Town's historic importance as the original settlement for the Latino/Hispanic community of San Diego is only marginally reflected in the area's built landscape. There are as many Anglo buildings as there are Spanish-Mexican ones. Prominent on the pseudo-townscape of the tourist district are the Wrightington House, built by Thomas Wrightington in the 1840s, and the Seeley stables, a replica of the stables originally built in 1867 to house stagecoaches and horses for Seeley's stage line, which made the trip from San Diego to Los Angeles in less than twenty-four hours. There is also the Whaley House, a two-story brick and wooden shingle-roofed structure that became the center of an Anglo-oriented Old Town in 1856–57. Old Town would quickly be eclipsed as a significant settlement when in the 1860s a furniture entrepreneur and developer from San Francisco, Alonzo Horton, came to San Diego and said of Old Town:

"I could not give you $5.00 for a deed to the whole of it—I would not take it as a gift. It doesn't lie right. Never in the world can you have a city here."[43]

In the short span of about twenty years, San Diego would pack up its town hall, its courthouse, bank, newspaper office, and other important city buildings and move lock, stock, and barrel down the hill onto the flat coastal plain. Only a decade before citizens had called this area "Horton's folly," because Horton the developer bought the coastal flatlands—later to be called Horton's Addition—with the intention of moving the city of San Diego there. He did. This marked the birth of "New Town," the new San Diego. Horton had achieved his main objective in coming to San Diego from San Francisco: to make good real estate investments. "Horton's Addition," much of which remains today, is visual testimony to late-nineteenth-century San Diego's transformation from a Mexican town built of adobe to an Anglo city of wooden Victorian- and New England-style architecture. Horton's Addition covers much of downtown San Diego today. Only a few of the original wooden structures, whose styles range from Western Stick to bungalow to Eastlake, remain. They are backdrop to layers of 1960s and '70s modernist skyscrapers and 1980s postmodern office buildings and retail structures. Multimillion-dollar investments have created waterfront villages, the redevelopment of the turn-of-the-century Gaslamp Quarter, a trolley network, and the centerpiece of the new downtown: a great postmodern shopping center. Its name: Horton Plaza, of course.

If Anglo San Diego wiped away the Spanish past in the middle of the nineteenth century, it also followed other areas of southern California in resurrecting the Spanish-Mexican heritage in a very different form a few decades later. San Diego did not ignore the Mission Revival frenzy that swept California in the 1880s and 1890s. In fact, one of the nation's greatest interpreters of that movement came to live in San Diego at the turn of the century. Irving Gill is generally recognized to be one of the twentieth century's visionary designers. He arrived in San Diego for health reasons in the 1890s. It didn't take him long to appreciate the simple beauty and meaning in California's mission past. He once stated that "the missions of California are beautiful because their builders could not but be honest. They had not the time, tools or skill to cover with ornament, or cut up into angle, so their works stand with undisputed dignity and superiority . . . their extreme simplicity holds the eye, resting and gratifying it, making an indelible impression of power and repose."[44]

Gill's gradual shift toward mission-inspired, industrially produced designs represents an amazing transformation from his origins, which consisted of working in the Chicago office of the early modernist skyscraper architect, Louis Sullivan. After leaving Chicago, Gill went to southern California, and surely what he found in California's mission architecture fit well with his strong be-

FIG. 4.13 Mission Revival, expressed in the work of Irving Gill, incorporated adobe-like walls, archways, and patios into an efficient, industrially produced modern building: Women's Club, La Jolla, California.

lief in the relationship between design and the natural environment. He quickly discovered that he preferred concrete and stone and tile, because of their advantages in the ecological setting: durability and insulation. He once noted that "we should build a house simple, plain, substantial as a boulder, and leave the ornamentation of it to nature, who will trim it with lichen, chisel it with storms, and make it gracious and friendly with vines and flowers and shadows as she does the stone in the meadow."[45] Two of Gill's greatest designs are in San Diego: the Bishop's School and the Women's Club, both in La Jolla. Both buildings demonstrate Gill's uncanny ability to design modern industrially produced structures that incorporate both functionally and artistically, mission elements. Both buildings were designed out of concrete over hollow tile with a light-colored stucco. The walls are adobelike, and there are archways, patios, arcades, pergolas, and bell towers.

The kind of buildings Irving Gill designed remain as remarkable curiosities and architectural treasures, rather than as part of a generic regional architectural style or movement. As mentioned earlier, it had been expected that Gill would be invited to head the design team that created buildings in Balboa Park for the 1915 Panama Canal Exposition. Instead, Bertram Grosvenor Goodhue was chosen, and his more ornate Spanish buildings were a big hit with San Diegans and spurred local enthusiasm for the Spanish Colonial Revival phase in San Diego. Ironically the Santa Fe Railroad Station in downtown San Diego had been built in majestic Mission Revival style, in preparation for the Exposition of 1915. During the two decades following Grosvenor Goodhue's designs for Balboa Park, building styles moved away from the mission-inspired design toward the ultra-Baroque Churriguera motif, similar to Goodhue's great California Building in Balboa Park. Goodhue's design of the Prado, or main avenue running through the park, was a grand axis around which he put in fourteen major complexes, many linked by Andalusian arcades, formal gardens, patios, and plazas. Along the Prado one could see towers, domes, arcades, and ornate building facades. The park entrance spanned the Cabrillo Bridge, a stately structure with great arches and a Roman aqueduct–like appearance that reminded viewers of the Alcántara Bridge at Toledo, Spain.

Balboa Park made a winner of Bertram Grosvenor Goodhue, and the Spanish Colonial Revival designs caught on like wildfire in San Diego through the 1920s. Entire neighborhoods were appearing in Spanish Colonial Revival style — among them Mission Hills, Hillcrest, Kensington, La Jolla, Point Loma, and later Rancho Santa Fe. San Diego's largest university — San Diego State University (at the time called San Diego State College) — took the big step of dedicating its campus design in the 1920s to the Spanish Colonial theme. The campus president during that period, Dr. Edward Hardy, was instrumental in this decision. Inspired by Bertram Goodhue's fine work in Balboa Park, many architects of the period were designing what were termed Spanish-Mediterranean buildings, which brought together architectural features from Italy, Islamic North Africa, as well as Moorish Andalusia in Spain, and Spanish neoclassic, Plateresque, and Spanish renaissance architecture. President Hardy at the state college wrote that the new campus design would be "an architecture reminiscent of Spain and Spanish art itself influenced by the Arabian and Moorish art, and in landscaping very like that of southern Spain." [46]

San Diego had moved from the missions to the Moors, from Mexican memories of the region to a lapse of Mexican memory. This period is notable for the confusion that seeped into the relationship between building and memory. United States architecture has always been shorter in span and more ephemeral than in Mexico. San Diego's memory was exceptionally short. San Diego forgot its missions, and the romanticization of a false past was transferred from Mexico to another exotic locale where they also speak Spanish: Spain. Thus San Diego State University was to become a vision of Andalusian colleges, with Moorish walls and arcades, bell towers, and lush landscaped courtyards. If it did not portray the memory of the region, at least it built on elements of that memory. After World War II, the campus would be invaded by the modernist styles in vogue through the 1950s and 1960s — brutalist, drab, formalist gray structures cut across the fabric of the past in libraries, a student center, or a health-services building.

To a great extent, the campus of San Diego State University was a mirror of

FIG. 4.14 The California Building in Balboa Park was architect
Bertram Grosvenor Goodhue's landmark design and thought to be
one of the catalysts for the Spanish Colonial Revival movement in the
southwestern United States.

the larger San Diego region, where the post–World War II period was ushering in functionalist, no-frills, modern structures. International-style glass-and-
steel skyscrapers dominated new freeway-scale corridors like Mission Valley in
central San Diego. Modernism also tended to move San Diego away from its
past even further; the whole philosophy of modern architecture seemed to do
away with references to the past, and many were concerned about its effects on

cities. There were, of course, creative and innovative modernist buildings, such as Louis Kahn's Salk Institute in La Jolla, but largely the modern era saw San Diego evolve as a highly eclectic modernist-built landscape in which the past was further erased both by the scale of the diffuse metropolis and by the uninspired, placeless landscape of modernism. Spanish-Mexican architecture's main function now became clear: either for tourism, for homes in wealthy neighborhoods where the "Ramona" myth could be propagated, or for commercial real estate developers convinced that Spanish style might attract more consumers. Where all this connected to some real sense of the Mexican-Spanish past had long since been forgotten.

Latino/Mexican Space Reconsidered: The *Barrio*

> *Barrio.* In Spanish it means neighborhood. In English, it means ghetto.

The concept of the *barrio,* or neighborhood, can be traced back to the Aztec zonification of the city into subcommunities where extended families occupied common spaces. In Tenochtitlan and other Aztec cities, the Spanish conquerers came across these urban neighborhoods, or *calpulli.* The term *barrio* may actually derive from the eleventh-century Roman use of the Latin term *barrium* to refer to a district or precinct within a town.[47]

The cultural landscape of Mexican American *barrios* in the southwestern United States can best be viewed as a dialectic clashing of two sets of forces: the external pressures of urban development, capitalism, and anti-Mexican sentiment, which tended to restrict Chicano populations to marginal spaces within the larger city—leading scholars to speak of a process of "barrioization"; and the internal response by people of Mexican heritage to create a homeland, a distinct ethnic space that is valued by those who occupy it—a notion that has been termed "barriology" (the ideology of the *barrio*).[48]

This gradual spatial concentration of the Mexican/Latino populations of the urban southwest border region into barrios has left behind a set of distinct cultural landscapes over the last century and a half. The emerging creation of valued social spaces has injected new landscapes into the fabric of Mexican American communities. The idea of barrio-ization cannot be traced to any single decision or conspiracy of actors, but rather to an unspoken theme that has unified all the built environment decisions made by powerful actors in the history of southwestern urban development over the last 150 years. One can view this process unfolding across three time periods: the late nineteenth century, 1900–1945, and the post-1945 period.

Because Mexican people dominated the towns of the southwestern United States until the Treaty of Guadalupe Hidalgo (1848), the period following this landmark shift in territorial political control marked one of cultural, political, and economic shock. It took several decades for the new economic landscapes and political policies of the Anglo system to begin to penetrate the townscapes of the Southwest. By the 1870s and 1880s, with the completion of the transcontinental railroad, the process of displacement and marginalization of Mexican communities began. As towns that Mexicans once dominated were transformed to fit the needs of Anglo economic development (oriented toward capital-intensive agriculture, irrigation, railroads, etc.), the Mexican community was abruptly impacted. Urban space was commodified—land became part of an intense market system, and real estate speculation began. Land was subject to a taxation scheme in a market system where anything not managed by the government was privatized. Mexican *pueblo* communal lands disappeared into private hands. New water, rail, and other technologies cut across the old townscapes, while the real estate frenzy, particularly in the boom of the 1880s, left Mexicans forced into ghetto spaces and marginalized politically.

On the West Coast, the Californio (Mexican) populations declined in the middle and later part of the nineteenth century,[49] while the construction of new towns was heavily influenced by East Coast architecture. The period 1850–1900 saw the secularization of the mission system, the breaking up of large Mexican owned *ranchos,* and the erosion of the sociopolitical culture of the Californio population that had dominated the scene for five or six decades.

In the latter part of the nineteenth century, new infusions of Mexican immigrants penetrated the southwestern United States. The new Mexican immigrants were not necessarily wealthy Californios of direct Spanish descent as had been the case before 1850; they were the first waves of Mexicans of mixed Spanish-Indian heritage (*mestizo*), the first of millions of people of Mexican descent who would begin to populate the mining towns, railroad centers, farming communities, and industrial cities of the American Southwest.

The earliest settlements of Mexican workers from the last decades of the 1800s were modest, simple clusters of adobe homes. The settlements were often referred to as Sonoratowns, since many of the Mexican migrants came from the northern Mexican state of Sonora. What is striking about the settlement process of Mexican immigrants, as early as the 1870s and 1880s, is that they were already forming their own spatially confined niches in the urban fabric. Thus began the process of Chicano barrioization.[50]

"Barrio-ization" can be said to comprise the second period of Mexican built environment history, from 1900 to 1945. During this period, the Southwest continued to grow, cities expanded, and more immigrants from Mexico arrived.

FIG. 4.15 Ghettoization in the Mexican American residential landscape: a street in decline in Tucson's *barrio* (R. Villa).

The experience of these immigrants was one of increasing segregation into less and less desirable parts of the city. The period 1900–1945 is notable as a time in which the process of ghettoization intensified. Various forces were at work. On the one side, increasingly larger waves of Mexican immigrants arrived in the American Southwest in the early decades of the twentieth century. As they flowed toward urban labor markets, a second force—economics—took over. Like other unskilled immigrants before them, Mexicans did not have the resources to pay very high rents. As cities like Los Angeles industrialized and developed, land values increased. Enclaves of low-rental housing formed, typically in the least desirable parts of towns: adjacent to the overcrowded factories, near noisy railroad stockyards, or on the far edges of town. Language also played a role in the ghettoization process. Mexican immigrants became more comfortable living near the old Sonoratowns or the emerging Mexican immigrants' enclaves where they could find others who spoke Spanish.

As cities such as Los Angeles, San Antonio, San Diego, Albuquerque, and El Paso became more densely populated, there was more competition for property, and the property market heated up. Greater hostility developed in the process of neighborhood formation. Dominant populations and their political power blocs create written and unwritten rules that discriminate against ethnic minorities.

In the southwestern cities of the early twentieth century, discrimination served to exclude Mexicans from some neighborhoods, further driving them toward their *barrios*. Discrimination had already become a way of life for Mexican immigrants, who had to endure severe backlashes during periods of economic recession. Discrimination in housing was just one more way some Anglos chose to scapegoat the Mexican immigrant population amidst a period of economic downfall.

Such behavior cannot help but manifest itself on the cityscape. The final period in the history of the Mexican American urban landscape is that of post-1945. By 1950, *barrios* were well entrenched in cities like Los Angeles, Santa Barbara, El Paso, and San Diego.[51] The cultural landscape of the *barrio* had been fairly consistent across the Southwest before 1950: communities of a few humble adobe structures, mostly in ruins, small wooden frame houses, low-rent tenements, family-owned markets in wood-frame buildings, and Catholic churches built of stucco or plaster. The 1950s and 1960s were a period of frenzied urban development, particularly in the largest southwestern cities, most notably in Los Angeles. Here the *barrios* that had existed for several decades were threatened by massive urban redevelopment. Land was seized for building freeways and other public facilities. Many unwanted and noxious developments—factories, freeways, stadiums—invaded what had been the primary living spaces for Mexican immigrants. The cultural landscape soon became one of distress: abandoned warehouses, heavily polluting factories, freeways, increasing crime, police.

Examples of this process of barrio-ization are evident throughout the southwestern United States. In East Los Angeles, the building of freeways substantially disrupted the landscape of Mexican American neighborhoods like Boyle Heights and Chavez Ravine. In San Diego, a freeway and bridge sliced the Barrio Logan neighborhood into fragments. Freeways were defended by some planners as evidence that cities were becoming more technologically sophisticated. Some observers even went so far as to argue that freeways allowed more freedom of movement, a truly democratic development.[52] But too many freeways destroyed the sense of place and endangered the quality of life of Mexican American neighborhoods.

In response to these conditions in the latter half of the twentieth century, we find an increasing shift in consciousness by the Latino population toward viewing their neighborhoods as a kind of valued cultural and social space. Some scholars argue that the period of the 1930s, in which the economic Depression spurred massive deportations of Mexican immigrants, served to spark greater determination on the part of those who remained, or those who returned, to construct permanent spaces in the Latino community.[53] This determination, which some call "barriology," began with the creation of symbolic activities—parades, holiday festivities, and cultural events—that ritually celebrated not only Mexican culture but also Mexican American place/community.

One specific form of intervention by Chicano community activists materialized as a battle to preserve park land being usurped by freeway and other development. In Los Angeles, activists and preservationists fought to protect several public spaces on the east side, including Obregon and Elysian Parks. In other cities of the Southwest, "Chicano Parks" and community centers were created in Mexican American neighborhoods. In San Diego, a former water tank lying in Balboa Park was transformed into a Mexican American cultural center called Centro Cultural de La Raza. On the otherwise uninspiring exterior, stark, colorful, powerful murals were painted. Nearby in Barrio Logan, the oldest Mexican American neighborhood in the city fought to create a neighborhood park under the Coronado Bridge. In 1970, the neighborhood mobilized a political action in the form of civil disobedience, when it learned that land under the bridge was to be given to the California Highway Patrol for use as a substation and parking lot. Latino residents responded by physically taking over the space, remaining on it, first, as an act of protest, and later, by way of constructing their own park. Eventually, the city and state governments backed off and allowed the community its park, a site that today commands enormous symbolic pride in the community.[54] Surrounding the park are vivid Mexican murals, covering the otherwise imposing pillars of the Coronado Bridge. Each spring, a special Chicano Day celebration takes place here to honor the history of the community's struggle to create this important place.

Thus "barriology" represents a kind of collective decision to find ways to Mexicanize the bland spaces that had become home to the Chicano population. This growing social place consciousness has produced a contemporary generation of artists, community organizers, architects, store owners, schoolchildren, and others determined to inscribe their cultural origins upon the built landscape of their neighbors. This impulse can be seen both as a response to the crisis of barrioization and marginalization, and as a way of enriching their community experience. It is noteworthy to remember that the neighborhoods occupied by people of Mexican descent usually consisted of buildings in the Anglo tradition—wooden bungalows, Victorian mansions, or simple brick-and-concrete apartment houses. Ironically, the buildings designed with Mexico in mind—the Mission Revival and Spanish Colonial Revival structures—were usually *not* occupied by people of Mexican descent. We have already seen that these turn-of-the-century building styles were largely created and financed by Anglo promoters and investors concerned not so much with the preservation of Latino culture as with the propagation of a romantic image of California that would draw would-be residents and consumers.

FIG. 4.16 Freeways invade the *barrio* landscape: Chicano Park's kiosk is overshadowed by the freeway ramps. Barrio Logan, San Diego.

Thus, although Latinos could not alter permanent buildings and large infrastructure projects, they could transform the landscapes to make their communities more livable. It would be a mistake to restrict discussion of Latino *barrio* landscapes to the buildings alone. Landscapes in cities are strongly defined by buildings, but the spaces between the buildings are often equally or more important to the overall cultural landscape. This is quite noticeably the case in the Latino *barrio*. As stated above, in most Mexican American *barrios,* the landscapes they transformed were not originally built by them; they were built by the dominant Anglo population. But as Mexican Americans established territorial control over these places, they also established their own cultural landscapes. They personalized many of these spaces, transforming them, in part, from hopeless ghettos into vital living spaces, moving from a condition of being "barrio-ized" to one in which they felt a sense of belonging, a sense of place, a "barriology."

East Los Angeles is an excellent example of a Latino living space transformed by Mexican immigrants. It is today the largest concentration of Mexican American *barrio* communities in the southwestern United States. More than a million people of Mexican and Latino heritage live in East Los Angeles. Mexican immigrants began arriving there in the early decades of the twentieth century, settling in and around the original plaza of the nineteenth-century Mexican town. When the old plaza "Sonoratown" core could no longer absorb Mexican immigrants in the 1920s and 1930s, there was, as in so many other immigrant reception areas across the Southwest, pressure for the neighborhood to expand physically. Studies have shown that ethnic communities often expand in wedgelike fashion out of the original downtown area toward the edge of the city.[55] For Mexicans, expansion to the north and west was blocked by high rents and discrimination. Expansion to the south competed with a growing black community. This left the more logical path of expansion to the east of downtown, and so the Mexican *barrio* shifted eastward in the 1930s, as did many factories that employed Mexican immigrants and a trolley system between the factory locations and the old downtown plaza.[56]

Late-twentieth-century East Los Angeles, although the largest ethnic enclave of Mexican Americans in the urban United States, has building types typical of most older sun-belt "inner suburbs" built in the 1930s and 1940s: wood-frame, bungalow-style single-family homes on narrow, deep lots with small front yards and deeper backyards (except where second homes have been added onto the back lot, not unusual in densely populated East Los Angeles). What makes East Los Angeles unique is the way its people have enlivened the setting by adding to it elements that reflect their cultural understanding of urban living space. One scholar terms this "enacted space," people of one culture acting upon their living space to adapt it to their needs.[57]

Chicano personalization of the *barrio* can take many forms but generally revolves around either the way physical space is utilized, or the way the landscape is decorated. Often overlooked is the importance of *people* in transforming the more static built environment. In the *barrio,* what stands out is not the geometry of the wood-frame bungalows on their rectangular lots but, rather, the way the spaces around the lots have been personalized: "In the residential streets of East Los Angeles, everybody is a proprietor of the street. Children control the street by playing in it. Teenagers (gang members) exhibit physical control of the street, which can be read by other gang members. Adults control the street by knowing who lives around it."[58]

Street vendors add color and flavor to the streetscape of the Latino *barrio.* The street vendor, or *ambulante,* is an important element of the landscape of Mexican and Latin American cities. Street vendors in Latin America are late-twentieth-century relics of urban life in earlier centuries when street markets and street vending were a regular part of the urban economy, when the scale of urbanity was pedestrian, and the scale of marketing limited by technology and local ownership. In the late twentieth century, the combined forces of global marketing and automobile travel have moved marketing off the streets. The street

FIG. 4.17 The enacted *barrio* streetscape: taco vendor in Highland Park section of Los Angeles (R. Villa).

vendors that survive in less developed nations are a product of economic adaptation. Millions of urban dwellers came from farms and, unable to find work in traditional sectors like manufacturing or construction, they turn to the informal or street economy as a source of income for survival. Public spaces—streets, plazas, church yards, and open markets—become the domain of the large, mobile street-vending population south of the border.

In the *barrios* of the American Southwest, street vending reflects the same kind of innovative response to economic conditions. Those who sell on the streets are simply trying to earn a living in a difficult job market. They adapt their trade to the setting, using innovative equipment and spatial strategies to make their products and services more marketable. It is not uncommon on the streets of El Paso or Tucson or East Los Angeles *barrios* to find items being sold from shopping carts, makeshift barbecues, aluminum trash cans, wooden crates, Tupperware, a van, spread across a chain-link fence, or on pegboard stands. One study of East Los Angeles vendors identified seven street vendor prototypes:[59]

— "*Los moscos*" (the flies), or Central American and Mexican immigrants who gather in groups, peddling their availability as laborers. They usually station themselves on strategic street corners by which potential employers know to cruise if they need workers. Mariachis travel on commercial streets, often near bars, selling their services as musicians. They also find places to congregate (certain street corners) where people know to come to look for their services if they wish to use them for private parties.

— "Asphalt vendors" are those who set up near freeway off-ramps, or on the median strips of major street intersections. Taking advantage of slow-moving vehicles or cars at stoplights, they, like their counterparts in border cities like Tijuana, try to sell everything from bags of peanuts or oranges, to flowers and newspapers.

— "Pushcart vendors" roam the streets of East L.A. selling exotic fruit cocktails and other food (tamales, ice cream, etc.). Again these same kinds of vendors can be seen in Tijuana or Mexicali selling fruit and fish cocktails, shaved-ice drinks, hot dogs, and *carne asada* (broiled meat).

— "Tent vendors" are usually clever female entrepreneurs who set up enclosed stalls by attaching fabric from poles, buildings, or other means of support. Tent vendors are usually wedged tightly between buildings and fences or other structural supports. They sell clothing and household goods.

— "Weekend vendors" sell odds and ends, used clothing, household goods, in a sort of Mexican version of a flea market. Vendors work mainly on Saturdays. They make use of fences to hold up items for sale and delineate their selling areas.

— "Auto vendors" sell out of their vehicles, which they move from location to location, often parking their trucks or vans near key roadside sites and setting up their temporary markets for new items like Mexican ceramics or homemade objects.

— "Roach coaches" are the large food trucks one sees near construction sites and factories in most cities; in East Los Angeles, the food trucks are often custom-built and have become a popular part of the neighborhood landscape.

Similar patterns are found on the streets of San Diego's Barrio Logan, the oldest and most important Mexican American enclave in the city. While the magnitude of the neighborhood dictates a much smaller number of vendors, their range of activities is similar to that of Los Angeles. The same can be said, with perhaps regional variations in food, for the *barrios* of Texas, Arizona, and New Mexico. What is interesting about all these forms of informal commercial activity is the way Mexican American vendors adapt to social space.

For example, although East Los Angeles has a more pedestrian scale than most suburban communities, it is still traversed mainly by automobile, and vendors have therefore adapted both their choices of vehicles and selling locations to the freeway, automobile orientation of the city. In San Diego's Barrio Logan

FIG. 4.18 Latino creativity is quite evident in the commercial built environment: a tire store in the south Phoenix *barrio*.

neighborhood, the freeway creates the main public space of the community—a park called Chicano Park that lies directly beneath the bridge that joins the mainland to nearby Coronado Island. Around Chicano Park, one finds food, fruit, ice cream, and clothing vendors, as well as those who sell out of their cars. Many more commodities are offered for sale than in most neighborhoods; street vending is a Mexican (and Latin American) phenomenon, and clever entrepreneurs experiment with what can be sold until they get it right. Chicano and Mexican immigrant sellers are careful to choose the right locations and the proper mechanisms to engage in street vending. They use fences and buildings to delineate their selling space, keeping in mind that, even when shopping, people feel more comfortable in a well-defined consumption space, rather than one that chaotically spills over into public space. Also, many vendors utilize artistic designs in decorating their vans, buses, or cars to attract public attention: crucial in an informal street venture, where advertising in traditional media isn't possible.

It may also be true that the lively commercial culture of the street found in the *barrios* of the U.S. Southwest reflects the longing among Mexican immigrants for the public market culture so dominant in their homeland. Mexican cities are dominated by lively public spaces: plazas, squares, markets, and a vibrant street life. In the more automobile-oriented and suburban American city, this sense of place is lost. Latinos are trying to re-create the sense of plaza and public life they left behind south of the border.

There are a number of other "props" used by Latinos to personalize neighborhood landscapes like East Los Angeles.[60] Gas stations are converted to taco stands. Balconies and front porches on turn-of-the-century homes are vividly personalized with family items ranging from potted plants to furniture, toys, and barbecue equipment. Storefronts are stylishly decorated to the whim of the owner's taste. In Barrio Logan, in San Diego, many stores around Chicano Park display individual art produced by their owners. These decorations are often cluttered juxtapositions of color and advertising text, in a style that has been called *amontonado* (literally, *stacking*).[61]

Mexican American homes are distinguished by the emphasis on the front yard, or *la yarda*. Anglo homes typically utilize the front yard in a decorative way that tells outsiders something about the social status of the occupant. The front lawns are neatly mowed, and there may be flowers in the garden beds, but, as landscape writer J. B. Jackson argues, the front yard is often an impersonal space.[62] In East Los Angeles, the front yard is highly personalized, an active space that is decorated for everyday use (fountains, play space for children, etc.).[63] One of the main decorative features of the front yard is religious: the Christian shrine, which can also be traced to the idea of building a shrine for a saint in Spain or colonial Mexico. Yard shrines apparently translate differently in different *barrios* of the Southwest, from the *nichos* of Tucson, to the *capillas* of San Antonio to *grutas* in East Los Angeles.[64] The ultimate function of the yard is that it provides a way for individual residents to connect with the larger community: "Nowhere else in the urban landscape of East Los Angeles is the Mexican use of space so illuminated and celebrated than in the enclosed front yard. As Mexican immigrants settled in their new homes, the front yard became a very personal expression . . . The Mexican brings a new interpretation of the American front yard because many homes in Mexico do not have them . . . The front yards reflect Mexican cultural values applied to American suburban form."[65]

Fences appear to be another kind of landscape element of Mexican American *barrios*. Fencing in the front yard makes it a more intimate household space. It can be adorned with flowers. The act of enclosing and decorating the front yard becomes a way of integrating it with the indoor space of the home. The idea of enclosing the front yard is probably derived from the tradition of the enclosed courtyard or interior patio which was brought to colonial Mexico by Spanish colonists. This tradition, in turn, can be traced to the architecture of Islamic houses in southern Spain.[66] In the *barrios* of Tucson, we find evidence of the original Spanish colonial enclosed house in the form of the Sonoran adobe, a walled house with an enclosed patio. After 1900, this form of enclosure was

FIG. 4.19 Personalized *yarda* (front yard) in East Los Angeles. Note that the fenced enclosure is transparent to allow communication with neighbors (R. Villa).

gradually replaced by the fenced front yard, which became dominant in Mexican neighborhoods, but not in Anglo ones. The main form of enclosure is the chain-link fence.[67]

In the San Diego *barrio* of National City, a former resident describes a more creative form of fencing:

In my old neighborhood there was a man we called the "can man." In the 1980's, he started building a fence in front of his house out of empty beer cans, soda bottles and aluminum cans held together with cement. He would place the bottles and cans on their sides, the bottoms facing out towards the street, cementing them together. By strategically placing different colors of bottles in circles, diamonds and waves, he created patterns in the fence. The project began to grow as he added more elaborate posts and arches. Most amazing was a tower which connected with the house. The house became a neighborhood landmark; for years we used to drive by slowly, checking on the progress, wondering what he was going to do next.[68]

Whereas an Anglo resident would consider that his or her residential space begins at the front door, in the *barrio,* the home can be said to begin at the front-yard gate: "Collectively, the enclosed front yards in the neighborhood create a very intimate atmosphere as opposed to nonenclosed front yards of typical suburbs. The fences along the streets break up the lawn space of each home and the street becomes more urban rather than suburban in character, because the fence reflects a personality of the resident on the street."[69]

In the end, Mexican American *barrio* residential space displays a great deal of vernacular artistry. Latinos customize and personalize homes that would otherwise be indistinguishable from many other residential landscapes in rapidly urbanizing regions of the southwestern United States. In the *barrio* it has been possible to transform the homes, not so much by remodeling, which would be more expensive, but by transforming the spaces around the homes and the relationship between the home and the surrounding space. The small wooden bungalows are enhanced by the fenced-in personalized yards. But, more than just enclosing the yards, this alteration speaks to the larger issue of the design plan of the house. In Anglo homes, the flow of space moves from front to back, with the most important space being the back patio and backyard. In many *barrio* homes, the flow of space may be from side entrance to front, and the most important spaces are the front porch and front yard.[70] Once again, in the absence of the traditional interior courtyard, some observers claim that Mexican immigrants use the fence to create the feel of the interior patio in the front yard. The wood-frame houses themselves are rarely altered structurally, but they are often painted in bright and unusual colors.[71] Color can be traced back to the Spanish-Islamic cityscape, where polychromatic tiles embellished palaces and churches in a style called *mudejar*. This was eventually passed on to architectural style in colonial Mexico. Of course, indigenous architecture was also noted for its striking color, so that if one believes that cultural practices regarding home and neighborhood design are fused from different influences over time, it would not come as a surprise to find that Mexican Americans often choose the best paints and brightest colors to adorn homes in the *barrio*.[72]

There are other ways Chicanos impose their signature on neighborhood landscapes. Graffiti, or "tagging," is an outlet for young people to express themselves graphically on the built landscape. The term *graffiti* was coined by archaeologists in the eighteenth century when the ruins of ancient Pompeii were excavated from under volcanic ash. The walls, which had been preserved by the volcanic debris, were covered with personal odes, vulgar jokes, and social criticism that had been spontaneously scratched upon them. Thus the Italian term *graffito*, or its plural *graffiti*, was used to refer to scribbling or scratching of rude drawings, casual writing, or social commentary on rocks or walls.

Graffiti are termed *placas* in the *barrio*. They typically have a specific purpose: a way for gangs or individuals to express territorial ambition.[73] Gangs use specific tags to mark off space. Public parks or other meeting places are tagged by a local gang to express intended control of turf. The edges of one gang's turf are

FIG. 4.20 Chicano gangs put their stamp on the *barrio* landscape: *placas* (graffiti) on an empty lot in East Los Angeles. Gangs often choose their names from place identifiers, in this case, the 101 freeway (R. Villa).

also marked off to suggest working boundaries between one gang and another. Tagging areas outside of one's turf can indicate a form of graphic challenge from one gang to another. Sometimes, one gang's marker will literally be crossed out to accommodate another gang's tag. In a culture that places so much emphasis on ownership of property, and on control of private space, it should not be surprising to city governments that *barrio* gangs often mimic the values of the larger society, in wanting to control space. "Tagging" may also be a way to protest and express anger toward the establishment. Graffiti is often spray-painted on public property, including freeway exit signs, stop signs, or storage bins. Severe fines and penalties are assessed when the authors are caught defacing public property.

But, there are also more positive sides to the graffiti phenomenon. Many *barrio* observers have suggested that graffiti is a way for young people to add color and liveliness to the often impersonal and institutional elements of their neighborhood landscape. The *barrio,* visually speaking, can be a bleak place, filled with abandoned buildings, rundown storefronts, and factories with blank gray walls. Graffiti is often more than just idle scribble; it is carefully crafted calligraphy from practiced, artistic hands. Many in the *barrio* feel that programs should be set up to channel this artistry in more positive ways, and in some cities, small social-service projects are doing exactly that, training gang members to become artists and to contribute to the beautification of their neighborhoods.

Perhaps the most striking element of the *barrios* of the American Southwest, during the past three decades, has been the emergence of art in public spaces in the form of murals. *Barrio* muralism emerged as part of the larger Chicano movement in the 1960s, which sought to air demands and gradually politicize the *barrio*. Both muralism and the larger political movement also represented a way of maintaining cultural pride and, more specifically, defending real neighborhoods from the threat of demolition, urban renewal, or deterioration in quality of life brought on by the location of noxious facilities (freeways, stadiums, factories, bridges, etc.). In a sense, *barrio* muralism was a response to negative impacts of urban development on Mexican American communities in the 1960s and 1970s.

The emergence of murals on the *barrio* landscape can also be traced to more general cultural and historic forces. Muralism was an artistic and political vehicle that had emerged after the Mexican revolution of 1910–17. It became a way to inform and educate Mexico's basically illiterate rural population of the 1920s about the ideals of a new society and the evils of the past. Postrevolutionary muralism in Mexico in the 1920s and 1930s served to build a new consciousness. Diego Rivera, the great Mexican muralist and avowed Marxist, who became an international celebrity, captured the flaws of his country's past in murals on some of Mexico's great public buildings. Rivera was commissioned to create a mural for Rockefeller Center in New York City in the 1930s, but the mural was ordered destroyed by the Rockefellers when they discovered he had included Lenin among the world's greatest leaders. Other muralists joined Rivera in painting new images on Mexico's urban landscape, images that challenged and confronted, that promoted a new ideology of workers, peasants, and revolution. For example, José Clemente Orozco, from Guadalajara, created giant caricatures of state, church, bankers, politicians, and the military.

Given this legacy, and the conditions they faced living in the urban Southwest of the United States, in the 1960s the Chicano movement was part of the larger political struggle of ethnic minorities in the United States to achieve a better place in American society. Muralism, as it had in Mexico some four decades earlier, became a vehicle for protesting and airing demands on the daily urban landscape. It was also a way for Latinos to reclaim their place on that landscape. A field survey of murals in the *barrios* of El Paso and Tucson showed that the vast majority of murals were located in valuable public places—community centers, parks, and on major retail buildings. The process of painting the murals is a community activity; the art itself is community oriented and, therefore, locates in the most publicly frequented places. The main themes in early mural work (1960s, 1970s) tended to include pre-Columbian and religious ref-

FIG. 4.21 *Barrio* calligraphy: mural on store wall, south Phoenix.

erences, as well as attention to ethnic identity. More recently, there has been a
shift toward recognition of larger themes: harmony with nature, the global system, the Americas, as well as an emphasis on local landmarks and place identity.
Images from the *barrio* itself frequently find their way onto the artists' murals.[74]

In California, some fifteen hundred murals were painted on bridges, walls,
and buildings. As in the case of Mexican murals, the communication of ideas
was as important as the aesthetic qualities of the murals. The murals engage and
challenge the viewer. They often tell a profound story, whose subject can range
from religion and death to indigenous themes, historic events, celebration of famous people, and memories of scenic landscapes. The murals represent a way
for people to beautify what would otherwise be a sterile and depressing landscape, as for example in the painting of murals on the pillars of the Coronado
Bridge which intrudes upon the Barrio Logan neighborhood just south of downtown San Diego.[75]

If one analyzes the principal Chicano murals in the state of California,[76] the
connection between public art and community politics becomes clear. Images of
the Southwest (desert, cactus, mountains, volcano) appear, reminding the viewer
that many view this region as a homeland of Chicanos, a place called "Aztlán."
Images of the barrio-scape itself (*barrio* homes, graffiti, lowrider [decorated cars
driven at slow speeds] folklore, skyscrapers looming over the *barrio*) seek to re-

mind residents that the *barrio* is their community and that it is unique, but also increasingly troubled. The muralists have not been hesitant to place images of their political oppression and urban living conditions on the walls for all to see: police brutality, drug abuse, prisons, gangs, labor strikes. But perhaps equally striking in the mural art are the images that connect both back into Mexico and to the larger world of developing nations, especially Latin America. In the California Chicano muralism movement, some of the most recognized murals are those with Mexican themes: Pancho Villa, La Adelita, Emiliano Zapata, *pulquería* paintings of outdoor landscapes on bars typical of rural Mexico, numerous references to the great Mexican painter Frida Kahlo, and frequent reinterpretations of Mexican indigenous culture.[77]

The murals found in San Diego's Barrio Logan offer a particularly poignant illustration of the connection between public art and politics. After the Coronado Bridge was completed in 1969, residents of the *barrio* fought bitterly to prevent the California Highway Patrol from building a police station under the bridge. Land was occupied, there was civil unrest, and finally, the neighborhood won the right to establish a community park, Chicano Park, there.[78] From 1970 to 1973, the idea of embellishing the unsightly columns of the bridge with community murals took shape. The first murals were done during this period, and two artists' groups formed. Early murals mirrored efforts elsewhere in terms of content: symbols of indigenous culture, references to history and politics, and some graffiti. A special holiday each spring commemorated the founding of Chicano Park. But by 1975, crime in the park had increased, and drug dealers, drunks, and rival gangs fought for turf. A kiosk and second set of murals appeared by 1978. The murals became much more literal than the early mystical works. In 1980, Chicano Park was declared a historic site by the City of San Diego. The murals had played a vital role in establishing a sense of place and history in the center of the oldest Mexican American community in San Diego.

The taking back of their urban space through the creation of murals on the cityscape has assisted in achieving recognition of Latinos as a powerful political force in the U.S. Southwest, particularly in the border states of California, Texas, Arizona, and New Mexico. But as many of the images wafting across the barrioscapes make clear, the problems are far from resolved. Air pollution in the ghetto, police brutality, gangs, drug consumption, and unemployment remain deeply embedded in the *barrios*. Zoning, a tool created in the 1920s by cities to control land uses, was not used to better organize the *barrio* until recently. The problems of these neighborhoods may even be more grim than the images conveyed by muralists. No one would argue that the murals themselves offer any solution to the deeper problems. But they represent a way in which the Latino culture has begun to demonstrate that it has pride in its role in the urban scene,

FIG. 4.22 Mural landscapes evoke themes of pride and hard work, and the traditional Mexican connection to the land: a mural on the pillars of the Coronado Bridge, Chicano Park, San Diego.

some of which consists of territorial pride in the traditional spaces within the city that Chicanos have occupied.

It is understandable that not all Latinos chose to live in the traditional *barrios* when given the choice. The post-1950 period saw the gradual dispersal of upper- and upper-middle-class Latinos out of the *barrio,* as they assimilated into the larger urban fabric. While many Mexican Americans chose to move away from the *barrio,* they remained loyal to it, dedicating time to help preserve the neighborhoods, fight government insensitivity, or beautify the Latino spaces with parks, community centers, landscaping, and murals. More recently, the *barrio* landscapes of the Southwest have begun to show the effects of their connection to the global economy. Previously dominated by Mexican immigrants, the Latino *barrios* of today are filled with Central and South Americans as well. Evidence of their connection with their homeland, both economic and cultural, is illustrated best by the growing commercial landscapes of "transnational services"—legal assistance for foreigners, travel agents, remittance services, and assistance with immigration and naturalization. These activities are splattered across the commercial landscapes of the *barrio* today.

Many of the *barrios* continue to suffer severe urban design problems. Aside from low economic status, *barrios,* like other ghettos in the United States, have suffered from inadequate or irresponsible urban planning decisions. Examples include locating noxious facilities such as factories that pollute near *barrios,* building freeways through them, or airports nearby, inadequate open space, inadequate access to mass transit, locating prisons or jails or other negative facilities nearby, too much public housing, traffic congestion, and inadequate transport planning.

Cantones and *Colonias:* The Crisis of Exurban Mexican Immigrant Barrios

Long-term settlement of Mexicans in the southwestern United States produced the inner-city *barrios* described above. These enclaves represented somewhat traditional forms of immigrant adaptation to the urban housing market. Another kind of adaptation has also characterized the landscape of Mexican immigrant settlement on the U.S. side of the border. In this second prototype of community formation, Mexican immigrants responded to the high cost of both rental and owner-occupied housing by seeking nonconventional living spaces, ranging from illegal occupancy of land in undesirable rural and topographically isolated spaces (canyons, arroyos, riverbeds, etc.) to illegally subdivided lots. In both cases, the settlement experience appears as an extension of the shantytown and squatter experience in urban Mexico, including its northern border towns, and Latin America, where lack of capital forces cityward migrants to squat or illegally occupy undesired lands, build their own makeshift housing, live without basic services, and generally exist in a marginal, undeveloped urban community.[79]

In southern California, the large influx of Mexican immigrant workers in the post-1960 period has put a strain on an already saturated and overpriced housing market. While southern California is heavily populated, its urban form tends to be low density and dispersed. At the edges of the urbanized region, and in some exurban and suburban areas, lie tracts of agricultural land. It is not surprising that Mexican workers, beginning in the late 1970s, began searching for housing in these less expensive real estate locations. Furthermore, many immigrants working in agricultural or landscaping jobs on the outskirts of the city found it more convenient to reside near their work sites. For example, in northern San Diego county, thousands of Mexicans work for the agricultural industry, as day laborers, landscapers, packers, farm workers for the strawberry, tomato, and avocado growers, or for large nurseries and flower farms. Northern San Diego is a vast, complex topographic region with mountainous terrain cut

FIG. 4.23 Makeshift wooden shacks, Rancho de los Diablos migrant camp, northern San Diego (N. Barnes).

up by canyons and valleys. Housing developments for the affluent snake across the flatland on ridges and mesas. Down below in the flood-prone canyons and riverbeds lie thousands of acres of unusable land.

In these canyons thousands of migrant workers constructed live-in camps on unoccupied land. They set up spontaneous living environments, built from the detritus of their nearby work sites: tents and shelters of plastic, tar paper, cardboard, packing crates, and discarded wood. Clotheslines weave their way through the sites. Tortillas are cooked on the rusty lids taken from discarded fifty-five-gallon drums. Makeshift grills or pots are created from discarded items found in dumpsters. Most of the campsites, which the migrants call *cantones*,[80] lack running water or plumbing. Water is carried in from irrigation spigots on nearby farms. There is no electricity.

Aside from the inhuman nature of these camps in terms of health conditions, they are distinguished by a high degree of impermanence and instability. Their architecture is makeshift not only because of their limited resources; it is also that way because, for many of them, their unresolved legal status in the United States makes it necessary to be prepared to hide from the U.S. border patrol, or the immigration authorities. Even those workers with legal immigration status exist in a state of uncertainty, since the land they occupy is not legally zoned for residential use, and since the living conditions there (lack of running water, plumbing facilities) are usually in violation of county health codes.

These *cantones* remind one of the way poor city migrants find housing south of the border: they illegally occupy nonresidential land they do not have title to. This leads to a landscape of uncertainty. Housing is built of the cheapest materials. It would not make economic sense to invest in more expensive housing construction materials, if their fate is eventually to be driven off the land. Even renters usually do not invest in the infrastructure of the spaces they occupy. The difference is that renters are protected by the state and local housing codes that require landlords to maintain certain minimal levels of building safety and hygiene. Such protections do not exist for the Mexican migrants, who are thus forced to occupy ephemeral living spaces in what have been termed "shadowed lives." [81]

The typical housing types within the migrant camps range from makeshift tents built of plastic tarps and scrap wood to holes dug into the ground and covered with wood. The crawl spaces have been referred to as "spider holes" in the local media,[82] giving the impression metaphorically that the Mexican workers living in the wild are far apart from mainstream "cultured" San Diego, which sleeps in conventional houses or condominiums. Yet, the "spider holes" offer the migrants the possibility of "crawling" away or remaining hidden from the border patrol, who often raided these sites during the 1980s. Of course, the "spider holes" are amazingly unpleasant spaces for human shelter, frequently invaded, not by immigration authorities, but by fleas, rats, or snakes.

The migrant worker camps are not unique to San Diego County. Similar living conditions have been found in other parts of California. During the post-1960 period, Mexican migrants who crossed illegally into the United States have been forced to endure unbearably inhumane living conditions because they occupied a bizarre world: one in which their labor was demanded by U.S. employers, but their presence in the United States remained illegal. Thus, the architecture of illegal migrants has been highlighted by instability, unsafe, unpleasant, and inhospitable shelter, and inadequate safety and hygienic conditions. Harassment by public authorities or by the so-called border bandits, criminals who prey upon illegal migrants,[83] has simply added to what has basically been an unpleasant architecture of survival.

A different scenario has unfolded in Texas. There, the new *barrios* are called *colonias*. The basic definition of a *colonia* is "unincorporated, quasi-rural settlements characterized by substandard housing, and the absence of running water, wastewater facilities, garbage collection and paved roads." [84] The *colonias* dominate the border counties of Texas and are also found in much smaller numbers along the Arizona and New Mexico borders. It was estimated that in 1995, there were about 1,400 *colonias* with some 340,000 residents in Texas.

While the *colonias* tend to give the appearance of being rural dwellings, they are decidedly urban in orientation. The majority cluster around cities, though usually just outside the limits of the city government boundaries, and its planning and taxation effects. Unlike the often illegal migrant camps in southern California, the *colonias* are usually settlements on legally owned and subdivided land. The legal problems lie in false claims made by developers about providing services, which frequently are never delivered, and in the means by which the land is sold. In Texas, developers tend to buy up cheap, unproductive agricultural land, or land in floodplains, subdivide it, and sell individual plots to Mexicans through a "sweat equity" contract. The developer retains ownership during a ten-year payment period until the last payment is made. The Mexicans literally "sweat" over loss of their property if they are unable to make even one payment before the end of the payment period.

One is again struck by the similarity between the landscapes of Texas *colonias* and those of many Latin American squatter settlements. Both are alternative residential living zones on the edges of the city, or in undesirable locations. Both often involve either the sale or occupancy of peripheral lands on unimproved lots, where the resident builds the house over a period of time. Both are vernacular landscapes that are changed over intervals as more capital becomes available. In Latin America, this gradual alteration of the residential landscape has been termed "in situ accretion."[85] And both lack infrastructure (water, sewer lines, electricity, paved roads). In Hidalgo County, Texas, for example, in 1992, it was estimated that 70.2 percent of the *colonias* lacked water, sewage lines, gas, and electricity.[86] In most Texas *colonias,* developers are able to keep total housing costs down by not providing the standard urban services required in most cities to develop land for residential use.

But, the lack of services has led to a landscape of terrible environmental degradation and health problems similar to those found in the shantytowns of Latin America. In the Texas *colonias,* lack of indoor plumbing, poor sanitation, and flooding of outdoor latrines have caused the outbreak of a number of diseases, including hepatitis, dysentery, tuberculosis, and even dengue fever.[87] Also, residents store their drinking water in fifty-five-gallon chemical drums, even though the drums are often marked with the warning: "Do not reuse for food and drink." This has resulted in rashes and gastrointestinal illness. Because so many of the *colonias* are located on flat, treeless fields near agricultural activity, residents are also exposed to dust and chemical insecticide spraying.

Some of the largest *colonia* populations sprawl on the edges of three cities in

FIG. 4.24 Trailers often represent the first stage of building a permanent residence in the *colonias* on the edges of Texas cities: *colonia* near El Paso, Texas (J. Pereau).

the Lower Rio Grande Valley—Laredo, McAllen, and Brownsville, the second, third, and seventh fastest-growing cities in the United States according to the census.[88] Other *colonias* are noteworthy on the outskirts of major border cities, including Del Rio and El Paso. These are all part of one of the poorest regions in the United States and what is ostensibly a peripheral region within Texas, where the economic and political power lies in the Dallas–San Antonio–Austin-Houston triangle.[89]

The landscape of the Texas *colonias* is one of isolation and intense rural poverty. This combination has much to do with the fact that the *colonias* are one of the least publicized phenomena of the region. One observer, speaking about the Lower Rio Grande River Valley, has noted, "It is quite possible to visit the valley and never really see a *colonia. Colonias* remain relatively invisible; many lie far from major highways and roads, squeezed between enormous fields of cotton, sorghum and corn, or hugging the edges of irrigation canals and citrus groves." [90] Treeless lots sweep across flat, open expanses of vacant land. The houses tend to be mainly of the single-family, detached type. Their architecture ranges from scrap wood shacks to wood-frame houses to mobile homes, discarded buses, and rebuilt railroad cars. Only rarely does one see a traditional brick or cement

FIG. 4.25 One should not forget that the *colonia* settlements in Texas represent a vast improvement over the poor state of housing in squatter settlements just south of the border: a *colonia* house in Ciudad Juárez (J. Pereau).

house. One study of the Lower Rio Grande Valley found that 5 percent of all housing units were ramshackle wood, 20 percent wood frame in poor condition, 45 percent wood frame in good condition, 15 percent brick/cement, and 15 percent mobile homes, including abandoned buses.[91] Another study of the *colonias* of the El Paso region shows how immigrants incorporate both U.S. and Mexican cultural traditions in their housing construction. For example, immigrants seem to prefer the use of the front gabled roof symbolizing the American house. They also favor the installed green grass lawn, a solid custom in the U.S. On the other hand, immigrants also prefer to fence in the front yard in a transparent manner, so as to maintain the Mexican tradition of social exchange through the front gate.[92]

Many of the Texas *colonias* are booming. An excellent example is Laredo, a NAFTA boomtown, at the hub of north-south transit and trade. Laredo has seen its population increase from 72,000 in 1970 to 155,000 in 1994. Much of this population increase lies in the *colonias*. Because so much of the growth is unplanned, the landscape of *colonias* is quite chaotic. It is not unusual, for example, to find a suburban brick house "surrounded by rusted trailers, and shacks nailed together with tar paper and packing pallets."[93]

The Texas government has begun to crack down on unscrupulous *colonia* developers. More than fifty lawsuits have been filed against them by the state government.[94] In 1992, the Environmental Protection Agency (EPA) in Washington, D.C., produced a comprehensive plan for cleaning up the border environment, including greater attention to the *colonias*. But many of the *colonias* exist in a kind of "catch 22" dilemma: until their plots are officially placed on city maps ("platted"), they cannot legally receive government assistance. But in order to be platted, *colonia* lots must have paved streets, lighting, and other normal services.[95] So even though the North American Development (NAD) Bank is putting some three billion dollars into border environmental projects, the *colonias* cannot so easily receive the benefits of these monies. Ironically, as the state makes it harder for developers to subdivide new *colonias* (a current bill before the Texas state legislature seeks to do this), the existing *colonias* will be forced to accommodate even larger numbers of newcomers, increasing population density, and causing further overcrowding and greater deterioration of the community quality of life.

In general, the living conditions of Mexican Americans and Mexican immigrants in the United States have consisted of segregation, discrimination into *barrios* and migrant camps, and a feeling of disenfranchisement from the larger society. Such living conditions have been reflected in the kinds of spaces Latinos in the Southwest have been forced to occupy. This is not to say, however, that Latinos have not fought back and tried to enhance their living conditions, or even improve the spaces they occupied. The migrant camps of southern California are distinguished by the ingenuity with which farm workers were able to build living spaces with limited materials and income. In Texas, *colonia* dwellers have struggled to achieve the dream of home ownership in the face of below-poverty-level quality-of-life conditions. The impressive rate of lot improvement and gradual construction of permanent dwellings attest to the overall accomplishment of these objectives.

The long journey of Mexico's urbanism to the northern frontier of the United States, as told in this chapter, is a complex tale of lost memory and borrowed memory. Nostalgia and marketing may have fueled Anglo use of Mexican themes in designing southwestern U.S. cities in the first part of the twentieth century. But the dominant Mexican demographic presence in the region today, on both sides of the boundary, suggests that a completely different kind of built environment is possible in the next century.

FIVE

High Tech?

The Cultural Landscapes of North American Economic Integration

When confronting its northern neighbor, history has taught
Mexico that it has few defenses.   —ALAN RIDING

What kind of cultural landscapes are produced in cities where Mexican memory collides with American "high tech"? If the borderlands encapsulate the meeting place of Mexican city-building traditions with those in the United States, they also bring together two cultures with strikingly different urban design traditions. These differences are borne out by the contrasting architectures, population densities, and city forms north and south of the boundary. Yet on the Mexican side, linkages with the U.S. economy did partly influence the evolution of border cities. And across the border in the United States, Mexican migrants brought their culture and created enclaves with distinct identity.

The ultimate fate of Mexico and of the region where Mexico and the United States physically overlap lies wrapped up in the process of integration—how the Mexican and U.S. economies and cultures intersect, and the resulting new cultural landscapes they produce. The previous chapters examined regional landscape elements for northern Mexico and the southwestern United States but did not address the collision of culture as it embeds itself in the built environment. This chapter seeks to explore this matter, focusing on the impact of U.S. culture on Mexico's border urban landscape. The timing of this discussion is most appropriate. A key phrase for the 1990s is "economic integration." Mexico has entered a long-term trade alliance with the United States—the North American Free Trade Agreement (NAFTA). The main debates concerning NAFTA in the early 1990s revolved around its impact on labor, work conditions, and the physical environment. But what will North American economic integration do to the physical plant—the cities, towns, and built landscapes—on each side of the border? Few studies on the impact of NAFTA have even mentioned this as an issue.

Embedded in the question of NAFTA are two larger processes threatening cultural landscapes in cities everywhere, and will be especially important in transformation of the Mexico-U.S. border region: globalization and modernism. The rise of a global economy undoubtedly represents one of the more potent forces contributing to the redefinition of urban space. Many urban activities— banking, manufacturing, the recruitment of labor, trade, marketing, and advertising—were once locally based but are now managed by global corporations. Because decisions that impact cities are made by managers from global headquarters in another city or country, the fate of the urban built environment is more uncertain than ever before. The U.S.-Mexico border may be particularly hard hit, since most of the key economic activities—tourism, manufacturing, and trade—are controlled by global actors.

Early in the twentieth century, modernism was embraced in Latin America, as well as the United States and Europe, as a system for incorporating the best elements of technology to design a better world. Utopian architects like Le Corbusier or Frank Lloyd Wright envisioned futuristic cities where architecture could solve the social and economic problems of urban industrial societies. The elevator, steel-frame skyscrapers, reinforced concrete, and sheet glass were to be the building blocks and materials of utopian cities. Le Corbusier revealed his plan in *La Ville Radieuse* (The Radiant City), which called for surgical removal of historic centers in cities like Paris and their replacement with "machine age" vertical communities where schools, shopping, work sites, and housing would be self-contained within each skyscraper. Yet, by the end of the twentieth century, we have come to recognize that these utopian visions were ill conceived. This is perhaps best illustrated in the failed utopian Brazilian capital, Brasilia, which was designed as a grand Le Corbuser-inspired modernist project but ended up overscaled, impractical, environmentally alienating, poorly utilized, and lacking in humanness.[1] In the words of one critic, Brasilia "is an expensive and ugly testimony to the fact that, when men think in terms of abstract space rather than real place, of single, rather than multiple meanings, and of political aspirations, instead of human needs, they tend to produce miles of jerry-built nowhere, infested with Volkswagens."[2]

Neither globalization nor modernism is entirely to blame for many of the ills of late-twentieth-century North American cities—overcrowding, pollution, gridlock, noise, crime, alienation, and loss of community—but they have certainly been contributing agents. The proliferation of books and studies of failed megacities such as Los Angeles[3] attest to the problems of globalizing cities. The prevailing model of urban development in these cities is one in which corporate profit is a driving force in the logic of the built environment. Thus, just as the bottom line dominates the ideology of global investors, so it impacts the landscapes of the cities they build.

North American economic integration must also be viewed through the lens of the cultural landscape. The integration of U.S. and Mexican economies is a long-term enterprise involving negotiation over fair trade, labor, and environmental impacts. It is also a renegotiation of the built landscape of North America. For Mexico, the potential losses may be greater. Mexico has an older and longer set of traditions brought to bear upon the built landscape. Its vernacular landscapes are rich and imaginative, even along the northern border, as we saw in chapter 4. Mexico, therefore, may have the most to lose in the transformation of landscapes brought on by North American economic integration. Mexico, it seems, will be forced to embrace North American–style modernity. Let us examine this prospect in two important layers of the built environment: the tourism landscape and public places.

Embracing Modernity? The Example of Tourism

The quickest way to douse itself in the kind of modernity that grows north of the border is for Mexico to embrace its tourism industry. At its worst, tourism ignores local culture; it tends toward generic settings that pacify anxious visitors. In Mexico, the tourism industry has long been on the front lines of cultural "North Americanization." More recently, this pattern has accelerated.

There is little question that, for developing nations like Mexico, tourism generates income, and more important, foreign income—dollars. As one writer stated about Mexico during the economic crisis of the early 1980s, "What might rescue Mexico, at least from the stigma of its incessantly predicted collapse? Not crude oil, but tanning oil. Tourists."[4] But tourism is no panacea; it can generate social tensions, exacerbate existing inequalities, and create overdependency.

These problems express themselves physically in the cultural landscape of tourism. Tourism is a global industry increasingly controlled by large, multinational corporations. Such global tourist enterprises exert a monopoly over the tourism industry in areas like transportation, travel agencies, advertising, and investment.[5] This authority manifests itself in the built environment in several ways. First, tourism is converted into a commodity for consumption in the world market. Just as in product marketing, global companies want to standardize the tourism experience. Thus, tourism "packages" are subject to mass marketing in the developed world. The basic infrastructure of tourism—airports, hotels, beach resorts, restaurants, boutiques, and commercial spaces—is designed to be homogenous and uniform. Tourists traveling to Cancún or southern Baja California confront familiar building styles, facilities, and tourism spaces. In Mexico, chain restaurants, hotels, and clothing stores (some U.S. owned or franchised) are gradually saturating the cultural landscapes of tourism zones.

The ultimate prototype of homogenized tourism is the Club Med, a generic style of vacationing that subjects tourists to standard experiences in different parts of the world. Club Med creates a "safe" exotic setting that is usually detached from the local surroundings. Club Med experiences are self-contained packages. Those who purchase these packages are provided with all the entertainment needed for the experience. Tourists need not "venture" out of the confines of the resort to experience the "real" Mexico. Their paradise is conveniently stored within Club Med's walls. That is a truly "placeless" form of tourism marketing.

The tourism industry, controlled from international command centers in wealthy nations, tends to promote distorted images of Third World nations like Mexico, the main destinations of their clients. Global tourism firms have little interest in portraying nations as they really are. For example, it is almost always the case that poverty is minimized or ignored, as are many local customs and practices. Instead exotic and romantic qualities of the landscape are amplified— lush jungles, white sand beaches, turquoise oceans, red-tiled roofs, and colorful markets, for example. Some tourist promoters even go so far as to imply that sexual liaisons with exotic locals are possible, and that the mind-set of host people is that they are there to make the tourist feel comfortable.[6]

The distinct marketing strategies of the international tourism industry thus lead to the production of placeless landscapes, devoid of culture and nature.[7] If tourism is more profitable in built landscapes that are homogeneous, then what incentive can there be for tourism developers to preserve the original landscapes of the places they invest in? Even in ecologically sensitive zones (jungles, mountains, etc.) or culturally preserved spaces (colonial downtowns), the demand for cosmopolitan infrastructure by tourists—luxury hotels, swimming pools, and plush shopping spaces—has the effect of diminishing the original landscapes which become overwhelmed by structures designed for consumption. Throughout Latin America, and especially in Mexico, the preserved ruins of ancient cultures or magnificent natural settings are gradually being overshadowed by the landscape of global consumerism—international chain hotels, restaurants, stores, and car-rental agencies.

The destructive impact of tourism development on cultural landscapes is

FIG. 5.1 Safe, familiar, and perhaps exotic architecture is one of the key features in the packaging of the tourist experience by global firms: a discotheque in Cancun, Mexico.

a worldwide phenomenon, and examples abound in Europe, the Polynesian islands, and Latin America. Even in the Hawaiian islands, massive tourism development, despite bringing greater affluence to the region, has also generated polarization between rich and poor territories and left a growing resentment toward the exclusive Japanese golf clubs (with membership fees over one million dollars), resorts, and condominiums. Suddenly, amidst beaches destroyed by dull high-rise hotels, politicians in Hawaii are being elected on growth control platforms.[8] In Latin America, tourism is also questioned. It not only displaces agriculture, industry, and land for housing; it also displaces culture.[9]

In Europe, the construction of Disneyland outside of Paris unleashed a massive critical response among the French public, much larger than the investors may have originally envisioned. Critics, among them the mainstream press, charged that Disneyland, located so close to the sacred cultural cityscape of Paris, was a distortion of French culture, an imposition of American cartoon characters and fantasy architecture on the French. One commentator went so far as to describe Disneyland as a "cultural Chernobyl." A general backlash seemed to emerge in Europe, centering on the contaminating effects of foreign visitors and typified by the example of one newspaper article with the headline "Europe Fumes at Tasteless Tourists."[10]

Another way that tourism manifests itself in the cultural landscape is through its "enclave" character. The ideology of tourism development is to create a consumable product for mass marketing; if the local culture interferes with the marketing of the product, then it is simply to be removed. The important thing is to provide the foreign tourist with an uninterrupted feeling of comfort and escape. It is believed that tourists want to forget reality. So reminders of the real country within which the tourism development is located are to be minimized where possible. A similar marketing strategy is employed by gambling casino developers in Las Vegas and Reno. The absence of clocks and the consistent seductive eveninglike lighting of the gambling parlors are architectural ploys used to create a timeless setting within which consumers can escape . . . and spend. Further, it is typically the case that tourism zones are physically separated from the host culture. Tourist districts often appear as self-contained clusters of Western-style hotels, restaurants, and shopping areas. Tourist enclaves tend to be a bubble of high-priced goods and services, thus enhancing the gap between the tourist district and the remainder of the host setting.

One of Mexico's leading architects, Ricardo Legorreta, has designed a number of important resort hotels, including the lavish Mayan temple–like Camino Real in Ixtapa. In describing his relationship with developers during the design of the Ixtapa hotel complex, Legorreta lamented that the investors failed to understand the importance of relating the architecture to the region. In one particularly upsetting example of the enclave mentality, Legorreta said, "the main attraction of Mexico's Pacific Coast is that it has the best climate in the world, but the builders wanted to seal all windows and put air conditioners in all 450 rooms."[11]

Mexico may, in fact, be the most important place in the hemisphere to examine the impact of tourism on a historically and culturally rich built environment. Mexico has become the "star" of international tourism in Latin America, receiving some 40 percent of tourists traveling to Latin America. It now welcomes more than six million visitors annually, generating revenues of some three billion dollars a year.[12] But these impressive numbers also point to Mexico's big dilemma: how to manage the impact of massive tourism development on its built environment, so as not to jeopardize the future value of the national patrimony, which requires conservation and preservation, two processes that are not universally supported by tourism interests within and outside of Mexico.

Along the northern border, the impact of tourism on the cultural landscape does not go unnoticed by native Mexicans. In Tijuana, parts of the city have been reduced to caricature. These caricatures partly play up to U.S. tourists' expectations of what kind of experience they will have on the Mexican border.[13] But not all Mexican border observers accept this transformation of their city and its landscape as a way of marketing for outsiders. "We've badly adjusted to

FIG. 5.2 Tourist knickknacks blend into the border cultural landscape:
Revolution Avenue, downtown Tijuana.

our tourism," comments one Baja California architect. "We've gotten into bad
habits. Our tourism is humble, it's lacking in educational qualities. The tourists
who come to Revolution Avenue come to bargain, to buy little knickknacks.
They lack any sense of art or architecture. The knickknacks they buy are like
the buildings. In the end, it is a form of art, a picturesque moment, a landscape
like your Las Vegas. But all architecture reaches a limit, and then begins to fall.
Revolution Avenue may be in its hour of decline." [14]

As its international debt has mounted over the last two decades, the Mexican government's need to generate foreign revenue accelerated. This tends to make government officials skeptical about the cost-benefits of protecting historic landscapes in potentially high-yield tourism zones. Recent governments have, in fact, made this increasingly clear. Shortly after taking office in December 1988, former Mexican President Carlos Salinas de Gortari, to the dismay of many citizens, announced that his administration would "restructure" foreign investment laws to bring in outside capital badly needed to jump-start the nation's economy. Two changes that were immediately put in place included: first, relaxing previous laws permitting a maximum of 49 percent foreign ownership of business enterprises to allow 100 percent ownership for certain kinds of economic activity; and second, doubling the leasing period for foreign possession of property, through the so-called *fideicomiso* (trust), from thirty to sixty years.[15]

These moves were, of course, a prelude to the Salinas administration's larger ambition of signing the North American Free Trade Agreement, which occurred four years later. But even as early as 1988, the Mexican government was actively courting the presence of U.S. investors. Enter the tourism industry. Tourism development represented, for Salinas, a much greater potential source of national revenue than previous administrations had tapped; but, foreign capital was badly needed for new infrastructure. Thus, as early as the spring of 1989, then–Minister of Tourism Carlos Hank Gonzalez embarked on a whirlwind campaign to attract North American investors. By the mid-1990s, the effects of these campaigns on the cultural landscape of Mexican coastal communities, the border region, and other tourism zones were obvious: U.S.- and foreign-owned hotels, retail outlets, and other enterprises, or their subsidiaries, are gradually displacing Mexican activities. Shopping malls, fast-food restaurants, golf resorts, time-share condominiums, and American real estate offices are becoming increasingly common south of the border.

The willingness of the Salinas administration to relax constitutional protections against foreign control of the economy raised questions about how far Mexico was willing to abandon control over its culture in return for the economic advantages of foreign investment. At a time in history when multinational corporations were imposing their "Western" models of economic development upon Third World nations, concerns about the long-term effects in such areas as the environment have been well documented. Some damage would, of course, be suffered in the cultural arena, through the more subtle and less publicized destruction of the cultural fabric of specific places—their architecture, community identity, flora, and fauna.

In Mexico, there are those who worry about cultural "North Americanization." It is said that such worries are not entirely new, that they have been around since the end of the Second World War. But, the trend toward North Americanization has accelerated with the onset of NAFTA. The Salinas administration operated under the rule that economic growth would take precedence over considerations of cultural preservation. In his third State of the Union speech in 1992, then-President Salinas stated: "Nationalism is that which strengthens the nation. It is not the longing for forms and traits of other times. Our culture is not, cannot and should not be a dead catalogue of past triumphs. Nor can it be impermeable to interchange with other cultures."[16] By opening the country to the greatest foreign influx in the nation's history, new questions have naturally emerged about Mexican culture and identity. As commentator Carlos Monsivais said recently about Mexico's cultural transformation, "It has been accelerated by the religion of globalization . . . private enterprise is the saint and free trade is the holy grail."[17]

What we have in Mexico is yet another case of a developing country grappling with exposure to the United States and the global economy in a moment of economic transformation. It is possible to view the transformation of Mexico's architecture and traditional landscapes in the context of global consumption. We know, for example, that transnational corporations (TNCs) seek to create in developing nations a mood of consumption that enhances TNC profits. TNC global marketing campaigns emphasize, as mentioned earlier, the importance of consumer recognition. Thus, global consumption tends to be enhanced by encouraging a world of uniform consumer tastes and values. For example, sales campaigns have been identified in which the consumption of white bread, confections, and soft drinks creates the idea that status, convenience, and sweet taste are more important than nutrition.[18] It follows that multinational corporations and their supporting interests not only create a *mood* for consumption but also a *built landscape*—buildings, architecture, cities—that reflects the values of Western consumerism.

How does this manifest itself in Mexico? One of the things neighboring territories—the U.S. Southwest and northern Mexico—share is a unifying element: growth. Northern Mexico has had one of the fastest population growth rates in the nation over the last three decades, mainly due to internal migration. The southwestern United States claims a similar distinction north of the border. On both sides, one of the key economic sectors feeding on the crescendo of population has been tourism. Tourism also sustains what has been called the "growth machine," the amalgam of development-oriented enterprises—land investors, real estate entrepreneurs, developers, banks, construction companies, architecture firms—that benefit from growth.[19] The U.S. "growth machine" has already shown that it is capable of penetrating the border. Economic forces that shape rapidly urbanizing areas of the United States, such as southern California, are now aimed squarely at Mexico. The development of the tourism economy along

FIG. 5.3 Global consumerism is becoming more conspicuous in the commercial landscape of Mexican border towns: Jack in the Box in downtown Tijuana.

the Mexican border offers an excellent example of how Mexico's need for a quick economic fix may be culturally disruptive in the longer run.

Development-oriented enterprises that operate along the Mexican border include land investors, developers, banks, construction companies, chambers of commerce, and architects. Mexico's growth machine is mediated through a different political system than in the United States, but in the end, the bottom line is the same: the growth machine (be it the main political party, or PRI, or the tourism-planning agency, FONATUR, aligned with private sector interests) has as its objective the maximization of profit per unit of land. Visual aesthetics, historic preservation, and environmental design do not readily enter the agenda of growth machine advocates. For example, when the global corporation Foodmaker, Inc., decided to open its third-largest Jack in the Box in the world on Revolution Avenue in Tijuana, the restaurant was designed in the standard Jack in the Box mold, including the red box with the words "Jack in the Box" resting on a tall pole. No one questioned whether this visual design might be incompatible with the more vernacular and whimsical streetscape of downtown Revolution Avenue.

"I don't think we should bring these establishments in the way we did," one architect commented, speaking of the new Jack in the Box and McDonald's restaurants opening in Tijuana. "The reason they built the exact replicas of their U.S. stores in Tijuana is this: Mexico is still trying to imitate the heavyweight and the heavyweight is still the U.S. But these fast food outlets distort our city."[20]

Further south, an entire village has appeared along the Baja coastline, a village whose existence and design are entirely devoted to the consumption of lobsters by North Americans. From its humble origins as a small village of five migrant families from the state of Jalisco, Puerto Nuevo has become a busy commercial town that houses some thirty restaurants and several nearby luxury hotels. Ironically, the town is really divided into two: the three or four main streets are lined with one- to three-story restaurants, some simple boxy stucco structures, others more elaborate and modern. At the edges of town, in sunken canyons or on abandoned lots, are the homes where the restaurant workers live. Puerto Nuevo is a kind of *hacienda* that produces lobster consumption for U.S. citizens. The town is basically oriented toward American consumers, with the housing for workers attached as an afterthought. In a sense, this reinforces a conceit that some North Americans have about Baja California: that it is a recreational park for their entertainment, and not a real place with a native population. It is derived from a long-standing notion that the United States should own Baja California, a conceit that in the 1980s was updated to imply that Mexico should sell Baja to the U.S. so it could pay off its national debt. The impact would be, in the words of one writer: "Gas stations, coffee shops and motels along the road; cities proliferating on the shore; coves dominated by towering condos; real estate signs polluting the landscape; traffic jams and auto wrecking yards; resort hotels with swimming pools, hundreds of square miles of tract homes, and an overnight burgeoning of slums for the 'aliens' who would flock to these glitzy oases for jobs as waiters, busboys and maids. In short, it would soon look like southern California."[21]

The commercial eclipse of Baja California culture is already under way. Baja California is a 55,000-square-mile peninsula dominated by desert and mountain wilderness. Its vast coastlines, east and west, have largely gone undeveloped in the twentieth century. Only its northern flanks, lying at the gateway to southern California, are heavily urbanized; the remainder of the peninsula is wildly pristine, a vast frontier comparable in magnitude to other great wilderness areas— Brazil's upper Amazon basin, or the Australian outback. This is changing at a sudden and swift pace. Geography—proximity to the postindustrial, megalopolan giant of southern California—makes Baja California highly vulnerable to the marketing interests of the U.S. growth machine. Several decades ago, writers glorified Baja California's isolation and pristine natural beauty.[22] It was inevitable, however, that a land so rich in beauty and so close to the exploding markets of southern California be brought within reach of the developer.

More than 25 million U.S. tourists visit the peninsula each year. Some 40,000

North Americans live permanently on the peninsula, and in one stretch of sixty-five miles along the coast between Tijuana and Ensenada, 25,000 North Americans occupy exclusive housing subdivisions in an enormous wedge of prime beachfront land. Only Guadalajara, Mexico, long a retirement destination for U.S. citizens, has more North Americans.

These statistics do not convey the full extent to which this peninsula is being swept into the North American cultural and economic web. The development of transport infrastructure linking the United States with Baja California is one example of growing integration. Several commercial airline companies are opening direct service routes into Baja. Today, direct flights connect Baja with San Diego, Los Angeles, Dallas, Denver, Vancouver, and Toronto, and the list keeps expanding. A second form of North American cultural penetration into Baja is seen in real estate and commercial development projects. Beaches from San Felipe to Loreto and Cabo San Lucas that were once isolated are now being overrun by time-share condominium developments, all-terrain vehicles, and recreational vehicle parks. To Californians looking south, Baja no longer seems distant, isolated, and empty, or far from the beaten path. Even Hollywood considers southern Baja within reach. In a 1989 movie, *The Boost,* members of Los Angeles's jet set flew their private airplane to Cabo San Lucas on the southern cape of Baja (over one thousand miles from Los Angeles) for dinner, apparently returning to Los Angeles the same evening. Hollywood often distorts distance and the nature of places, but this kind of scripting also reflects California's changing perceptions of its southern neighbor. Mexico has moved into Hollywood's line of vision, and her exotic shores lie within reach of the affluent.

A century ago, *filibusteros* (freebooters) saw in Mexico the possibility of earning great wealth quickly, if not illegally. The American William Walker sailed into the southern Baja California port of La Paz in 1853 with an expedition of two hundred armed men and captured the city. For a short time, Walker lived out his fantasy: he declared himself President of Lower California. Today's *filibusteros* are North American investors and real estate entrepreneurs who want to convert Baja's wilderness into an international tourist mecca. The costs of selling off the coastline to tourist developers are many, not the least of which is the destruction of *authentic* culture.

Acapulco was Mexico's original flirtation with the tourism model, the first large-scale, palm tree–lined, tropical resort south of the border. Created after the Cuban revolution in 1959, it grew in two and a half decades from a small town to a giant metropolis of one-half million people. At its peak, Acapulco boasted over twelve thousand hotel rooms and some 1.5 million yearly foreign visitors. But it also spawned one of Mexico's largest shantytowns, and the massive incoming migration generated high unemployment, housing shortages, and more recently, serious problems of contamination and air pollution. The beach-front today is clogged with high-rise hotels, leaving little space to view the once-pristine beaches. Acapulco is the first example of catastrophic spontaneous tourism in Mexico.

Acapulco was also the first case of a beach resort that completely over-whelmed its natural setting. Since then, the Mexican government has attempted several large-scale "planned" tourism developments at Ixtapa/Zihuatanejo and Cancún. In 1972, the Mexican government tourism development agency Fondo Nacional de Turismo (FONATUR), in a partnership with the World Bank, sys-tematically designed Ixtapa/Zihuatanejo on the Pacific coast in the state of Guer-rero. The idea was to convert the marshes, coconut plantations, and mangrove fields into a modern tourist resort at Ixtapa, while the small town of Zihuatanejo would be converted into a service city via an urban renewal plan. The plan was not without controversy. *Ejido* (state communal farm) lands were seized by the government under protest by local landowners. Observers believe that the gov-ernment did not adequately provide for the needs of local residents; the biggest insult was that more than six thousand construction workers were brought in from outside the region, leaving the locals underemployed.[23]

Cancún, on a peninsula off the coast of the Yucatan, was also a planned city designed by FONATUR with the Inter American Development (IAD) Bank. It was created using a similar model of a resort paired with a service city. Cancún has been criticized for being destructive of both the physical and the socio-cultural environment. When Cancún was designed, FONATUR's planners did not utilize a comprehensive environmental protection plan; as a result, man-grove wetlands and tropical forests were destroyed. Quarries were dug, creating water-filled holes that would become mosquito-breeding areas. Wildlife sanctu-aries were destroyed and picturesque lagoons filled in for condominium sites. On the sociocultural side, tourism workers were supposed to live in Cancún City, adjacent to the resort. But the price of housing became so high there that many were forced to live in giant squatter settlements down the road in Puerto Juárez (population over thirty thousand), an embarrassment to FONATUR.[24]

Meanwhile, the architecture of Cancún itself erases one's memory of Mexico rather quickly and forcefully. The resort zone is filled with U.S.-style mini-shopping malls, which sell T-shirts and generic cuisine. Hotel architecture is largely of the glass international style and rather uninspired, with only a few exceptions. Cancún City is bustling, chaotic, and commercial, like Hong Kong, filled with K-mart-type stores for workers and street vendors selling household goods. The *zocalo* (main square) is bare and underwhelming, a wasteland that people walk across to get to the next store. Cancún City has been smothered by global consumerism.

This legacy awaits Baja California. Tourism development, while offering short-term, measurable benefits, can create serious long-term problems. In Mexico, tourism facilitators are handing over ownership of property to foreign interests. Tourism development can be destructive to the physical environment, as is already clear in the cases of Acapulco and other large-scale resorts. It can also deface the cultural artifacts of Mexico's regions (such as Baja California). It gives foreign interests, in concert with a class of elite Mexican "facilitators"—lawyers, bankers, financial consultants, engineers, architects, and government officials who are paid to assist in setting up North American investment projects—the power to reconstruct places like Baja California in the image of their choice.

The presence of the North American growth machine in Baja California is escalating. A landscape of small towns, farm communities, fishing villages, and wide open spaces is slowly being transformed into "tourist architecture"—white and pastel stucco resort complexes and generic theme parks for tourists. One of the first things one notices on arriving at the new population centers on this desert peninsula—San Felipe, Loreto, or Cabo San Lucas—are the highway signs announcing, in English, the sale of land for single-family housing, golf villas, or condominium development. The fishing villages and farming towns with their antique central plazas are brushed aside, and in their place are new commercial streets lined with boutiques and high-rise hotels. Baja's unique sense of place is sacrificed in favor of mass production of all-purpose exotic resort paradises for foreign tourists.

The tourism landscape was central to Tijuana and other border town economies for much of this century. The border imagery—sombreros, taco stands, and donkey carts—may be artificial, but it is universally recognized. It is part of the fantasy architecture, as in Las Vegas or Disneyland, that makes the border marketable. "What's behind tourism is money," says Jaime Venguer, a Mexico City architect who practices in Tijuana. "Tourists come to Tijuana to buy things cheap, drink beer and have fun. Mainly, they come to buy, not to look around and be educated. The guidelines given to tourists have nothing to do with what actually happens here. Ninety percent of all tourists—the ones that fear Mexico—arrive by tour bus, enclosed, like any tour bus anywhere in the world. Enclosed, alienated, segregated. They're taken to the tourist traps, and told to buy their gifts there. They're given a half hour, and then, it's off to the Jockey Club for lunch. Basically that's how it works."[25]

Mexico's Brush with Disneyland

In the spring of 1991, an unusual tourist attraction made its debut in Mexico, along the northern border with the United States. It was called "Mexitlán—The Land of Mexico." According to promotional brochures, it promised to be the ultimate tourist experience in the Americas, a theme park that combined culture and amusement, a kind of Mexican version of Disneyland. Several entrepreneurs from Mexico City conceived of the twenty-four-million-dollar theme park idea. Its main feature would be hand-sculpted Mexican cities in miniature, 1:25 scale models of ancient and modern national architectural treasures—Indian pyramids and temples, colonial palaces, churches, basilicas, plazas, boulevards, and skyscrapers. The exhibits would be enhanced by expensive high-tech light and sound shows, continuous live entertainment, and seven restaurants. The project would cover an entire city block on the edge of downtown Tijuana.

There were similar scale model exhibitions in the Netherlands, Denmark, Switzerland, Spain, and Taiwan. The head designer of Mexitlán was Pedro Ramírez Vázquez, one of Mexico's top modern architects, whose celebrated works, mainly in Mexico City, included the Aztec Stadium, the National Museum of Anthropology, and the Mexicana de Aviación (Mexicana Airlines) skyscraper. Ramírez assembled a team of architects, sculptors, artists, and craftsmen to re-create the miniature cities whose buildings would average five to six feet in height, and whose tallest structure, a replica of the Mexicana Airlines skyscraper, would be about twenty feet high. Teams of workers spent three years photographing and videotaping buildings, and studying original drawings, to build the replicas. At times, as many as a thousand artisans worked on the project.

If Mexitlán was a meeting of Mexican and U.S. culture, it was also something of a collision. From a marketing perspective, it seemed to make sense to put a Mexican theme park on the edge of the theme park capital of America—southern California. But Mexico had a tradition, long reinforced by the government, of preserving the cultural patrimony. It was supposed to keep Jack in the Box and Disneyland out of its urban landscapes. Would a U.S.-style theme park represent a sell-out to *gringo* culture?

Absolutely not, said the designers. Mexitlán wasn't inviting Mickey Mouse or Donald Duck or Walt Disney in. There wouldn't be any Tomorrowlands or Matterhorn bobsleds or roller coasters in Mexitlán. What there would be was a space of celebration, in miniature, of the built landscape of Mexico. Mexitlán would be an affirmation of one of Mexico's greatest assets—its architecture. This, they insisted, was definitely not a mini-Disneyland on the border. "Only in a generic sense, is Mexitlán a theme park like Disneyland," said Julian Souza,

FIG. 5.4 A combination museum and theme park of miniature cities
was created to celebrate Mexican architecture: Mexitlán in downtown
Tijuana (J. Ozorno).

Director of Operations for Mexitlán. "All theme parks offer permanent exhibitions. At Disneyland, you've got mechanical rides and animation. In Sea World, it's animals doing shows. Here in Mexitlán, there will be monuments from all over Mexico, combined with movement, light, and music."[26]

American theme parks interject onto the urban fabric a world of fantasy and escape. Southern California is perhaps the national heartland for theme parks in the United States, and Disneyland is its centerpiece. Disneyland, the quintessential choreographed space, is what architect Charles Moore once described as a place where "people have a sense of being somewhere and being special."[27]

There are those who believe that simulated spaces such as Disneyland have become the new core areas of late-twentieth-century American cities. In one architectural guide to Los Angeles, Disneyland is viewed as important enough to merit the second chapter of the book, just after downtown Los Angeles. Disneyland is presented, if not as a real place, then as a vital part of the landscape of Los Angeles, "an energetic collection of environmental experiences." It is argued that Disneyland offers important lessons about urbanity in the modern age, from the relationship between community and reality to that of memory and inhabitation, to propinquity and choreography. Its virtue lies in "kinesthetic excitement," in which forms and spaces constantly change as the visitor moves through the theme park in different modes of travel (rail, roller coaster, etc.). Also, its design is praised in its clever juxtaposition of disparate places (different theme subareas within the park).[28]

But the idea of Disneyland as a force in the making of the North American urban landscape, in particular in places like southern California, can also be quite disturbing. Whereas some would promote Disneyland as "a medium sized city with a crime rate of zero,"[29] others correctly point out that, in fact, Disneyland is a metaphor for everything that is wrong with late-twentieth-century U.S. cities. It appears as a technocratic utopia, a completely simulated high-tech space entirely devoted to the production and consumption of leisure. It attracts because it offers an escape from the impersonality and alienation of North American urbanism. But in the end, it isn't real at all; it is a completely artificial space. Its workers aren't mere laborers; they're the "cast," somewhere beyond the edge of real urban life. Disneyland is reduced to theater, a "cult empire."[30] And, lest we not forget: No one *lives* in Disneyland.

Aware of the cultural pitfalls of aligning their new creation with North America's Disneyland, the creators of Mexitlán went out of their way in the early stages of promoting their project to offer a clear distinction between the aims of Mexitlán and those of the southern California theme park.

"We're trying to show who we are," commented Juan Miramontes, one of the four project architects. "Mexitlán shows our roots through our architecture. It isn't just scale models of buildings, it's a way of seeing art, color. We're showing a culture and a way of being. Mexitlán has a different message than Disneyland. In Disneyland, you climb, they move you around physically, they shake you up and jolt you. You see pirates from a boat, you ride the bobsleds. It's very beautiful, I like it. But it's a diversion. You don't think much. Mexitlán is not a small version of Disneyland. We're not trying to compete with it. This is a window to Mexico. We're trying to offer a sample of what Mexico really is. A lot of people in the U.S. think they know Mexico because they've been to Tijuana. Tijuana is not Mexico."[31]

When it opened, the first visitors to Mexitlán saw a dazzling display of craftsmanship and artistic detail. The pyramids of Teotihuacan and Gran Tenochtitlan, the Mayan city of Chichen Itza, colonial Tazco, and contemporary Mexico City looked unmistakably real. The *maquetas* (scale models) were crafted from a mixture of stone, often taken from the original building sites, and acrylic resin. They would need to withstand exposure to the elements in a permanent outdoor space. The scenic representations included lifelike miniature hand-painted human figures. Over seven hundred thousand such figures would eventually be found in the park.

But despite the Mexican rejection of the idea of Disneyland, great care went into creating the feeling of a "show" around the two hundred different scale models. Each was set on a raised platform surrounded by speakers. Music, delivered through a computer-operated sound system, would create moods in different settings throughout the park: tropical music for the coastal regions, Baroque sounds for the colonial towns, ancient pipe instrument melodies for pre-Columbian cities. At night, the mini-towns and -cities were lit up like real ones, thanks to a sophisticated fiber-optics system. Other theatrics included a mini–roller coaster, like the *montaña rusa* (literally Russian Mountain) in Mexico City's Chapultepec Park, cruise ships sailing along the Mexican Riviera, authentic-looking crowds in the Olympic Stadium replica, cheering on a re-creation of the 1968 Olympic ceremonies. There was talk of installing sound booths where visitors could listen through headphones to lifelike audio experiences, such as Mayan athletes playing on the Ball Court at Chichen Itza, as they did a thousand years ago.

"Mexitlán is a meeting of the First and Third Worlds," said the chief architect, Ramírez Vázquez. "The labor, the handicraft, is pure Mexican. But the fiber-optic illumination and omni-sound systems are of the twenty-first century."[32]

The problem for any theme park is attracting tourists. The problem for Mexitlán was the American tourist. The investors estimated that 16 million U.S. citizens cross the border into Tijuana each year, many by foot. But most don't come to visit indoor museums. "The Americans come here for the sun," said the architect Miramontes. "They come to walk, browse, eat their taco or hot dog."[33] The investors' plan envisioned a market of one and a half to two million visitors a year at a $12-per-person entry fee. To bring in crowds of this size, they knew they had to build more than just a museum.

The Mexitlán group also guessed that one of its largest target populations might be the growing community of Americans of Mexican ancestry. "In the

United States, there are many people of Mexican descent, but they don't know the land of their parents," says Miramontes. "There is such an absence of information about Mexico in their lives, it's a shame. Many of them haven't even been to Mexico City. What's sad is that sometimes when you meet a Mexican American, there is a culture clash. They'll say, 'We've already been to the moon, and you're just a Totonac (Indian).' But life is more than just landing on the moon."[34]

Eight months after opening, Mexitlán had attracted only a little more than a hundred thousand visitors. Winter and the spring rains had combined with the recession to slow the flow of tourists to a trickle. The owners tried lowering prices, adding new entertainment, and creating Disneyland-like characters called Emiliano (as in Zapata) and La Adelita, who would walk around the park greeting young children. Still, by the late summer of 1992, attendance was so low that the park was closing earlier and staying closed more often. Many employees were laid off, and there were rumors that the park might shut down.

Why was Mexitlán unable to succeed in a prime location in the most heavily visited Mexican border tourist city? It appeared to have all the ingredients for success as a tourist destination: good parking, excellent advertising, a strategic location on the pedestrian route from the border to the downtown Tijuana tourist zone near Revolution Avenue, good restaurants, stores, and a competitive admissions price. Even the owners couldn't understand. When they did exit surveys they found that people were satisfied with the experience they had once they came inside. The problem was getting them inside.

Mexitlán is a metaphor for all Mexican cities, as they face cultural integration with the United States. Mexico must decide how it wishes to embrace modernity. In Tijuana, the owners of Mexitlán wanted to create a tourism park for the American market, but they assiduously avoided any connection with Disneyland. Disneyland, of course, is perhaps the most successful tourism recreation model north of the border.

The architects of the Mexitlán concept wanted to create a distinctly Mexican version of a tourist theme park. Mexitlán proudly reproduced Mexico as a real place sculpted in miniature. This did not intrinsically interest American tourists, because they do not necessarily come to the border to experience Mexico as a real place. They come to be in the Mexico they have long associated with its border towns, where the focus is on the spectacle of carnival: horse racing, bullfights, nightlife, and immediate gratification through drinking and eating. They come to the border to be tourists, not of the serious museum-going type, but in a way that may have as little to do with experiencing authentic places as our simulated cybernetic suburbs have to do with their earlier inner-city incarnations. For Mexico, a nation wedded to memory, the path to modernity in this hemisphere means coming to terms with this.

The Death of the "Plaza"

If tourism represents one way in which Mexico is struggling to embrace modernity in its cities, it is not the only struggle. There is a paradox associated with Mexican border towns like Tijuana. Despite a history of dependency on the United States, Mexican border towns, as early as the late nineteenth century, had strived to connect with their Mexican roots.[35] By the late twentieth century, as technology brought the border in closer touch with central and southern Mexico, the core areas of Mexican culture and decision making, this process appeared to be more likely. Yet just as the possibility of greater Mexicanization lingered near, there was also the specter of global culture and the global market, and in Tijuana, a modern cityscape that, in part, began to look not like modern Mexican cities but like modern American ones. A local architecture critic describing Tijuana's new buildings in the 1980s wrote: "Modular panels of steel and glass and concrete stamped in the same patterns used in Kansas City were glued to painfully copied arrangements of landscaping found in Sorrento Valley (in San Diego) office parks. These things threaten to turn Tijuana into Anywhere, Mexico/U.S.A." [36]

How would Mexican cities along the border embrace high technology? Would the discotheques and glass-and-steel towers, the shopping malls and strip developments erase the last vestiges of Mexican imprint on the urban landscape? Such large questions cannot be answered in a short period of time, nor in one stroke. A Tijuana architect once stated: "It took the heartland of Mexico more than a thousand years to establish an identity. In Tijuana, we are pregnant architecturally speaking. We are barely one hundred years old." [37] If Tijuana is pulled between two cultures, one Mexican and traditional, the other global, American, and futuristic, a good place to monitor this process is in its open spaces and parks. Public space has always been one of the more Mexican elements of its city life in the nation's interior, but what about along the border? How is Mexican border public space influenced by the proximity of the United States?

Traditions regarding public space in the United States are tied mainly to Europe. In European preindustrial cities, private residential spaces were notoriously overcrowded and cramped. By contrast, public squares, parks, and boulevards during the same period were open-air, spacious, and elicited a feeling of excitement. Public space in preindustrial urban Europe thus was viewed as healthy and desirable, as opposed to dark, oppressive private living quarters.

The early nineteenth century and the beginning of the Industrial Revolution in European cities yielded mass housing and more cramped tenement districts, leading one urbanist to call settlements of this period "cities of the dreadful night." [38] Obviously, the attraction of open streets and public space continued to remain strong during the early industrial period. In England and other European nations, the second half of the nineteenth century was devoted to crafting new forms of urban design, such as the garden suburb, that would address the problems of urban overcrowding and slum tenement living.

The late nineteenth and early twentieth centuries saw similar developments across the Atlantic Ocean in North America. U.S. cities were spatially dispersed through mass transit. While some experimentation with garden cities and green belts was done in U.S. cities, automobile suburbs began to dominate urban space by the 1960s. With the evolution of highway-induced, multicentered suburban sprawl, public space and public life would take a clear backseat to the importance of the private realm—the suburban residence, the automobile, and private commercial shopping centers.

In U.S. metropolitan areas in the second half of the twentieth century, the town squares, pedestrian street spaces, and other public places would begin to lose their primacy as the city became dominated by amorphous highway sprawl. Sociologists have noted that in modern U.S. cities, people lose their incentive to utilize public spaces—town squares and parks—because of reports of increasing crime and gang-related violence.[39] People retreat further and further into the private realm and into the perceived safety of the automobile and the home. Public life slowly disappears.[40]

But, as mentioned earlier, some have argued that it is old-fashioned to promote urban public life in the form of people meeting on town squares. These kinds of public spaces, they claim, come from a traditional Eurocentric model of urban space that should not be forced upon contemporary U.S. cities. Instead, they call for a model that addresses the "new public realm" of urban life, where residents connect with one another through "virtual space": interactive media, computer exchanges, fax communications, radio talk shows, and voice communications.[41]

But such arguments are not entirely satisfactory. One has to worry about the kind of urbanism we find in southern California, a place typified by the comment that "phone and modem render the street irrelevant," and that Main Street has been reduced to either a fantasy space in the simulated world of Disneyland or a place somewhere between the airport and a multinational corporate headquarters, along a fiber-optic cable line or on a fax machine link.[42]

In southern California, the few celebrated places where people can meet in public are theme parks and shopping malls. In fact, neither are public spaces at all but are privately owned. Shopping malls in the late twentieth century, many urbanists agree, are the public squares of one hundred years ago. Their design normally is manipulated to enhance consumption, rather than public life. For example, entrances, escalators, fountains, and benches are carefully designed

FIG. 5.5 One of the few places where southern Californians celebrate public life—the shopping mall: Horton Plaza in San Diego.

to heighten consumer access to retail establishments, particularly large anchor stores. Time, space, and even weather can be altered or suspended to ensure consumer comfort. Noise from the "real" city is neutralized by the ubiquitous white noise—Muzak.

Meanwhile, on the "mean streets," [43] public space is either destroyed or privatized. Benches are designed so that users remain there only a short time. "Street person" has become an unfriendly term in urban life. Downtown redevelopment leaves the street abandoned, as high-rise corporate towers and hotel com-

FIG. 5.6 The Spanish Renaissance public square historically anchored colonial towns in Mexico; it is still a presence in most Mexican cities: the *zocalo* (main plaza) of Mexico City.

plexes create private interior spaces disconnected from the pedestrian avenues and squares. We are witnessing the death of the Olmstedian vision of public space.[44] Frederick Law Olmsted was the late-nineteenth-century landscape architect who designed the great urban parks of American cities, including Central Park in New York City. Olmsted envisioned public landscapes and public spaces as social safety valves, places where people of different social classes and ethnicities could meet and mingle in a positive, open environment. But this vision is being crushed under the weight of late-twentieth-century U.S. urban life, where spatial decentralization, suburban formation, and the decline of inner-city life have created a pattern of privatization of the public realm.

For Mexico, architectural expressions of public life are deeply rooted in the history of its cities. The first great "plazas" of the Americas, vast public spaces surrounded by temples or towering stone pyramids, were prominent features in pre-Hispanic indigenous settlements, especially those crafted by the Olmec, Toltec, Mayan, and Aztec cultures. The sprawling open plazas of the ancient Zapotec city of Monte Alban in the valley of Oaxaca have been described as "one of the loveliest civic areas ever created by man, and certainly the most beautiful in America."[45]

The Renaissance public square on the Iberian peninsula took the form of the *plaza mayor,* and was officially recognized as a high-status location during the period of Spanish colonial rule in Mexico. King Philip II of Spain, in his Royal Ordinances passed on to the colonists in 1573, decreed that the central public square, or Plaza de Armas, would serve as the fulcrum of colonial town life, and the main nexus for important public and religious buildings. For more than three centuries, the plaza became the most vital arena for public life in Mexican and Latin American cities.[46] In the late nineteenth century, when Mexico embraced European neoclassical trends, especially those from France, plazas were embellished with kiosks, park benches, fountains, trees, and surrounding arcade-covered sidewalks.[47] Even as the pressures of population expansion combined with changing transportation technology to alter urban structure in the twentieth century, public life and the public plaza, or *zocalo* as it came to be called in Mexico, continued to thrive. Public space—plazas, parks, and the street—remains embedded in the civic conscience of contemporary urban Mexico.

But, along the northern border with the United States, Mexican cities have struggled to create and preserve traditional public spaces. In northern Baja California, during the first three decades of its largest city—Tijuana's—growth, it became clear that the 1889 plan, anchored by five central plazas, would not conform with the emerging commercial character of the city. By 1921, Tijuana had become a dynamic center of trade and consumption of tourist services by its northern neighbor. These influences caused the settlement to reconfigure itself. Commercial uses began to cluster in the northeastern corner of town, near the international border crossing, rather than around the main plaza that had been designated in the plan of 1889. Radial streets leading out of town fell into disuse. So did the plazas. In the Tijuana of the Roaring Twenties, traditional Mexican public spaces were quickly forgotten, as the emphasis shifted to the service economy and tourism circulation. Revolution Street, lined with wooden cantinas and dancing halls, became the functional center of town. It had originally connected two public plazas from the 1889 design. But now the plazas were disappearing and only one public space—a park called Teniente Guerrero, to the west of the downtown area—would survive the fervent tourism boom of the 1920s.

The eclipse of the traditional plaza has occurred in most of the Mexican border towns and cities. One study notes that "it seems clear that the relative appeal of the plaza is eroding. This appears especially true in larger cities among the middle class as the process of suburbanization accelerates and as alternative and quasi-public spaces such as shopping malls become available.[48] In Tijuana, much as in U.S. cities, in the second half of the twentieth century the quintessential arena for public life lies on the new private plaza: the shopping mall. The shopping mall was one of the great North American inventions of the postwar,

baby-boom era. Megamalls—a million square feet-plus of commercial space—
became the icons of suburban America in the 1960s. Thirty years later they're
still the vital organs of the megalopolis. Safe, compact, self-contained pockets
tucked away in U.S. freeway hyperspace.

In the newly created automobile-age city, shopping malls offered a refuge
within the sprawling, faceless checkerboards of suburbs that stretched out into
the farmland. In southern California and elsewhere, the malls and freeways and
cookie-cutter tract homes were built where lemon groves and avocado farms
once stood. The American city became a place built for machines, not pedestrians. Walking threatened to become a lost art. Asked to compare San Diego
and Tijuana, a Mexican architect commented: "I don't see people walking in
this part of the United States. In Tijuana, you see people walking in the streets,
meeting in cafes."[49]

However, by the 1980s, Tijuana seemed to be following in the footsteps of its
northern neighbor. Baja California discovered freeways. Tijuana discovered the
shopping mall, and called it a plaza. Tijuana became a city of mini- and mega-
plazas—with names such as Plaza Río Tijuana, Plaza Fiesta, Plaza del Zapato,
Pueblo Amigo, and Viva Tijuana, all built in a feeding frenzy of commercial real
estate expansion that started during the 1980s real estate boom and hasn't finished.

In Mexico, the plaza was not only the town square. It was once a stage
upon which some of the greatest acts of Mexico's history unfolded: the sighting
of the symbolic eagle and snake by the Aztecs; proclamations of independence
and revolution; great battles and hangings and the facing of firing squads; fiery
speeches from the likes of Emiliano Zapata and Pancho Villa. But for Tijuana,
a late bloomer on the stage of Mexican history, the great plazas never achieved
the same presence as they did in cities of central and southern Mexico. Tijuana's
fate lies in the next century. "Tijuana was born with its roots in the American
dollar," an official from the Mexican Ministry of Industry and Commerce said
nearly two decades ago.[50] Its destiny lies in shopping, in a Mexico of superhigh-
ways and plazas—Mexican shopping malls.

The Plaza Río Tijuana is Tijuana's largest mall, not exactly a megamall by
U.S. standards: it has about 150,000 square feet of commercial space, compared
with San Diego's Fashion Valley Center (1.4 million square feet) or Mission
Valley Center (1.3 million square feet).[51] A giant mall in San Diego like Univer-
sity Towne Centre in La Jolla can accommodate seven thousand cars. Tijuana's
River Zone mall receives about two thousand cars on a peak day. The Plaza Río
Tijuana has some 110 stores, comparable in size to two large malls in San Diego:
Fashion Valley (125 stores) and University Towne Centre (135 commercial ten-
ants). But, the commercial real estate market is expanding south of the border,

although it's still small when compared with its neighbor, southern California. In Tijuana, say mall administrators, a good shopping plaza can charge about four or five dollars per square foot to commercial tenants. Across the border in San Diego, mall commercial rentals range from eighteen to thirty-six dollars a square foot, according to several real estate brokers.

Built along the lines of a modernist southern California outdoor regional shopping mall, Plaza Río Tijuana is anchored by three large department stores (two of which are Mexican companies, the other a Sears), a Triplex movie theater, restaurants, and an array of smaller shops that, as in the United States, sell everything from designer clothing, books, and records to shoes, athletic equipment, and pastries. The design of the mall allows mostly middle- and upper-class shoppers, who arrive mainly by car, to actively utilize open-air public spaces within the shopping center. These spaces consist of sunken plazas and courtyards decorated in two-toned brown tile, all with ample seating and landscaping. The spaces are carefully maintained and tend to be heavily used for casual eating, with food supplied by numerous concessions. Plaza Río Tijuana's tremendous success may have less to do with its design, than with the fact that it offers the kind of stores and quality of goods that Mexican consumers learned to prefer from their shopping experiences in the United States.

Built in 1982, Plaza Río Tijuana is your basic American-style shopping center. It boasts a Denny's, Sears, and Pizza Hut. Its travel agencies advertise package tours to Hawaii and Las Vegas. Its ice cream parlors sell malteds and banana splits. In the 1990s, large posters of Magic Johnson, Michael Jordan, and Shaquille O'Neal hung in its shoe stores. The plaza is typically filled with well-dressed shoppers in Guess? jeans and T-shirts that say *Mazatlan*. They come from the new suburbs east and west of town, or from posh old neighborhoods called Chapultepéc or Cacho, nestled in the hills above the old downtown. They mill about in stores or rest on brown tile benches, while children play tag nearby. Public telephones seem to be continually in use. *Cumbias* and *musica ranchera* or loud rock music blasts from music stores with names like Discoteca Alta Tensión. For a mere $17.50, that album can be yours on CD, or for $4.50 you can have it on cassette tape. *Tijuananenses* seem to like this low-lying, sandstone-colored mall. In the past, studies have shown that Mexican shoppers favor malls that look like the ones in the United States.[52] Plaza Río Tijuana qualifies in that regard. It could be moved to the corridor of shopping malls in San Diego. Most users will tell you that it is clean, well run, and has many good shops.

But not all modern Mexican border shopping plazas work. A different mood greets the visitor to the shopping center just across the Paseo de los Heroes. Plaza Fiesta consists of an outdoor mall and, at the south end, an attached indoor mall called the Plaza del Zapato. There is an empty, almost eerie feeling here: not the eeriness of an abandoned Mayan city—more like a deserted circus or an amusement park relic. Plaza Fiesta also lies in the heavily traveled River Zone. It sought to re-create the ambience of a colonial town in a space dominated by outdoor cafes and restaurants. The buildings are of white or lime green or pink pastel–shaded stucco, with pseudo-arcaded facades and second-floor balconies with iron railings and lanterns. Iron or wooden grilles cover second-floor windows, as they would in a colonial town. The public areas have kiosks and fountains that are mainly decorative rather than used. There is very little public seating; the few users of these spaces are primarily those who sit at costly outdoor cafes or restaurants. The designers of this commercial center envisioned a lively ambience; they placed brightly colored awnings and umbrellas in front of the many restaurants serving international cuisine—Greek, Italian, French, and Yugoslavian. The center offers live entertainment in the evenings. But it has become a largely underutilized, claustrophobic, and not very public place. It is cut off from the rest of the city by heavily traveled boulevards surrounding it. It is a commercial island filled with provocative colonial forms that creates neither a sense of place nor a feeling of community.

The Plaza Fiesta, built in 1986, is smaller than the Plaza Río Tijuana. The outdoor mall has some forty-five stores and offices and fifteen restaurants in a two-story village design. The stucco buildings, the iron grilles and lanterns above wooden doors, the neo-cobblestone streets and alleyways are supposed to make it look like a colonial Mexican town, like Guanajuato or Taxco, old silver-mining towns. It looks like a Hollywood set.

At the Cafe el Griego, on weekend nights, young women gyrate and slither their way through belly dances set to Greek music. A man balances a large wooden table in his mouth. Before 1989, business was brisk here, and on weekends, Tijuana's young and restless packed the cafes and bars. By the early 1990s the "village" had become a ghost town. The public fountains were dry. The cafes and outdoor seating areas empty, even on a Friday night in midsummer. Many stores and restaurants began closing down. *Se Vende* signs were posted in the windows of abandoned businesses whose nameplates—Supersnack, Riconcito Tapatío, or Video and Piano Bar Karissma—had already begun to fade.

Neighboring Plaza del Zapato consists of twenty-five shoe stores on two levels. The stores are all Mexican, with names like Moda Bella, Watanabe, Bianca, 3 Hermanos. A half dozen have gone out of business. The mall's one blue-tiled public fountain has running water and is surrounded by a jungle of terra-cotta-potted plants. The floors are of red Mexican tile. Blue and white stained-glass skylights filter in a soothing, subdued light. Few people are here to enjoy all this.

How is it that the Plaza Río Tijuana, on one side of the boulevard, can be

FIG. 5.7 In northern Mexican border towns, attempts to create new public spaces in the form of shopping malls have often failed: this pseudo-colonial, postmodern commercial center in Tijuana's River Zone is an example.

packed with shoppers, while, on the other side, the Plaza Fiesta and the Plaza del Zapato are almost empty? According to officials, the Plaza Fiesta has a commercial vacancy rate of 25 percent, while the Plaza Río Tijuana is only 1 percent vacant. If the Plaza del Río has two thousand cars in its lot at peak consumer hours, the Plaza Fiesta might only have a few hundred.

The nightlife may explain why it went downhill. "Three years ago, Plaza Fiesta became saturated with restaurants," says Miguel Ravelo at the Chamber of Commerce in Tijuana's River Zone. "The restaurants attracted a lot of young people and created a clientele of diversion rather than of consumption. The place became chaotic and noisy with people drinking and partying until six in the morning. This was not a family place. Too much disorder. If I want to go to disorder, I don't bring my family, I go alone."[53]

The nightly festivities in the plaza had driven out a lot of other businesses. Apartments that were originally built on the second floor above the stores were now almost all vacant. Drug dealers were rumored to be regular customers in some of the bars. In 1989, an argument one night between two patrons, reportedly over a romantic triangle, got out of hand. Guns were pulled, and in the ensuing shootout, one person died. The bar where the incident occurred shut down. The plaza had reached its lowest point. People began to view the commercial center as a place controlled by drug dealers and criminals.

Since 1989, things have continued to go downhill. On a Friday evening late in the summer of 1991, business is slow on the plaza. Music from one of the bars bounces across the empty cafes and off the stucco walls. A few Mexicans are drinking at one of the outdoor tables, and their laughter resounds in the otherwise silent space. "Right now the plaza is bankrupt," says Javier Esponda, the owner of the Brazilian restaurant Oba Oba and the new administrator of the shopping center.[54] But Esponda believes that better advertising and maintenance can improve business. He's hoping to tap the American market.

But you wonder if these shopping malls disguised as colonial towns really belong at the northern frontier of Mexico. The fake kiosks and false arcades, the red-and-white-checkered Italian tablecloths, the pink-dyed cement planters, the turquoise awnings. A shopping developer's postmodern fantasy dropped onto Tijuana like a UFO. One Mexican architect, asked about these kinds of places, said:

The architects and builders who come to the border from Mexico City think American tourists want to go to Mexico and see mariachis walking around in typical colonial scenes. So they end up building mini-shopping centers that are poor imitations of small authentic towns. They end up creating a misery of space. And the tourists often don't even go to these places. Plaza Fiesta is so depressing. It's a poor imitation of reality. There is no landscaping. In Tijuana, you need landscaping, you need trees and little plazas with trees around them that create shade. You don't see a tree in any of these mini-shopping centers. It's like going to the desert. Everything is dead. The buildings are like shacks. They have no dignity. The shacks you see in the *colonias,* the poor areas, are far more dignified. They have little pots filled with plants. Plaza Fiesta just doesn't work as a concept of space. They try to use every square inch. But, the streets don't lead anywhere. In Taxco or Guanajuato, the streets are even narrower, but they open onto little plazas. There's mystery in real colonial towns and in their streets. When you walk around, you discover things. In Plaza Fiesta, there's nothing to discover. It's blasé. If small towns in Mexico were really like that, my God, the people in the towns would be dead by now.[55]

There may still be hope for the memory of spontaneous public life in Tijuana, though. A fine example of contemporary public space is the outdoor plaza in the Centro Cultural de Tijuana museum complex designed in 1982 by architects Pedro Ramírez Vázquez and Manuel Rosen. The architects believed that the museum would be more exciting if it included a usable outdoor space. The one they created has touches of the indigenous ceremonial plazas, empowered by the massive concrete walls of the museum and a globe-shaped amphitheater. The space is generously used by pedestrians, by schoolchildren and museum visitors. Taxis stop and pick up nearby, while vendors sell tacos, hot dogs, sand-

FIG. 5.8 The one authentic public space in downtown Tijuana—Parque Teniente Guerrero—is a vital meeting place for the neighborhoods surrounding the central business district.

wiches, ice cream, and juices. Unfortunately, it is mainly utilized as a function of the presence of the museum. It lies in the city's River Zone, a linear wedge of office buildings and shopping centers with high-speed traffic corridors running through it. It is difficult to reach the Cultural Center on foot.

The one truly significant public plaza in downtown Tijuana is the Parque Teniente Guerrero, which emerged near one of the original secondary plazas from the 1889 urban plan. The park was expanded to cover an entire city block early in the twentieth century; its radial pedestrian paths leading into a central square within the park mirror the design in the original town plan. The park no longer serves the larger city. It is a well-maintained neighborhood public space, used by residents of the downtown zone. In a city largely devoid of open space, Teniente Guerrero remains essential. At dusk, it comes alive with children on bicycles, young couples, pigeons, vendors selling *elote* (corn on the cob), and shoe-shine stands. It is Tijuana's throwback to the colonial *zocalos* that have generally been well preserved in Mexican cities in the interior.

It is disappointing that Mexican border town plazas and the spontaneous urban public life they symbolized disappeared in the first decades of the twentieth century when an architecture of North American consumption emerged.

In the 1950s and 1960s, the automobile arrived, and in the next two decades Tijuana's public life moved into the private shopping mall or onto the downtown shopping street. Like that of its southern California neighbor, modern Tijuana's is a highly fragmented space where no continuous pedestrian movement is possible. Communities and pedestrian zones are arrayed like islands floating on the superstructure of a diffuse, highway-oriented commercial metropolis. The town square has disappeared, and the only hope for public life lies with those who choose to re-create it through design commissions for public or private complexes.

The loss of traditional spaces is being lamented in cities worldwide, but it is particularly noteworthy in the borderlands, where a developing country with a rich heritage of urban design is contemplating its future as an economic partner with a nation that looks more to the future than to the past. Both the erosion of cultural landscapes as a result of tourism development and the privatization of vital public space are examples of the potentially destructive effects of NAFTA on Mexico's built environment. We have seen that these effects are intensified in the Mexico-U.S. borderlands. In the next chapter, we confront those who design the cultural landscapes—architects working on either side of the international boundary. Their perspective offers a measure of the current state of uncertainty over the future of the built environment at the meeting place of Mexico and the United States.

SIX

Culture and Place

The Border Architects Speak

Mexico is a country of architects. We Mexicans are builders;
we are all architects.   —RICARDO LEGORRETA

The twenty-first century may be the century of the transfrontier metropolis—single city-regions that sprawl across international boundaries. Such
places already exist in Asia, Western Europe, and North America. In an increasingly globalized economy, it becomes necessary for inhabitants to create
unified regions to better compete in the world system. If those regions happen
to overlap international boundaries, so be it. The Mexico-U.S. frontier may be
the place where this kind of settlement prototype is crystallizing at the high-
est speed, due to the magnitude of cross-border flows of workers, shoppers,
and tourists, and the cross-border synergy of the North American Free Trade
Agreement (NAFTA). Transborder marketing, advertising, and manufacturing
are common to the frontier regions of Brownsville-Matamoros, Laredo–Nuevo
Laredo, El Paso–Juárez, Calexico-Mexicali, and San Diego-Tijuana.

It may now be possible to speak of "transfrontier architecture," architecture
around the international border that is shaped by two cultures. Few studies acknowledge the role of architects in shaping cultural landscapes. Yet architecture
is a profession that demands sensitivity to the built environment. While some
architects may design structures out of context with their surroundings, most
professional designers seek to integrate their work with the surrounding land-

scape. Architects represent, therefore, a vital source of information about the making of a region's landscape.

The View from the South

Jorge Ozorno, an architect, lived in Mexico City all his life. In 1984, he came to the northern border, to Tijuana. "When I first arrived," he says, "and the taxi from the airport snaked through the streets of some older neighborhoods near downtown, I took one look and almost got on the next plane back to Mexico City. The city seemed chaotic and vulgar." [1] But Ozorno chose to stay. He became part of a dramatic influx into northern Mexico of talented young designers — the new border architects — from the cultural heartland of south central Mexico.

The new architects form part of a larger wave of some of Mexico's most talented professionals — doctors, engineers, university professors, lawyers, architects — surging onto the shores of Tijuana and other northern Mexican cities from the large cosmopolitan centers of the nation's interior. Lured by the promise of economic gain and by the amenities of the Pacific Ocean and nearby southern California, most of the new professionals are from Mexico City and want to put behind them memories of pollution, overcrowding, and earthquakes. Tijuana has often greeted them skeptically. To some, they are invaders — *chilangos*, a derogatory term for the Mexico City newcomers.

Most of these young craftsmen were trained in Mexico City. As they sketch their designs on this strange bicultural stage that is called the borderlands, the new architects are anxious to undo what the previous decades left behind. "A lot of Americans want to discover the real Mexico without going any farther than Tijuana," says Guillermo Barrenechea, an architect who has practiced in Tijuana for thirty years. "A lot of Mexican Americans come to Tijuana searching for an identity. We've got to offer them a better environment. We don't have to build spectacular things, but we've got to inject a different Mexico down here, something that foreigners can appreciate." [2]

Barrenechea is principal architect in a multimillion-dollar project that will create a new downtown in the eastern part of Tijuana. He wants the new design to capture what is embedded in older Mexican cities farther south. "Our new project will be like a typical, modern Mexican city," he notes. "It will be simple, modest. It doesn't have to be spectacular to attract the Mexican consumer. No glass towers. The Mexican consumer is scared off when it's too sophisticated. It's got to be simple. A plaza with streets leading into it. Horse and buggy. A kiosk with a band playing in it. A place where you can have a typical Mexican encounter, where someone will say, "It's been a long time since I had a real

Mexican conversation." We're talking about Mexicans wearing white pants and big hats; a conversation over a bottle of tequila." [3]

"The essence of Tijuana can still be Mexican," states Jaime Venguer, another Tijuana architect originally from Mexico City. "Rapidly built houses. Patio schemes. Mexican labor is our strongest Mexican element." [4] NAFTA promises greater prosperity along the border in the next century. But there is also the risk of further cultural contamination from the north. Already, American-style fast-food restaurants are invading the cityscape, and not all Mexicans are happy about it. "We Mexican architects are looking to discover our roots," adds Venguer. "We want an architecture that is Mexican, but also that is sensitive to the border, to its materials and technological advantages. The border is like a zone of transition. Since we are in a transition space, from one culture to another, we need an architecture of transition. The border should be like an Escher drawing where there are humans on one side and ducks on the other side, and in the middle humans turn into ducks. That's the border to me, when there's a mixture of both sides, and it produces a third thing." [5]

Mexican Architecture and Pride

Eugenio Velásquez, born in the United States but brought up in Mexico, is of Spanish and Mexican ancestry. He studied architecture in Guadalajara and came to Tijuana in the early 1980s. Stylishly dressed, wearing a short leather jacket with fur around the collar, Velásquez likes to frequent Tijuana's elegant discotheques at night. He could easily fit in in any global metropolis: Mexico City, London, or New York. Principal architect in the firm Arte Proyecto, Velásquez prefers to do his design sketches alone, finding inspiration in music and poetry.

In Tijuana, we're not in the best position. We're far from our roots; we're very close to a culture that isn't ours, that we don't understand, but that interests us. We know that in the north, they look toward the future, toward excellence, the perfection of things. The Latino carries in his heart the romanticism of things. So since we're neither from the north nor from the heartland of the south, things become difficult here in the hour of architecture. We're disoriented.

As architects our Mexican designs are more human, but yours are more efficient. Our designs have flavor, sentiment, weaknesses. Some are ugly and some are beautiful. They incite passion, they attract interest. American designs are about perfection; they're cold, they lack feeling. North of the border, I like Michael Graves's Hyatt Hotel in La Jolla because, even though it's postmodern, it has an Italian touch, it has the romantic language, natural colors, the color of rocks; I feel that it is closer to us. I like the Salk Institute of Louis Kahn with its robust, brute materials, its meditative quality, its connection to the sea. I also like the buildings of Balboa Park because they reflect part of our culture.

FIG. 6.1 Tijuana's discotheques epitomize the eclectic cultural landscape of a young border city: like Caesar's Palace in Las Vegas, the entrance to Marko Disco draws from the theme of ancient Rome (J. Ozorno).

No one in Tijuana has the confidence yet to say what the city's identity should be; we're growing so rapidly that we just improvise. The government could help more, but unfortunately, it's not like the United States where laws are laws. Here the relative of someone can come in and build whatever he wants. If he wants to design a French Provincial house or build Japanese style, he does it. And no one can say anything. We're not a city that has much culture to begin with. Eventually, it comes back to haunt us, through visual contamination. There are badly proportioned buildings constructed with inferior materials. We need to better maintain our buildings. Architecture is a discipline; what we're doing is not disciplined.

There are fifty-two discotheques in Tijuana today. The most important ones are Marko Disco, Baby Rock, Flash, Viva Tijuana, News, Iguana, Banana Rana, and Senor Frogs. They can add to our urban architecture, but sometimes the opposite is true. Some builders lack imagination. There's a lot of piratry. You design and build your business, and if it goes well, others begin copying it all around you. That's why you see so many discotheques near each other; they used to be farther apart, but over the years they moved closer. People would say, "Where's the party?" It was easier to move them closer.

The Free Trade Agreement is going to dramatically change our lives. If we put in our romanticism, our art, and we utilize what North Americans know, which is the perfection of things, we'll arrive at a new style of architecture that is unique, different. We want a situation where we can learn from you and you from us, only it's faster if we learn from you, than you from us, because you have the recipe, the practical side. Understanding *el romanticismo* of the Latino is more difficult.

In Tijuana, we still have a lot of deprivation in our landscape. High in the hills, you see tires, cardboard, beer crates—all used to make architecture. But we also have all the materials from the other side: cement block, brick, Spanish tile. If we combine both traditions—Mexican and American—we can have a better architecture." [6]

Emergency Architecture

Jorge Ozorno studied architecture and grew up in Mexico City. He came to Tijuana in 1984. He began designing what he calls "emergency architecture," buildings for moderate-income neighborhoods. He was a professor at and, in the early 1990s, director of the School of Architecture of the Tijuana branch of the Ibero-American University.

When I arrived in Tijuana, two strong images influenced my designs: the land invasions in the Tijuana area and the earthquake I had lived through in Mexico City. When large portions of Mexico City collapsed, in a very short time, and with very little money, it was necessary to create new works of architecture and engineering. I realized that it was partly a question of will. When the catastrophe hit, and there were urgent needs, it forced the imagination to develop solutions, that, although they weren't always definitive, served to propel architects to a higher level.

In Tijuana, I saw a city whose rhythm of growth was out of sync. The government takes the attitude: We're going to build a great municipal palace, to have a gala inauguration, where photographs are taken, so in the history books they can record these "great" moments. And they spend outrageous amounts of money. You see in other parts of the world, like in Kuwait, that they declare a state of war, and then build a city for three hundred thousand inhabitants in less than two months. With schools, training centers, airports, and hospitals. You start thinking that maybe what is needed in Tijuana is to declare a state of emergency and say, on this day, we are going to think about what to do for Tijuana.

Emergency architecture consists of a series of transitional steps that must be taken to address the urgent needs of the city. I've gone out on weekends to the poor *colonias* where people are just arriving to take possession of their land. They can build a house in a single weekend, with tires, wooden poles, and plywood. They literally raise the main structure of the house in four hours. The imagination of the squatters is a maximum expression of creativity. With three pieces of plastic, they build an entire house. The government has not been sufficiently helpful. With a policy of emergency or transitional architecture, we would bring back the value of the *barrio* (the neighborhood) to the city. People would organize from within, with the support of the government, and be able to deal with the needs of their immediate environment.

In Tijuana, the housing initiatives already exist. What's missing are the resources the residents should be receiving: paved roads, schools, hospitals, etc. In Tijuana, the unem-

FIG. 6.2 Vernacular residential architecture in the *colonias* incorporates creative informal design: recycled tires used for fencing or terracing on the steep hillsides of Tijuana.

ployment rate is low. Once people find a source of income, they buy a car, their house begins to grow. A system of emergency architecture would address the problem of providing public buildings. We architects have little to teach migrants about housing. They have shown they can build, even on steep embankments. We can guide them on how to maximize the use of plywood, or how to design a latrine, but they've demonstrated that they have a capacity for the spontaneous construction of housing.

So what I'm talking about is designing schools, libraries, recreation centers, social service centers, and fire stations, which is what the *colonias* don't have. They arrive and construct their houses — twenty thousand or fifty thousand people attach themselves to a parcel of land, but they don't have a medical facility, they don't have a child-care center, and in the end, they don't have control of their lives. We need to help these families feel rooted. We can do this by building rapid, ephemeral buildings — low-cost, flexible structures that can be easily assembled and disassembled. Emergency architecture.[7]

Border Condominiums

Jaime Venguer lives in La Jolla, California, but is originally from Mexico City. He studied architecture at Cornell University in the United States, and is the owner of Venguer Associates, an architectural design and building firm in

Tijuana. Venguer commutes each day from La Jolla to his office in a modern tower adjacent to the Cultural Center in Tijuana's modern River Zone. He designed and built the luxury Ventura condominium complex, a fourteen-story concrete tower with a high-tech glass-cube facade. Marketed as *la gran aventura* (the great adventure) it features two- and three-bedroom units with balconies

FIG. 6.3 The optimistic landscapes of NAFTA: advertisement for a luxury condominium project that was never built (by permission of architect, Jaime Venguer).

and sweeping views of the region, Jacuzzis, spas, saunas, cable television, and a gymnasium.

I started out doing luxury condominiums in Tijuana. We designed and built two luxury towers with ocean views and golf courses in Rosarito. We built the luxury Ventura Condominiums on the golf course in the Chapultepec area of Tijuana. These were designed with the idea of creating a superbuilding directed toward a special clientele in Tijuana: a lot of privacy, excellent views across the golf course, in the best neighborhood of Tijuana, with the best services, luxury services. But we found that the market really isn't there yet. We weren't able to sell all the units in this building. We completed the project in 1990 and two years later the building was only 50 percent occupied. Some people bought in as investors, others have rented their units. But it wasn't the business project we expected.

We're just finishing the condominium towers on a peninsula south of Rosarito. The clientele was American. Our business fell off after some disputes about land ownership. The units go for $125,000 to $150,000 (U.S.) for about 1,250 square feet. It's a very special setting: the waves crash against the rocks down below; we built a pier and put in a Jacuzzi.

We switched out of this luxury architecture because the market just isn't there right now. We had thought Tijuana was in a boom, as everyone expected. We thought we'd tap the *maquiladora* clientele, let's say: the clientele from the interior of the country. But they never materialized. In Tijuana, there was a change of governments, and then the U.S. economy went into a recession. All of this meant that the border economy weakened; it became static. And those of us with money tied up in property investments, we had to leave them, and I realized we could not continue to move our business in this direction.

Today we're developing a lot of moderately priced housing for people who live here in Tijuana. For a long time, people here haven't had the chance to buy their own homes. We're building small individual homes for people in the La Mesa area, and we're helping the consumer get a loan and buy a house where the monthly payments on their mortgages are about the same as what you would pay to rent a house or apartment. It amounts to about $400 a month with a fifteen-year mortgage and 20 percent down payment (paid in installments) for a 750-square-foot house with a small private patio and separate parking. The houses are very basic: two bedrooms, kitchen, dining area, bathroom, all made from cement block with plaster inside and tiled bathrooms. They are terraced one above the other for privacy. They're not architectural masterpieces, but they are dignified.[8]

High Tech Meets Tradition

Architect Luis Licéaga's office in Tijuana is crisp, modern. The centerpiece is a large computer system. Digitized architectural drawings hang nearby. Another of the young architects originally from Mexico City, Luis studied at UNAM (the National Autonomous University in Mexico City) and came to Tijuana in 1978. Soft-spoken, and a behind-the-scenes professional who does not seek the limelight, Licéaga has established a reputation for his creative designs for modernist

FIG. 6.4 Mexican border architects seek to create modern office buildings that are respectful of the past: The Torremól building (Tijuana) incorporates elements of a traditional cathedral, according to its architect (by permission of architect, Luis Licéaga).

office towers and apartments in the River Zone. His gray Torremól office tower, across from the high-profile Cultural Center, is admired for its strong presence as a modernist high-rise building in the booming River Zone area near downtown Tijuana.

When I arrived here fourteen years ago, there was nothing in the River Zone. Nothing. There were maybe two buildings here. Some of our new buildings, the glass towers and so forth, may be a bit exaggerated, but they stand out as landmarks. They are symbols of the new city.

Torremól was originally going to be a luxury office building. When the demand for offices was high, we were talking about plush offices with private suites, kitchens, saunas—it was something else. But when Mexico's economic situation started to change (in the early 1980s), the original idea died. Eventually, the investors put together a different package: the commercial part of the building—the base—was expanded, and there would be only six floors of offices. We moved the elevator off to the side, so the businesses could have an entire floor to themselves.

I worried a great deal about the building's relation to its site, a block corner. I wanted to integrate the exterior to the nearby CECUT (Cultural Center). The CECUT has strong, separate geometric elements, and we employed a similar strategy with Torremól. In our building, the emphasis is on the sphere and the pyramid, one geometry accentuates the other. I also tried to integrate the past into the building. I was preoccupied not to design a glass edifice without identity.

In Torremól, there are three elements—base, tower, and window—inspired by the colonial church. The base is functional, for commercial purposes. The tower is familiar in our culture, like the towers of churches and indigenous structures. The windows try to adapt to the region's climate—they are tall to allow ample light in.

A lot of Tijuana's new development is out of the hands of architects. It has to do with politics and economics at the national level. The scenography of Tijuana—for commercial and tourist purposes—is like a cancer that spreads over the city. We have a discotheque in the River Zone that looks like a pile of rocks, and near there a restaurant with a strange flying object attached. It's visual pollution. We have to ask: What is Tijuana's reason for being? Is it cinematography, creating an amusement park to bring in tourism?

But Tijuana is Mexican. It has vernacular architecture: what the common people build. They use sheets of metal, tires, stones, and adobe. Their neighborhoods are colorful and improvised. These areas are, in a sense, more authentic than downtown or the River Zone.[9]

City of the Future

Guillermo Barrenechea has been practicing architecture in Tijuana for thirty years but has lost neither exuberance nor vision nor a sense of humor. Originally from the state of Sonora, he studied architecture in Monterrey. He has designed restaurants, stores, parking garages, beachfront condos, and private homes in Tijuana, Mexicali, Ensenada, and Mazatlán. He is currently the principal architect on a large multimillion-dollar urban-development project that proposes the creation of a new commercial and civic "downtown" east of the current city center in what is called the third phase of the River Zone. Barrenechea thinks Tijuana's future lies in the purchasing power of its nearly two million inhabitants, a potential he believes has gone largely untapped. Using maps hand-drawn on the backs of paper cafeteria placemats, he sketches giant concentric circles to plot the projected market areas for hundreds of thousands of consumers living in the eastern and southern outskirts of Tijuana. Tijuana's future, he notes, lies in a series of mega–shopping centers—not of the southern California suburban-mall type—but rather as a series of "new downtowns," high-density, pedestrian-oriented commercial districts, following the contour of the Tía Juana River. The Tijuana of the twenty-first century will be a linear city, with high-speed trolleys and computer-powered monorails moving people among the downtown districts. To succeed, he thinks the new commercial and civic centers must recapture the spirit of old Mexican cities. The new eastern "downtown" will begin breaking ground in two years.

This city needs an identity. When you're in a city like Oaxaca or Puebla, walking through the main square, there are vendors all over, selling chiles or tomatoes, or whatever, on street corners. Walking through these spaces gets your blood flowing.

Zacatecas, an old silver-mining city, is very poor. But it's a very beautiful place. We were sitting one night in a cafe and heard a pleasant musical sound off in the distance; so we went out to see what it was. There were seventy young girls, twelve to fifteen years old, all playing the clarinet in the middle of a street near downtown Zacatecas. The music drifted through the streets of the old neighborhoods. Flowers were in bloom all around. There were arched doorways and cloisters, and even some of the modest houses, from colonial times, had silver handiwork in their exterior walls.

That's the mood we want to create in our new project. The old Tijuana, with its scenography, is vulgar. Vulgar. Some of the new glass buildings in the River Zone? Scary. Badly thought out. One has little high-tech glass mirrors, another a hole in the concrete facade. Every imaginable element in the modern repertoire of commercial architecture seems thrown into one building.

The authentic American architect is designing beautiful things, while the Mexican architect in Tijuana has been sleeping. It's not that there isn't talent. There's talent. But the objectives here aren't always clearly defined. People get distracted. It's like a river; you have to channel its energy in the right direction.

But, in one hundred years, Tijuana will be an interesting place. Most Mexican cities in the interior have always been beautiful. You go to Michoacán, all the towns are beautiful. There isn't an ugly town in Michoacán. Here it seems that Tijuana has always been ugly. Here there is a temporary quality to everything. People come here and are constantly on the move. There's no sense of settling down, no sense of posterity.

The significance of Baja California lies in its indigenous cultures. But they are often forgotten. The descendants of Baja's native cultures are a beautiful people, tall with great big smiles. We worked together on a project in Ojos Negros. They would cook these dinners with clams, which they pried open first, poured in spices, then closed them again and cooked them on branches over an open fire. With mezcal or tequila and a guitar we got blissfully lost out there in the hills. Magnificent. The nights in Ojos Negros.[10]

Stone Walls of Mexican Architecture

Manuel Rosen is an architect from Mexico City who moved to the Tijuana–San Diego border area in the mid-1980s. In Mexico City, he studied at the Academy of St. Charles (now the National Autonomous University of Mexico, UNAM), and was raised in a family that socialized with some of Mexico's great artists—Diego Rivera, David Siqueiros, Luis Barragán. He designed Tijuana's landmark building—the CECUT—with Pedro Ramírez Vázquez prior to moving to the border.

Architecture in the United States is an imposition by the mass media, developers, and builders. Nobody worries to teach the people what good architecture is. I'm not just talk-

FIG. 6.5 One of the striking qualities of Mexican border townscapes is the people
(J. Ozorno).

ing about Mexican architecture; I'm talking about architecture in general. I don't think
there is a knowledge of what architecture is, what design is, except what we see in magazines and through promotion on TV. It's a pity.

We can never forget that the United States and Mexico are two very different cultures,
with different concepts of time, family, and space. In Mexico there is tremendous poverty,
and you see a lot of people in the streets—children, everything. But they're always with
someone else. They're never alone. In the United States, the homeless are on the streets,
and all alone. You never see them with anybody, with children, friends. You see homeless
people passing each other on the street, and, even then, they don't say hello to each other.
People in the United States are afraid to interact in the public arena. There's no touching
in public, no hugging, no caressing of children. The consequences of this are dreadful.
You're becoming dehumanized.

Latin people have a different concept of home. Home is the place where they throw
down their roots and have children. They want the children to be together with them
until they marry. Even after they marry, they want them to remain nearby. In the United
States, people are more mobile. They move from city to city. The concept of children is
different. Once they grow up, they're on their own, and let them do the best they can.

In the United States, the way people specialize limits creativity. An architect is not a
specialist. An architect is a creator of spaces, and I don't care what the spaces are, whether
they're hospitals, theaters, office buildings, or penitentiaries. Here in the United States,

you have architects who specialize in bathrooms, others in kitchens, or in windows. I'm not sure Americans want to make a statement with their architecture. Everyone is trying to get a commission, then do it as soon as possible, as fast as possible. During the building phase, except on the really big projects, architects don't even supervise their own work; they turn it over to the builder. So when changes are made, there's often no consultation with the architects. The architect disappears. He becomes a draftsman.

Its different in Mexico. In Mexico, we have shame. Architects are ashamed of doing something they don't like. I don't see that as much here in the United States. There is a total lack of respect toward the architect. There seems to be a tremendous misunderstanding about what the architect is and what he does. In the United States, when a real estate agent sells a house, he makes 6 percent. For that same house, the architect, who went through hell to do it, with all kinds of fights and aggravation, he probably makes 4 or 5 percent. Out of that he has to pay off his consultants. It's ridiculous; it just doesn't pencil.

Tijuana's identity crisis is exacerbated by Americans who come there looking for "original" Mexican things. There's a story told in Mexico about an American who went to Cuernavaca, Mexico. A large skull was offered to him for sale. It was the skull of Cortes, he was told. He asked, "Is it original?" And the Mexican vendor said, "Of course it's original." So he bought it. Then, a few days later in a different town, a different boy approaches him with a small skull for sale, and says, "This is the skull of Cortes." The American says, "Is it original?" The Mexican boy replies, "Yes." The American says, "But how can it be original, if this one I already bought was the original?" The boys answers, "But this is the skull of Cortes when he was young!"

So, in Tijuana many people think, if you build something that is typical, the Americans will go crazy about it. That's who they cater to. Is Mexico relinquishing the border to the United States? Remember, we're always eager to have foreign things come in to visit us—people, culture, and so forth. But we're also eager to see them go away and take everything with them. To penetrate the stone walls of the culture of Mexico is not easy.[11]

The View from the North

North of the border, architects have begun to take notice of Mexico. In California, especially southern California, architects recognize the inevitable connection to Mexico, but many are still groping to understand what those ties mean in their cities and in their own work. For many residents of the U.S. Southwest, Mexico's presence has two vastly different implications. On the one side, Mexico is a foreign nation with severe economic problems and potentially volatile political conflicts. It could be a burden to the United States, particularly along the Mexican border, where drug smuggling and illegal immigration show no signs of disappearing. On the other hand, many Americans seek a heightened relationship with their southern neighbors and are fascinated by the rich cultural heritage they associate with Mexico. Some architects in southern California live and work far enough from the border that they feel disconnected from Mexico.

Others benefit professionally by practicing design on both sides of the border. Many of the U.S.-based architects interviewed for this book (more than a dozen) insisted that they want to understand Mexico better. They believe Mexico will be a prominent part of southern California's future, and it is time to work more closely with Mexican ideas about the city and its design.

The Scale and Power of Mexican Architecture

Rob Quigley is nationally recognized for his innovative hotels and other buildings in downtown San Diego. He has been a leading advocate of well-designed, efficient, low-cost housing for low-income populations in downtown areas. He is also a thoughtful advocate of preservation in design and of the importance of context in architecture. In 1996, Quigley won an international competition to design the new public library in downtown San Diego.

All architecture ought to reflect its time and place. Anything built that's impacted by the social dynamics of the border ought to reflect that in its architecture. I'd like to think that everything we build is influenced by the locale—by being close to the border—but I'm not sure how.

We recently designed a community center in the Sherman Heights neighborhood for a predominantly Hispanic clientele. The requests from residents were really sophisticated. They were very concerned about respecting the past of their immediate neighborhood: Victorian structures; Hispanic-influenced structures, arches, courtyards; the mass and weight of buildings. But they were also clear about building for the future. They didn't want a nostalgic reinterpretation of Hispanic buildings. That's very advanced, much more insightful than what you get from the engineering department.

The arch was important as a symbol. Most interesting of all—and what broke with what an Anglo client would have done—was their attitude toward the garden. This was different from anything I've been requested to do before. They saw the garden as being more important than the building itself. A total reversal of the Anglo tradition, of the relation of the building to the landscape. When we finish the project, the building not only turns into a backdrop for the garden; it actively turns into an aspect of the garden—there's a seamless interface between the building and the garden.

They clearly did not want a Mexican building. There was not even any discussion about it. In fact, when they pointed to examples of Mexican influence, it was filtered through influence in the neighborhood. It was not first generation out of Mexico but interpretations of Mexico by further generations.

Mexican architects I admire are doing modern architecture. But they use materials that connect to the past. They're one of the few countries that's been able to create an identifiable *national* architecture in the modern movement. Mexico has a strong identity. There's a clarity in Mexican architecture that does not exist in the United States. It has a scale and a power to it. A wonderful mix of European and Mestizo. Architecture of the

FIG. 6.6 The arch and the Victorian house were two elements a Latino community in the U.S. chose to incorporate into the design of a new neighborhood center: Sherman Heights Community Center, San Diego (architect, Rob Quigley).

desert, of pyramids, architecture of scale. I feel like an insignificant dabbler after seeing the muscular nature of the Mexican architect.

In Mexico labor is cheap, materials are expensive. That dictates a certain type of architecture. You can use handcrafted materials; you can actually lay a big building up in block. You can create mass—thick walls and heavy things that are labor-intensive. You can't do that in the United States. Here we have the opposite situation, relatively less expensive materials and very expensive labor. We just can't afford the labor to do certain things, and yet we have technology to do things differently—light framing kinds of things, steel with panels, for example.

In Mexico, the architect still seems to have quite a bit of respect, as an artist. The architect's decisions have great weight and great prestige. In this country, architecture is thought of as a business commodity only. The concern is not with how wonderful a building is but that it make money fast—the short-term capitalist ethic, you might say. In other words, the artistic component of architecture is devalued here, whereas in Mexico it is highly valued.

What I like about Tijuana is its pedestrian vitality, its sense of color. There's an architectural abandon that happens on a small scale there, with people and their houses, and is very confident, and doesn't happen here. You sense that there are no rules in the residential districts. And here in the United States there are thousands of rules: what you can do, what you can't do, zoning, front yard setbacks, fence heights, restrictions on the design of front doors, community groups telling you that your house must be white, zoning commissions telling you how high you can build. We just seem to thrive on restrictions here. In Tijuana, with a lot less rules, there is a more coherent result. You get a vibrancy, a spontaneity.

Part of what makes it this way is that it's not self-conscious. The result is something quite wonderful, if you extract that out of the issue of poverty. The cliché that Mexicans work with their hearts and Americans with their heads is true. Americans feel they've lost the mandate to be creative. We have to charge four times as much because of all the regulations. After you get done jumping through all these hoops, you're lucky if there's any creativity left because it has all been homogenized.

Developers in the United States are like tuning forks. They respond to the vibrations of the city. The tuning fork is tuned to society, and society is tuned to dollars. Developers will tell you, "Whatever you do, don't win any architecture awards or prizes on my building." In their minds, there is functional architecture, that sells, and aesthetic architecture—that doesn't. If a building wins an award, they think it's an ego trip and it won't work in the market.[12]

At the Mercy of Something Else

Mark Steele, originally from Michigan, has been an architect in San Diego since 1978. Steele's recognized designs include shopping centers, housing, and a bay-front urban design plan in San Diego. He is a visiting professor at the New School of Architecture, San Diego. His office is a Quonset hut–shaped building he owns in downtown La Jolla.

Whether we like it or not, our cultures are becoming blended at the border. There's a real opportunity down there to design projects that integrate the two societies, instead of drawing a line between them. But a lot of designs reinforce the border by putting up spiffy, juicy stuff on the U.S. side without paying attention to the Mexican side.

The border zone itself is very utilitarian, with freeways and such. There's not a significant entrance to the countries from either side. There's no ceremony. It's very abrupt, impersonal. It's actually hostile. The whole area. In Detroit-Windsor, you have the river. Across the river is Canada. Down here, it's across these gullies and that wire fence is Mexico.

The border entrance is a very seedy kind of place. There's no elegance to it. When you cross the border into Mexico, you feel like you're going into a second-rate place. And it really shouldn't be. Tijuana is becoming one of the major cities of the world, and most people don't realize that because of the way it is dealt with. There's no sense of demarcation at the border and no elegance to the transition.

I don't know Tijuana very well. I mostly think of it in terms of Third World problems. Mud streets. That's what I see. I've never thought of Tijuana as having any real identity or cohesive quality. I've been to Mexico City and it had a real elegance about it, but also

FIG. 6.7 One U.S. architect's perception of the border: "Across these gullies and that wire fence is Mexico."

a despair. Tijuana has very little quaintness. I've been to Durango. It's quaint. Tijuana seems to be at the mercy of something else.

I'm all in favor of more discussion about our relationship with Tijuana. But this is probably the first discussion I've had with anyone about Mexican architecture or about Tijuana. I don't know that many people who are interested in it. It's been hard to sustain any kind of regional or Mexican influence in architecture here. This region is interesting because of its climate, but I think the proliferation of Mediterranean architecture is kind of trite; it really isn't like we're on the Mediterranean. A lot of it is real pastiche kind of stuff, which is corny and made up.

In San Diego, historically, there's been a lot of Victorian architecture, and then today, it's contemporary architecture. One of the things that's happened to architecture, which is the same thing that's happened to food, automobiles, and clothing, is the inability of the mass media to support regional styles. Our designs are influenced by the region in the sense that we take advantage of being outside—courtyards, French doors, atriums. In my own house, every room opens onto an atrium. The atrium goes back to Egyptian designs, thousands of years before Christ. It has gone through pretty much all the cultures in the southern climate, and it always works well. To me the atrium house is a perfect San Diego house.

Europeans are, in general, more quality-oriented, and I suspect Mexicans are too. If you go to Europe, a lot of architecture is very simple, but it's much more highly detailed and better quality. There's a sense there that high-quality things—food, architecture, cars—enrich your life. In the United States, there's an emphasis on jobs and earning money. Our designs end up looking cheesy and goofy-looking. Somehow, the attention to detail, an awareness of the world and how it enriches you, has escaped Americans. And I don't know why. I mean, except for Native Americans, we're all European or something. I think it's about quality. The real difference between us and Japan or Europe or Mexico is quality. We just don't understand it; we just don't make a commitment to it. If people are oblivious to the quality of life, they're oblivious to architecture.[13]

The Quantum Leap

Joseph Martinez is a native San Diegan who studied architecture at Berkeley and Harvard. He is one of the principals in the firm Martinez, Cutri & McArdle in downtown San Diego. Martinez has been active designing hotels, offices, commercial space, university buildings, and housing on both sides of the border. From his office high in the Symphony Towers Building, you can see all the way to Tijuana on a clear day.

Too often in the United States, architecture looks only at buildings. Ninety percent of the architects in this country are object builders. The building is abstracted from the surrounding environment. We've also forgotten about culture. We've subtracted culture and tradition out from our lifestyles because we've gotten caught up with the computer, freeways, traffic engineering, environmental systems, marketing experts, real estate brokers, developers, politicians, and the media. We've lost our sense of the richness of culture.

So the real issue when you look at the border is how the border is being erased. Culture can be realized through aesthetics, through the arts. It might be realized through landscape architecture. This is one region; the air, the ecology doesn't stop at the border. There's no reason the landscaping could not pass through the border. Then there's transportation. There's no reason you should have to wait two hours at the border. Birds don't stop at the border. The whales migrate north and south. Air passes. Look at the demographics. By the twenty-first century, in the state of California, maybe 25 percent of the population will be Latino. Minorities are going to be the majority. Whether you talk about Mexico, or the United States, the movement of people is changing the grid. It will have to be a transparent border.

I'm not enamored of the politics of Mexico. I'm not enamored of their pollution; I'm not enamored of their violation of civil rights; I'm not enamored of the strong dominance the Catholic Church has on Mexicans and the poor; I'm not enamored of the government policies toward the poor people. I'm disgusted with the way indigenous people—the Indians—are treated there. I am enamored, though, of culture, and the history of culture, starting with the Olmecs and working up to the Zapotecs, Aztecs, Mixtecs, Toltecs, and to the present day. That opportunity is important, and the border offers the bridge from one world to the other.

My work as an architect focuses on culture and aesthetics. I've subtracted out things that relate to technology, computers, and construction systems. Exclusive materiality. We look at how culture generates form. If you look at 1970s modernism—steel and glass—it's acultural. It was cultural in its time frame, but it doesn't tell the whole story. I believe in some designs, we can incorporate a more indigenous perspective—in materials, in heaviness of the base, in rustication and ornamentation (jaguars, serpents, eagles, or warriors). Those kinds of details. Also, intense textures of materials and colors. If you walk down the streets of Dolores Hidalgo (Mexico), it's like walking down a color swatch in a paint store. Every building is a different color and they're vibrant, intense. You might have one building with individual units, and what distinguishes the units is just the color of paint. The plaster, the bearing walls, run straight through, but it's the paint that separates one from the other. We're trying to use that principle in our designs here in San Diego.

In Tijuana, they designed the Zona del Rio, and they got it right! They built the great boulevard first, when nothing else was there. They put double rows of trees on both sides, and a median in the middle, plus wide lanes, big open traffic circles, big fountains. That's how you build a city. It's no different in Rome or London or Tokyo or Mexico City or Washington, D.C. That's how you build great cities. It's better to have good streets and mediocre architecture than it is to have spectacular works of architecture and lousy streets. The problem is you will get every kind of building and they won't relate to one another, because everyone is trying to outdo the other. But if you have a street that's organized, everything else will fit.

Good streets will neutralize things. Revolution Avenue in Tijuana is one of the most exciting streets in Tijuana. It's alive. Whether the architecture is there or not is almost irrelevant. I can't tell you a single building on Revolution. I can't. But I can tell you: The sidewalks are really wide; the stores are really animated; the width of the street is good for the height of the buildings. There's music. It's lively. Sunlight comes down onto the street all parts of the day. The Jai Alai Building is there. I can't tell you about most of the buildings. I can't tell you there are works of architecture you should go see. But you do have to go see the street.

San Ysidro (the border crossing) could be the center for free trade in the twenty-first century. San Ysidro could be San Diego's future. You look at its variable character. On one side, east of I-805, there's so much retail—Payless shoe stores, Kentucky Fried Chicken,

FIG. 6.8 Great spaces rather than buildings are the mainstay of great cities. In Mediterranean and Latin American cities, great streets and squares abound: Piazza San Marcos,
Venice, Italy.

Church's Chicken, fast food — that has high-intensity uses, not too different from Tijuana.
The architecture that's developed there is the second generation of buildings; the next
level will be second stories — it will densify to something like Tijuana. Wouldn't it be interesting to see how you could make that connection? Revolution to San Ysidro Boulevard.
Using trolley, high-intensity uses in the *barrio*. Tie the two urban environments together,
and then let the architecture come, then the graphics, then the landscaping. We need a
new urban vision — it's in a valley, it's all connected. It's one region.[14]

Yearning for Mexico's Freedom of Expression

Ken Kellogg was born in San Diego's Kensington neighborhood and has
practiced architecture in San Diego since 1958, after studying at three universities, the University of Colorado, U.C. Berkeley, and the University of Southern
California. He is well known in southern California for his unusual designs,
working with natural materials like stone.

The kind of architecture I do is "Spanish" in style but the kind that was original back in
Spain. In Mexico they like me because I'm a ditchdigger, I don't wear all the fancy ties
and the suits and all that, like these guys up here do. My work is site specific. It's not out

of the drawer. You don't scrape your lot. You take into account sun, neighbor, street, and landscape. You come up with an unusual design that will fit the circumstances. I favor wood and stone. A lot of people don't use stone anymore, but I'd say I've designed with stone in five or six different ways, usually indigenous to the area.

I've been going to Tijuana since the 1930s. I've seen Tijuana probably closer and better than any architect born here. I remember going across the old bridge and seeing people lined up bathing in the river. I like the uninhibited aspects of Tijuana, its people, its humanity. The way people try to make a living on their own. I like the parts most people don't like—the guy trying to pull you into his shop to do a paint job or an upholstery job on your car. Sure they may have slums, but what do we have here but sanitary slums?

You go down the street and commit a traffic violation. Most people don't stop at stop signs here. Over there, they slow down. There, if you break a traffic law, a cop comes up and tells you, you pay him ten dollars, and it's over with. He takes it home and feeds his family. Here, with all the integrity involved, the ethics (and I'm an ethical person), you spend a hundred dollars to go to court—plus the time you take off from your business—and you don't know if you'll win, and it ends up costing a lot more here.

To hang on to archaic ideals about architecture, like the city of Santa Barbara, with all that technology out there, it doesn't make sense. You can't even build two-story adobe because it's not considered seismically sound. So what you end up with is all pseudo, superficial. So why do we need to create a future of pseudoism, rather than allow for individual creativity?

All that Spanish-style building in Santa Barbara is a matter of economics. They think they have the market there. But I don't like it. What I do like is the foliage, the trees, the eucalyptus, the gardens, and the topography. The old Spanish buildings, including the mission, are great. But to try to make a landmark district, then have a group of ten or twelve people tell you that there're fifteen styles of Mexican architecture that are allowed in the area. They don't know what the hell they're doing. Look at their buildings. Fake metal windows made to look like wood. They're not real. The real stuff is the old stuff. Preserve it, but don't try to duplicate it, because the more you duplicate it, the more you ruin the old stuff. You're trying to do something that isn't there. What's real is the old stuff that was built in a certain time with a certain technology. It was built by hand, by Indians. I'm a hands-on guy, and there're not too many of us left in this business. I appreciate the old buildings, but now we're in a new ball game. Let the originals be distinctive and allow the new areas to flourish on their own.[15]

Mexican Modernist in the United States

Alfredo Larín lives in San Diego but was born in Mexico City. After studying architecture at Cornell University, he has lived and worked in both the United States and Mexico. Truly a binational architect, he's been practicing in the San Diego–Tijuana region for more than thirty years. Among his well-known designs are the Twin Towers of Agua Caliente, the Plaza Patria commercial center

FIG. 6.9 Some Mexican architects are pure modernists and reject historic references altogether in their designs: the Twin Towers of Agua Caliente, Tijuana (by permission of architect, Alfredo Larín).

and the Chapultepec Country Club in Tijuana, the Chicano Park kiosk in Barrio Logan, and the Celadon Restaurant in San Diego.

My designs are very modern. I don't necessarily try to inject Mexico into my designs. I try to adapt to each client. In Chicano Park, they wanted a typical colonial kiosk, like every town in Mexico. So I said, "Something's wrong here." They wanted a circular kiosk with a red tile roof. I said, "That doesn't fit here. This should be more Indian." I showed them my proposed drawings for the kiosk. They loved it. The city government didn't like it, but they accepted it because they wanted to please the residents.

There was a lot of architectural freedom in the United States thirty years ago. In Mexico, you never hear of a client suing an architect. Here, it's daily. I'm sick of it. Any little mistake you make—in a joint, a doorknob—you get sued. When we draw plans now, we're not trying to do our best design, we're trying to keep from getting caught, getting sued. We have to have $20,000 a year insurance. I don't like it.

The United States is going down the drain with this. Legal constipation. Everything is boxed up in legalities here. Products and materials are way overpriced because you've got to cover your legal fees. You can't compete with anybody. In Mexico, I can do anything I want. Anything. Height. I can build right up to the property line. You look at the River Zone area, considering Mexico is a developing country, there's less money for government supervision, but it's a beautiful area. Landscaping, trees. And here in the richest country in the world? Slums. If I don't go to Tijuana once a week, I can't stand it anymore. In Tijuana, they have monuments. They inspire people. They look good, they create landscaping, lighting at night. People walk around and say, "Here's my city." In San Diego, you walk on Broadway in downtown, do you feel good there? You might get mugged or something. Tijuana, you can walk anywhere at four in the morning, you won't get mugged. They check the teenagers from the United States coming across the border into Mexico, rather than vice versa.

The difference between Mexico and the United States is this: If you're in a restaurant in Mexico, and the air-conditioning goes off, people say, "Oh it's getting warm in here. Let's open the windows." If you're in a restaurant in the United States and the air-conditioning goes off, they say, "Oh, do you think the thermostat is on, or do you think the compressor in the air conditioner went off, or did the power shut off?" [16]

In this chapter, I have reconstructed only a small sample of the voices of Mexican and U.S. architects whose work is transforming the landscape of the Mexican American border region. Yet this sample offers a good cross-section of the dominant themes in the collision of culture, place, and landscape. One is struck by the keen sense of awareness that Mexican and U.S. architects have of each other, no doubt a product of greater cross-border integration of economy and lifestyle. Of the six Mexican architects interviewed, two live on the U.S. side of the border. Of the five U.S. architects interviewed, one is a Mexican living in the U.S., and one is Mexican American. One cannot draw a strict dividing line separating the cultural origins of architects working along the border. The designers of the border region are slowly reinventing themselves as a transboundary collective force.

Yet there is a palpable tension among these architects, anchored by their different world views acquired in distinct cultural settings on either side of the border. Mexico is seen as a culture with a strong attachment to the home. Its cities can claim a pedestrian life that thrives in streets, plazas, and other public spaces. It is idealized as passionate, warm, and romantic, while Mexican architects tend to view the United States as cold, efficient, and even dehumanized. If Mexico's political history makes the application of law appear to be unpredictable, the United States suffers from overregulation. Among architects, these differences lead to a sense that the two cultures diverge in the way urban built environments are constructed—color, spontaneity, and innovation reign south of the border; order, technology, and homogeneity dominate north of the line.

While most border architects agree that they work in a world of overlapping U.S. and Mexican cultures, they remain quite aware of their differences. Mexican architects vehemently defend preserving their traditions in the face of U.S. culture. They fear that perhaps in being so far from the center of Mexican culture, they will lose touch with it. Yet at the same time, many admire the modernism of North America.

U.S. architects worry that architecture in the United States is so controlled by profit that it stunts creativity and hinders attention to detail. They fiercely admire the vitality in Mexico's built environment. They respect the fact that architecture is a profession that appears to be taken far more seriously in Mexico. And also, they appreciate the way Mexican designers strive to preserve the role of the street as public space.

A second unifying theme emerging from the interviews is tied to the contribution of designers to making the border region a unique place. The borderlands encapsulate a number of troubling images for architects—vulgarity, visual pollution, deprivation, commercialism, lack of identity, and a feeling of chaos. This identity crisis causes Mexican architects to worry about piracy of original designs. U.S. architects lament the seedy, hostile, and generally dismal condition of the boundary landscape at the physical zone of contact: the boundary line, border gates, and crossings. This harsh, abrupt, and somewhat militarized corridor of space produces a landscape—of barbed wire and metallic fences, police and border patrol cars, guard towers, migrant dirt paths and trails, and abandoned buildings—that is out of sync with the political reality of free-trade accords, the opening of political boundaries, and the formation of a cross-border ecological and functional community.

Yet the border is also seen as a region in transition, with many new forms of emerging opportunity. Border architects view the 1990s as a strategic time to move beyond political boundaries, an opportunity to create a vital, bicultural landscape and eliminate superficial scenography, fake "Hispanic" architecture, or politically insensitive landscapes. NAFTA therefore represents an opportunity to rethink how landscapes are made in the United States, how they are made in Mexico, and what kinds of cities both nations want in the future.

Yet the question remains: Should the border be a zone of transition, an expression of the meeting of two different cultures, perhaps even a region where experimental landscapes of economic and cultural integration can take form? The borderlands offer a unique and timely laboratory for pondering different sorts of overlapping landscapes.

But, on the other hand, the borderlands might also be viewed as a place where each culture reinforces and protects its unique identity. For example, one of the subtexts of the border landscape is the tension between Mexicans and Mexican Americans in the area of the built environment. When Mexican Americans were given the opportunity to design their own community center in the Sherman Heights neighborhood of San Diego, according to the lead architect, Rob Quigley, they rejected Mexican building traditions, favoring local and more neighborhood-oriented designs, such as the Victorian house, an Anglo form brought to San Diego from the East Coast of the United States. A Mexican

American architect like Joe Martinez of San Diego admires Mexican architecture but also speaks critically of its politics. This tension between Mexican and Mexican American architects is echoed in the words of a Mexican architect (Juan Miramontes) interviewed in an earlier chapter of this book, who commented about American Chicanos: "There are many people of Mexican descent, but they don't know the land of their parents . . . when you meet a Mexican American, there is a culture clash. They say, 'We've already been to the moon, and you're just a Totonac (Indian).' "[17] While some writers have alluded to conflicts between Mexicans and U.S.-born Chicanos,[18] few have considered whether these differences might be expressed in the built environment. Mexican Americans may seek to construct neighborhoods north of the border that express their unique identity, but what exactly is that identity? It borrows heavily from Mexico yet rejects Mexico at the same time. This seeming contradiction may be one of the important tensions embedded in the built environment of the border region in the next century.

SEVEN

From Aztec to High Tech

Cities like Tijuana and Los Angeles, once socio-urban aberrations, are becoming models of a new hybrid culture, full of uncertainty and vitality. —GUILLERMO GÓMEZ PEÑA

In a world in which satellite communication and global markets increasingly shape modes of behavior, it is not surprising to find cities and regions that are products of more than one national culture, particularly along international frontiers. Barcelona, on the Spanish-French border is a hybrid city of northern Spanish/Catalan and French influence; Geneva, Switzerland, owes its formation to both Swiss and French forces. Cities have become maps of competing cultural forces imposing their wills upon the urban landscape.

The landscapes of cities in the United States are products of the immigrant cultures. Yet discussions about American urban landscape traditions typically focus on the theme of European culture. Most books written about American cities and their architecture concentrate on European traditions. Native American culture is usually covered in a few pages early in the book; Mexico is often entirely left out, or it merits only a brief mention in the section on "Spanish style" architecture.

In fact, as the previous chapters in this book have sought to argue, the Mexican-U.S. border urban landscape offers a glimpse into an emerging prototype of cities in the next century—transcultural cities. A new "Mex-American" landscape is being produced in an environment where Mexican people, whether U.S. citizens, immigrants, or Mexican nationals, are leaving their imprint on the cultural landscape. The diffusion of Mexican architecture and urbanism into the

United States is occurring while the international border fades as a barrier to social interaction. Whether by a formal North American free-trade agreement, through cross-border marriage, or common geography, Mexico and the United States are becoming integrated, and so are the nearby (and in some cases distant) cities.

The journey "from Aztec to high tech" will not be an easy one. The new landscapes of the borderlands reflect a collision of Mexican tradition with the forces of North American modernity. Those who live in the vortex of two different cultures are finding new ways to cope with this collision. Consider Mexican artist Armando Muñoz García, a native of Tijuana who has lived on both sides of the border. Muñoz García, like early-twentieth-century Barcelona architect Antoni Gaudi, is convinced that the tide of history must be inscribed upon the landscape of his native city.

In 1989, while Tijuana was celebrating its one hundredth anniversary, Muñoz García approached his city government about building a monument to the approaching millennium. Mexico is a nation wedded to monument building. But the monuments usually appear in the form of Baroque, equestrian statues honoring national heroes. Muñoz García had in mind something quite different: a giant building in the shape of a nude woman. A year later, with his own funds, Muñoz completed La Mujer Blanca (The White Woman), six and one half stories high, eighteen tons of concrete and plaster, wire meshing, and steel-reinforced columns, looking like a Mexican Statue of Liberty in the form of a six-story house.

The statue-building is symbolic of the kind of landscapes that will result from Mexican and U.S. integration. In Mexico, there will continue to be a push to maintain that which is Mexican. The border is the first line of defense against U.S. cultural invasion. As Muñoz put it, "People visit our city (Tijuana), and they just trash it. They have these stereotypes in their heads. That Mexico is dirty. So they don't care."[1]

So Muñoz García would launch his edifice in the face of Americans: a tall building shaped like a woman, painted a bright white color. "White represents purity," says the artist. "It contradicts the stereotyping of Mexican history, of Tijuana's history and of our women. We are not a city of prostitutes."[2] The woman stares out at America from across a canyon of proletarian homes that cling precariously to the steep slopes leading to the canyon bottom. Garbage lies scattered at the bottom, and chickens and dogs sift through it. Dark, polluted waters form a trickle of a stream. Mexico's cities remain blanketed by *colonias*, neighborhoods of the poor.

The irony of Muñoz García's Mujer Blanca must not be missed. A Mexican-born artist chooses as the symbol of his homeland a naked white woman? The

FIG. 7.1 Landscape as cultural message: a Tijuana artist employs the image of women as a sculptural theme in the urban landscape.

artist has taken a piece of American culture, the slickness of TV, the Calvin Klein-like obsession with female youth and nudity, and given it a Mexican spin. If you look more closely, the woman is *mestiza*. Her features are hard, and proud, like that of a Mexican *campesino*. She is not serene.

At the meeting places of cultures, Mexicans may feel overwhelmed by the massive consumerism of the United States. One result is that Mexico begins to search for meaning, even in the border towns.

The architect Jorge Ozorno says, speaking about the border:

We have to invent a history for ourselves. There are several layers to it. It begins with the rock paintings in the caves of Baja California, the first murals of the border region. Then we have the portable architecture of Baja's first missionaries, from La Paz to San Luis Obispo. They often had to build their structures quickly, based on memories of the missions and churches of central Mexico and Europe. There is also our local industrial architecture—assembly. The first tall buildings were assembled in Europe in the nineteenth century: the Eiffel Tower in Paris, the Crystal Palace in London. Here in Baja, the church of Santa Rosalia was designed by Eiffel—it arrived in boxes by boat and was assembled, a graceful building on an inhospitable, uninhabited, arid land.

When you walk down Revolution Avenue, with its multiple themes—a sixteenth-century *hacienda,* a great Moroccan bazaar—there are touches of the past, of other cultures. The shopping *galerias* are like Arabian bazaars. In Teotihuacan, in Mayan cities, the markets were open-air. When the Conquest came, there was the memory of St. Peter's Basilica, one of the largest covered spaces of its time. Imagine the Spanish conquerors who came upon a culture where there were no closed spaces. The conquerors had the closed-space idea in their blood. So they must have taken an intermediate position—open-air markets with canvas overhangs. Markets that can be moved around quickly, as they are in Mexico City.[3]

But, there is also a certain inevitability that American values invade Mexico. "My clients don't want to live in a house designed with recycled metal or

FIG. 7.2 A sunken shopping gallery brings the feeling of an Arabian bazaar to border cities: *galeria* in downtown Tijuana.

junk parts, even if it is excellently designed," says Ozorno. "They want a California tract house, with a picture window and a garage. A lot of people can't afford to buy a house in the United States, but they buy the magazines, and then they find a photograph they like, they bring it to the architect in Tijuana and say 'I want a house like this.' But in Mexico, our lots are smaller and narrower. We don't have a lot of freedom to design houses with ideal lighting and ventilation. To conform to our clients' wishes, we have to design caricatures of American-style houses in miniature. The scale is changed, and the house is distorted and out of proportion."[4]

"Our clients travel to the U.S., to California, and they are affected by what they see," adds architect Jaime Venguer. "They want to copy from the other side, they want to say, 'I live in an American-style house.' The technology of the United States is important—appliances, for example. You buy them in the U.S. and bring them across to Tijuana. So the idea is to copy what you see on the other side and transport it across to your house. With a good mason you can transform your home."[5]

The Risk of Placelessness

A favorite joke the Mexicans like to tell along the border with California goes like this: Two Mexican dogs traveling in opposite directions pass each other at the international boundary. One dog has been living in the lap of luxury in the United States but is heading back to Mexico. The other has been in Mexico for a very long time but is crossing the border because it is hungry. "Why are you leaving the United States when you have it so good here?" asks the dog coming out of Mexico. "Because I want to bark again," says the other dog.

What we find along the border—at the intersection of cultures—is a tension between Mexican and North American, between memory and futurism, between "Aztec" and "high tech." This tension is embedded in the urban landscapes which become metaphors for the transcultural nature of the larger region, where image and reality flow back and forth between the two dominant cultures. A Mexican scholar visiting the border at Tijuana reported that residents interviewed there, when asked what images best reflected their city, chose those strongly associated with the United States: the Revolution Avenue tourist street, the old Casino Agua Caliente, and satellite dishes, for example.[6] He describes the border as a "postmodern" place; it follows neither the strict cultural rules of the United States nor Mexico. It is something in between, or something beyond, a new form of identity. It calls for a new way of looking at the world.

Ultimately, Mexicans living along the border cannot ignore the impact places like southern California have on their cities. Like other global consumers, Mexi-

FIG. 7.3 High-technology landscape on the Mexican border: satellite dish in Tijuana.

cans have become enamored of the late-twentieth-century American cityscape, as expressed in the American-style shopping mall. Marketing studies have shown that Mexicans on the border prefer shopping in the U.S., not only because of the lower prices and, in some cases, higher-quality goods, but also because they simply like the American shopping malls better. As a result, the Mexican government has taken to building U.S.-style shopping malls on its side of the border. Yet the fascination with the southern Californian shopping mall remains. Shopping malls create a new sense of space and place, within an artificial, consumerist world that is admired north and south of the border. It would not be surprising in the next century to find that the landscapes of border cities like Tijuana become dominated by simulated, consumer-oriented spaces like shopping malls.

If Mexican memory is being eclipsed by global consumerism, it is illustrated by the fact that a theme park, Mexitlán, that sought to re-create in miniature the greatest architectural feats of Mexico failed, while just down the block, the tourist avenue of striped donkeys, curio shops, and high-tech disco bars decorated with serapes is thriving. Simulated Mexico—not the real place—becomes the preferred destination for tourists.

The quintessential simulated landscape can be found in the heart of every Mexican border city—the main commercial street built during the first tourism boom of the 1920s. Revolution Avenue in downtown Tijuana is to the Mexican border what Main Street, USA, is to Disneyland—a grand promenade that sets the mood for a carefully choreographed tourist experience. There are few places left where southern Californians can walk. Disneyland is one of them. Revolution Avenue in downtown Tijuana is another. If the experience of Disneyland begins by walking from parking lot through entrance gates onto Main Street, USA, the experience of Tijuana moves from the tourist parking just north of the border crossing at San Ysidro, through the pedestrian border gate, and along the path that leads directly onto Revolution Avenue. Few consider the irony of a street name (Revolution) that speaks of rural peasants fighting for land ownership at the turn of the century. Here, "Revolution" is carnival—buildings decorated like zebras or Moorish castles, flags and colorful blimps floating overhead. Revolution Avenue belongs to the American tourist. Its architecture ranges from romantic to gaudy to silly to downright hideous.

"The owners of establishments on Revolution Avenue have a funny way of thinking," says Eugenio Velásquez, Tijuana architect. "They think that by making things ugly, that will attract Americans. Americans are tired of seeing everything so perfect and well made on their side of the border; they want to have a moment of relief. So they come here to take refuge. They come here to feel rich, to spend a little, because here, even with what little they might earn over there, here they're like millionaires."[7]

"Revolution Avenue is theater," adds architect Jorge Ozorno. "It's a stage set that shows how *gringos* came in and built up the town. Today, you see a life-sized yellow school bus on the exterior of a building—it's oriented toward the market of American students eighteen to twenty-one years old who just got out of high school; since they can drink beer in Mexico (the drinking age is eighteen), they come here, and subliminally, they're delivered certain images—'Now, get on your school bus where you can drink.' They can make fun of it. It's all an exercise of border craftsmanship—all of the buildings on Revolution Avenue are carefully crafted. They're built for a party, with their friezes, their carvings, their adornments—it's a much more vulgar architecture than what we have in the rest of Mexico."[8]

One landscape scholar claims that "the essence of places lies in the largely unself-conscious intentionality that defines places as profound centers of human existence."[9] Authentic places must be contrasted with "placelessness," a condition that makes it less and less possible to have a deeply felt sense of place or to create places authentically.[10] Tourism development in Mexico, especially along the border, often is noteworthy for its tendency to create homogenous architecture and synthetic landscapes. What we might term "placeless tourism" becomes a strategy to remove the tourist, as much as possible, from the actual geographic and cultural setting. This "enclave" mentality, we observed earlier

FIG. 7.4A AND B Two examples of the carnival-like landscape of Tijuana's downtown tourism strip: Red Square, a discotheque with playful Russian-Byzantine architecture theme, and Bananas-Ranas Bar, with an American school bus on second-floor building facade.

in the book, is best illustrated by the Club Mediterranean, which is certainly not unique to Mexico. Club Med detaches itself from local culture, by creating an autonomous space within which the tourist can remain without ever having experienced the real place. Club Med instructs the arriving client to give up all money and traveler's checks (which are placed in a vault). While on the premises, Club Med clients are given "beads" to use to buy drinks or gifts. The food served at Club Med may not even reflect local products; at the Club Med near Guaymas, Mexico (the shrimping capital of the Pacific coast), the main regional cuisine—shrimp—was reportedly not served once over a seven-day period.[11]

At the border, there will always be a temptation, among those who invest in construction and development, to build an entirely fantasized environment where Americans will come to consume. A landscape writer once coined the term "other-directed architecture"[12] to refer to architecture deliberately pitched toward outsiders, spectators, and above all, consumers.[13] Using exotic decoration, grotesque facades, and outrageous colors, other-directed places are created to announce themselves as "vacationland" or "consumerland" for outsiders. Disneyland is an obvious other-directed place, "a world without violence, confrontation, ideological or racial clashes, without politics . . . a world that is white, Anglo-Saxon, and Puritan-Protestant, often redneck, void of ethnic cast."[14] It would be easy to write off other-directed places if they were confined to amusement parks like Disneyland. But the Disneyland idea is incorporated into tourist developments in Mexico, particularly along the U.S.-Mexican border, where

FIG. 7.5 The donkey cart—a decorated stage set for tourism photos dates back to the 1950s in Tijuana—and is the quintessential "other-directed" landscape element of Mexican border towns.

developers try to create an idealized "Mexicoland," a fantasyland that is a caricature of what Americans might think Mexico is (land of bullfights, sombreros, burros, and mission-style churches), insulated from the real Mexico, but with just a touch of a veiled sense of mystery and foreign intrigue.[15]

North of the border, mythmaking has also surrounded Mexican architecture, materializing in the form of reconstructed missions and imagined Spanish-

Mediterranean courtyards, arches, plazas, and quadrangles. The southwestern United States's "Mexican" urbanism became part of its larger frontier architecture, tied to the land, but also to the imagination of its new settlers.

The history of border towns like Tijuana is instructive. Tijuana began as a placeless landscape, a gritty gambling and drinking town for Americans. But gradually, Mexicans took their city back and over the last four decades of the twentieth century slowly transformed it into a more Mexican city. At the same time, Mexico, beginning after 1950, began to open its arms, culturally speaking, to the United States. This opening was felt first along the border, and, as cultural integration accelerated in the 1970s and 1980s, the Mexican border towns found it quite easy to accommodate the shopping mall, the fast-food restaurant, the freeway, the golf resort, and, in coastal areas, oceanfront condominiums. Mexican border towns became a metaphor for the larger nation, struggling between tradition and modernity.

FIG. 7.6 Here lies the future: The bilingual commercial landscape will be part of the built environment of the transfrontier metropolis along the Mexico-U.S. border in the twenty-first century.

Landscape and Culture Clash

On the U.S. side of the border, Mexico's presence in the landscape illustrates its larger struggle to find a harmonious peace with its northern neighbor. In U.S. cities near the border, the experience of trying to absorb Mexican architecture and urbanism has been distorted. While on the surface, the southwestern United States may seem to have "Hispanic influence" in its urban landscapes, a deeper examination shows this influence to be hollow, a "fantasy heritage," as one California writer described it.[16] Developers have created "old towns" and tourist spaces that attempt to re-create a Mexican past, and there are regional styles of "Spanish Colonial" and "mission" architecture, but in the end, the landscapes of the urban southwestern United States have not resolved their connection to the Mexican past.

The tensions of cultural integration are perhaps best expressed by the architects themselves. Mexican designers are evenly divided between those who embrace the past and seek to preserve Mexican culture on the landscape, and those who are prepared to modernize. Many are troubled by the invasion of American consumerism south of the border but must survive by accepting design commissions for condominiums or discotheques. Most Mexicans are facing the onslaught of "high-tech" consumerism with a kind of nationalistic pride that leads them to aspire to create forms that preserve traditional elements of Mexican architecture.

American designers view Mexico as a refreshing example of what their own culture is missing: respect for architects as professionals. In the fast-paced world of real estate development, U.S. designers believe that good taste in architecture is disappearing on their side of the border, while it remains more intact in Mexico. Yet too frequently, when attempts are made to borrow Mexican design themes and inject them north of the border, the results are disappointing—fake, pastiche forms that trivialize authentic Mexican design.

Mexico and the U.S. still have the opportunity to contemplate how their cultures and their architecture will overlap in the next century. The relationship for most of this century was one of tension; perhaps in a climate of free trade, the question of cultural integration can be addressed more appropriately. Architecture and landscape represent one piece of this larger tapestry of cultural integration. It is inevitable that Mexico will "North Americanize," and give up some of its unique attributes in architecture and urban design.

The "search" for authentic Mexican cityscapes north of the border leads into immigrant *barrios* like East Los Angeles, which have a rich vernacular expression but enormous economic and physical deprivation. There are signs of emerging social tensions in the U.S. sector of the borderlands, fueled by troubling tides of anti-immigrant and anti-Mexican sentiment. Perhaps most emblematic of Mexico's presence in the United States are the temporary landscapes of the Mexican migrant camps that lie on the outskirts of cities from El Paso to Los Angeles. They remind us that, at century's end, Mexicans are still "aliens" in too many places north of the border. Mexico continues to teeter on the edge of the American urban landscape.

NOTES

Preface

1. The reader will note that the title of the book—*From Aztec to High Tech*—alludes to the evolution of influences on Mexican urbanism, from its origins in the cultural heartland of central Mexico (*Aztec*) to its integration with the United States (*high tech*). Obviously, as I explore the northern borderlands, the term *Aztec* is not meant to apply literally to the region, since the influences of indigenous architecture never reached the northern frontiers in the pre-Columbian period.

2. I have not addressed the question of gender in Mexican-U.S. cultural landscapes. Gender was not a central theme in my research, but it is certainly an interesting topic that deserves attention in the borderlands. See, for example, Bennett 1995, Sklair 1989, and, more generally, Hayden 1995.

One. Introduction: Landscapes of the Transcultural City

Epigraph: A popular saying in Mexico, usually attributed to President Porfirio Díaz.

1. See, for example, Sklair 1991, for an excellent book on the subject.

2. Relph 1976.   3. Tuan 1977.

4. Hiss 1991.   5. Altman and Low 1992.

6. Hayden 1995.   7. Hiss 1991.

8. Logan and Molotch 1987.   9. See Sklair 1991.

10. Rybczynski 1989, 93.   11. Ibid., 88.

12. Sorkin 1992.   13. Davis 1990.

14. See Zukin 1991.

15. Two important summary works are Jackson 1984 and Meinig 1979.

16. Meinig 1979; Hough 1990.   17. Hayden 1995, 3–6.

18. Ibid., 3.   19. Tuan 1977, 107.

20. Lozano 1990, 21.   21. Relph 1987, 7.

22. Ward 1990, 179–80.   23. Knox 1987.

24. Ford 1994, xii.   25. See Arreola and Curtis 1993, 7.

26. Ibid.   27. Murray 1989.

28. See Arreola and Curtis 1993 for the most detailed and comprehensive review of the landscapes of Mexican border towns.

29. See Sklair 1991 for a review of border industrialization and the assembly plant program.

30. See, for example, Herzog 1990b; Young 1986; Christopherson 1983.
31. I make this point in Herzog 1991a.
32. Sklair 1989.
33. See Canclini 1990.
34. An excellent work on culture and urban space is Rotenberg and McDonogh 1993.
35. Tuan 1977, 123.
36. Hall 1969; Rapoport 1982; Agnew, Mercer, and Sopher 1984.
37. See, for example, Sale 1975; Sawers and Tabb 1984.

Two. *"Aztec": The Mexican Urban Landscape*

1. Paz 1961, 208.
2. Russel-Hitchcock 1955.
3. Wolf 1959; Kubler 1975.
4. González de León 1990.
5. Ibid.
6. Ibid.
7. Ibid.
8. See Ward 1990.
9. See Kandell 1990; Ward 1990.
10. Fischkin 1988.
11. For a discussion of national urban movements in Mexico, see Bennett 1995.
12. Bataillon 1979.
13. Hardoy 1968.
14. Stierlin 1964, 97.
15. See, for example, Stierlin 1964; Heyden and Gendrop 1980; Sabloff 1989.
16. Stierlin 1964, 179.
17. Riding 1986, 286.
18. Paz 1990, 13.
19. Gasparini 1981.
20. In theory every town would follow the Royal Ordinances; in practice they often did not.
21. Janson 1991, 295–302.
22. Kandell 1990.
23. See Lear 1996.
24. Ibid.
25. Ibid.
26. Ward 1990.
27. Escobedo 1989.
28. Sanford 1968.
29. Orozco was said to be less fervently involved, however.
30. Ward 1990, 161; Escobedo 1989, 68.
31. See X. de Anda 1987, 186–94.
32. Bullrich 1969, 29.
33. Ramírez Vázquez 1988.
34. Ward 1990, 221.
35. Suzuki 1983, 10.
36. Toca and Figueroa 1991.

Three. *The Journey North: A History of Mexican Architecture on the California Border*

Epigraph: Tijuana, Mexico, chemist Luis Tames in Romero 1992.
1. See Herzog 1990b; Morales and Tamayo 1992; Arreola and Curtis 1993.
2. Meinig 1971.
3. Martinez 1977.
4. House 1982.
5. Morales and Tamayo 1992, 60.
6. See, for example, Demaris 1972.
7. Arreola and Curtis 1993.
8. Sklair 1989.

9. Some of the border cities, like El Paso–Ciudad Juárez have always been connected.

10. Herzog 1990b. See also Reiniger 1997.

11. See Schmidt and Lloyd 1986; Herrera Perez 1989; Arreola and Curtis 1993.

12. Wilson and Mather 1990.

13. This is argued in great detail in Arreola and Curtis 1993.

14. See Ramírez Lopez 1983a and 1983b.

15. For Mexicali, see Meade 1983; UABC 1991.

16. Arreola and Curtis 1993.

17. Jackson 1970.

18. Arreola and Curtis 1993.

19. See Piñera 1991.

20. These are reviewed in Ward 1990.

21. See Gritzner 1983; Arreola and Curtis 1993.

22. See, especially, Arreola and Curtis 1993, 183–215.

23. Wilson and Mather 1990, 72.

24. A number of writers, notably Castellanos 1981, believe this permeates the overall nature of modern Mexican society.

25. See Arreola and Curtis 1993.

26. Ibid., 207.

27. Wilson and Mather 1990, 68.

28. For Ciudad Juárez, see Young 1986; for Mexicali, see UABC 1991; on Tijuana, see Herzog 1990b.

29. Wilson and Mather 1990, 94.

30. Demaris 1972, 4.

31. Ibid., 6.

32. Ibid., 7.

33. Rodriguez 1987, 45.

34. Demaris 1972, 10.

35. Ibid., 230.

36. Hoctor 1984, 19.

37. Mills 1986.

38. Miller 1981, xii.

39. Price 1973.

40. Light 1988.

41. Maciel 1990.

42. Iglesias 1985, 39.

43. Maciel 1990.

44. Miller 1981, xii. See also Garreau 1981; Moyers 1986.

45. Krich 1989, 23.

46. Rodriguez 1987, 43.

47. Ridgely 1966–68.

48. Wayne McAllister was also the architect for one of the first hotels on the Las Vegas strip.

49. Argote 1992.

50. Ibid.

51. Ibid.

52. Romero 1992, B-2.

53. Rendon Parra 1972.

54. Acevedo 1972. A more recent discussion on this subject can be found in Díaz Castro 1992.

55. Padilla 1989.

56. Ibid., 74.

57. Ridgely 1966–68.

58. Rendon 1990, 95.

59. Ridgely 1966–68, 58.

60. MacLachlan 1991.

61. Gordon, 1968.

62. Acevedo, Pinera, and Ortiz in Pinera 1985, 99.

63. Ibid.

64. De Baca 1991, 180.

65. Gordon 1968, 52.

66. Britton and Crosby 1964.

67. De Baca 1991, 130.

68. Ridgely 1966–68, 111.

69. Ibid., 108.

70. See Bustamente 1985, 316–31.

71. Ibid.

72. Piñera 1985, 144.

73. Price 1973, 60.

74. Herzog 1990b.

75. The use of the suffix *landia* (as in *Cartolándia*) is an Americanization. With so many places ending with *land* north of the border (Disneyland, for example), perhaps it is not surprising to find this usage in Tijuana.

76. Britton 1960.

77. Britton and Crosby 1964.

78. Ozorno 1992.

79. Ibid.

80. Ibid.

81. Ibid.

Four. El Otro Lado: In Search of Mexican Landscapes in the Southwestern United States

Epigraph: Rosen in Herzog 1991b.

1. Southern California is usually considered to be the part of the state more linked to the Southwest.

2. While some include the states of California, Arizona, New Mexico, Texas, and parts of Colorado, Utah, Nevada, and Oklahoma in a definition of this region, others reduce the Southwest to the states of New Mexico and Arizona, on the basis of defining a region where there is a strong presence of the three native cultures: indigenous, Mexican, and Anglo. See Meinig 1971. More generally, the U.S. Southwest is considered to lie primarily within the confines of the four border states of California, Arizona, New Mexico, and Texas.

3. Scully 1988, 16–24.

4. Price 1992, 28.

5. See Engelke 1993.

6. Predock 1992, 23.

7. The focus of this book is on Spanish and Mexican cultural landscapes, but obviously, the Native American influences, particularly of the Anasazi/Pueblo culture, are extremely important.

8. See Portes and Walton 1976.

9. See Sanford 1968.

10. Kandell 1990, 182.

11. Ibid., 143.

12. Scully 1988, 19.

13. Ibid., 23.

14. These ideas are developed by various authors in Markovich et al. 1990.

15. See Bunting 1976.

16. Wilson 1994.

17. Parachek 1967.

18. See Poster 1993.

19. A fuller discussion of Texas culture regions is found in Meinig 1969.

20. Robinson 1981.

21. For example, see the photos and narrative on El Paso in Garcia 1981.

22. See Kearney 1986.

23. Hinojosa 1986.

24. Henry 1993.

25. See R/UDAT 1988.

26. Wilson and Mather 1990, 86.

27. Pitt 1966.

28. Parachek 1967, 51.

29. Gleye 1981.

30. Kirker 1986, 6.

31. Davis 1990.

32. Kaplan 1987.

33. Starr 1990.

34. Davis 1990.

35. McWilliams 1964.

36. Kirker 1986, 125.

37. Starr 1990, 204.

38. Ibid.

39. Ibid., 300.

40. Banham 1971, 61.

41. Moore et al. 1984, xiv.

42. Ibid.

43. Morgan and Blair 1976, 15.

44. Kamerling 1979.

45. Andrews 1978, 270.

46. Hardy 1929, 3.

47. Griswold del Castillo 1979.

48. I am grateful to my colleague Raul Villa for both written and verbal clarification of this dichotomy. See Villa 1998.

49. Pitt 1966.

50. Garcia 1975.

51. Griswold del Castillo 1979; Romo 1983; Camarrillo 1979; Garcia 1981; Herzog 1990b.

52. Banham 1971.

53. This is argued in Villa 1998.

54. The details of this story are recounted in the film *Chicano Park*. See Barrera and Mulford 1988.

55. Yeates and Garner 1980.

56. See Romo 1983; Griswold del Castillo 1979.

57. Rojas 1991.

58. Ibid., 31.

59. Ibid.

60. Rojas 1991 uses the term *prop* in his work.

61. This term was introduced to me by Villa. See Villa 1998.

62. Jackson 1987.

63. Rojas 1991.

64. Arreola 1988.

65. Rojas 1991.

66. Arreola 1988.

67. Arreola 1981.

68. Teaff 1995.

69. Rojas 1991, 69.

70. Ibid.

71. Arreola 1988.

72. Ibid.

73. See Ley and Cybriwsky 1974.

74. See Arreola 1984.

75. Ford and Griffin 1981.

76. See Cockcroft and Barnet-Sanchez 1990.

77. Ibid.

78. See Barrera and Mulford 1988; see also Herzog 1990, 174–180.

79. See, for example Mangin 1967.

80. Chavez 1992.

81. Ibid.

82. Ibid., 67.

83. Wambaugh 1984.

84. Davies and Holz 1992, 119.

85. Griffin and Ford 1980.

86. Lewis 1992.

87. Myerson 1995.

88. True 1996.

89. Davies and Holz 1992.

90. Maril 1989, 2.

91. Davies and Holz 1992.
92. Pereau 1996a; 1996b.
93. Myerson 1995, F-14.
94. Ibid.
95. True 1996.

Five. High Tech? The Cultural Landscapes of North American Economic Integration

Epigraph: Riding 1986, 458.

1. Holston 1989.
2. Hughes 1991, 211.
3. Davis 1990; Soja 1989.
4. Shacochis 1989, 43.
5. Britton 1982; Jenkins 1982; De Kadt 1979; Urry 1990.
6. Britton 1979.
7. Eckbo 1969.
8. Conrow 1991.
9. Rodriguez 1991.
10. Krushelycky 1991.
11. Legorreta 1989.
12. Chant 1992.
13. This point is developed in Arreola and Curtis 1993, 77-117.
14. Velásquez 1992.
15. Herzog 1990b.
16. Miller 1992, A-8.
17. Ibid.
18. Sklair 1991, 92.
19. Logan and Molotch 1987.
20. Velásquez 1992.
21. Smith 1988, 6.
22. Krutch 1961.
23. Reynoso y Valle and de Regt 1979.
24. Bosselman 1978.
25. Venguer 1992.
26. Souza 1992.
27. Moore et al. 1984, 38.
28. Ibid.
29. Sorkin 1992, 231.
30. Ibid.
31. Miramontes 1991.
32. Ramírez Vázquez 1992.
33. Miramontes 1991.
34. Ibid.
35. The varied experiences of different border towns in this regard are outlined in Arreola and Curtis 1993.
36. Kaiser 1986, 1.
37. Ozorno 1992.
38. Hall 1988.
39. Lofland 1989.
40. Sennett's work on the evolution of public life hints at this process. See Sennett 1976.
41. Brill 1989.
42. Sorkin 1992.
43. Davis employs this term in his critical study of the militarization of space in Los Angeles. See Davis 1990, 223-63.
44. Ibid.
45. Hardoy 1968.
46. Arreola and Curtis 1993 point out that plazas in Latin America were probably not as standardized as is commonly thought.
47. Ibid., 136-38.
48. Ibid., 141.
49. Rosen 1992.

50. Economic Development Administration 1978, 57.

51. It should be noted that most of these shopping malls were undergoing expansion and remodeling in the mid-1990s. The figures refer to the malls before expansion was completed.

52. Economic Development Administration 1978.

53. Ravelo 1993.

54. Esponda 1992.

55. Rosen 1992.

Six. Culture and Place: The Border Architects Speak

Epigraph: Legorreta in Mutlow 1997, 8.

1. Ozorno 1992.
2. Barrenechea 1992.
3. Ibid.
4. Venguer 1992.
5. Ibid.
6. Velásquez 1992.
7. Ozorno 1992.
8. Venguer 1992.
9. Licéaga 1992.
10. Barrenechea 1992.
11. Rosen 1992.
12. Quigley 1992.
13. Steele 1992.
14. Martinez 1992.
15. Kellogg 1992.
16. Larín 1992.
17. See chapter 5, p. 164.
18. See Paz 1961.

Seven. From Aztec to High Tech

Epigraph: Gómez Peña in Byrd and Byrd 1996, 102.

1. Muñoz García 1992.
2. Ibid.
3. Ozorno 1992.
4. Ibid.
5. Venguer 1992.
6. Canclini 1990.
7. Velásquez 1992.
8. Ozorno 1992.
9. Relph 1976, 43.
10. Ibid., 80.
11. Author's observation and anecdotal interviews with tourists.
12. Jackson 1970.
13. Relph 1976, 93.
14. Ibid., 95.
15. Arreola and Curtis 1993, 92.
16. McWilliams 1968.

REFERENCES

Published Sources

Acevedo, Conrado. 1972. *Monographic Essay on Tijuana*. Tijuana.

Acevedo, Conrado, David Piñera, and Jesús Ortiz. 1985. "Semblanza de Tijuana, 1915–1930." In *Historia de Tijuana*, ed. David Piñera. Tijuana: UNAM-UABC.

Agnew, John, John Mercer, and David Sopher, eds., 1984. *The City in Cultural Context*. Boston: Unwin Hyman.

Altman, Irwin, and Setha Low, eds. 1992. *Place Attachment*. New York: Plenum.

Andrews, Wayne. 1978. *Architecture, Ambition and Americans*. New York: Free Press.

Arreola, Daniel. 1988. "Mexican American Housescapes." *Geographical Review* 78: 299–315.

———. 1984. "Mexican American Exterior Murals." *Geographical Review* 74: 409–24.

———. 1981. "Fences as Landscape Taste: Tucson's Barrios." *Journal of Cultural Geography* 2: 96–105.

Arreola, Daniel, and James Curtis. 1993. *The Mexican Border Cities*. Tucson: University of Arizona Press.

Banham, Reyner. 1971. *Los Angeles: The Architecture of Four Ecologies*. London: Penguin.

Barrera, Mario, and Marilyn Mulford. 1988. *Chicano Park*. Video documentary. New York: Cinema Guild.

Bataillon, Claude. 1979. *La Ciudad de Mexico*. Mexico: D.F. SEP/Diana.

Bennett, Vivienne. 1995. *The Politics of Water*. Pittsburgh: University of Pittsburgh Press.

Bosselman, Fred. 1978. "Mexico Reaches for the Moon." In *In the Wake of the Tourist*. Washington, D.C.: Conservation Foundation.

Brill, Michael. 1989. "An Ontology for Exploring Urban Public Life Today." *Places* 6: 24–31.

Britton, James. 1960. "The Promise of Tijuana." *San Diego Magazine* 12: 40–46.

Britton, James, and Harry Crosby. 1964. "The Beauties of Tijuana." *California Review* 4.

Britton, Robert. 1979. "The Image of the Third World in Tourism Marketing." *Annals of Tourism Research* 6: 318–29.

Britton, Stephen. 1982. "The Political Economy of Tourism in the Third World." *Annals of Tourism Research* 9: 331–58.

Bullrich, Francisco. 1969. *New Directions in Latin American Architecture*. New York: George Braziller.

Bunting, Bainbridge. 1976. *Early Architecture in New Mexico.* Albuquerque: University of New Mexico Press.

Bustamante, Jorge. 1985. "Surgimiento de la Colonia Libertad." In *Historia de Tijuana,* ed. David Piñera. Tijuana: UNAM-UABC.

Buttimer, Anne, and David Seamon. 1980. *The Human Experience of Space and Place.* London: Croom Helm.

Byrd, Bobby, and Susannah M. Byrd, eds. 1996. *The Late Great Mexican Border.* El Paso: Cinco Puntos Press.

Camarrillo, Albert. 1979. *Chicanos in a Changing Society.* Cambridge: Harvard University Press.

Canclini, Nestor. 1990. *Culturas Hibridas.* Mexico, D.F.: Grijalbo.

Canter, David. 1977. *The Psychology of Place.* New York: St. Martin's Press.

Carlson, Alvar W. 1990. *The Spanish-American Homeland: Four Centuries in New Mexico's Río Arriba.* Baltimore: Johns Hopkins University Press.

Castellanos, Alicea. 1981. *Ciudad Juárez.* Mexico, D.F.: Editorial Nuestro Tiempo.

Chant, Silvia. 1992. "Tourism in Latin America: Perspectives from Mexico and Costa Rica." In *Tourism and the Less Developed Countries,* ed. David Harrison. New York: Halsted Press.

Chavez, Leo. 1992. *Shadowed Lives.* Beverly Hills: Sage.

Christopherson, Susan. 1983. "The Household and Class Formation: Determinants of Residential Location in Ciudad Juárez." *Space and Society* 1: 323-38.

City of San Diego. 1978. *Barrio Logan/Harbor 101 Community Plan.* San Diego: City Planning Department.

Cockcroft, Eva, and Holly Barnet-Sanchez. 1990. *Signs from the Heart.* Los Angeles: SPARC.

Conrow, Joan. 1991. "Paradise Lost." *These Times.* April 10-16. 15: 11-14.

Coppock, Marjorie. 1995. "Education and Lifestyle Aspiration of Secondary Students in Border Colonias of Laredo, Texas." *Journal of the University of Massachusetts School of Education* 28: 14-19.

Crawford, Margaret. 1992. "The World in a Shopping Mall." In *Variations on a Theme Park,* ed. Michael Sorkin. New York: Hill and Wang.

Cuamea Velázquez, Felipe. 1986. "La Actividad Turistica en Tijuana." *Economia Informa.* July–August: 142-43.

Curtis, James, and Daniel Arreola. 1989. "Through Gringo Eyes: Tourist Districts in the Mexican Border Cities as Other Directed Places." *North American Culture* 78: 19-32.

Davies, Christopher, and Robert Holz, 1992. "Settlement Evolution of 'Colonias' Along the U.S.-Mexico Border." *Habitat International* 16: 119-42.

Davis, Mike. 1990. *City of Quartz.* New York: Verso.

De Baca, Vincent. 1991. "Moral Renovation of the Californias." Unpublished Ph.D. thesis. La Jolla: University of California, San Diego, Department of History.

De Kadt, Emanuel, ed. 1979. *Tourism: Passport to Development?* Oxford: Oxford University Press.

Demaris, Ovid. 1972. *Poso del Mundo.* New York: Pocket Books.

Díaz Castro, Olga V. 1992. *Leyendas de Tijuana: La Tía Juana*. Tijuana: Instituto Tecnologico de Tijuana.

Duncan, James, and David Ley. 1993. *Place/ Culture/ Representation*. London: Routledge.

Eckbo, Garrett. 1969. "The Landscape of Tourism." *Landscape*. Spring-Summer. 18: 29–31.

Economic Development Administration. 1978. *Economic Problems of the California Border Region*. Washington, D.C.: U.S. Department of Commerce.

Engelke, James, ed. 1993. *The Nature of Regionalism in the Southwest and Northern Baja California*. San Diego: New School of Architecture.

Escobedo, Helen, ed. 1989. *Mexican Monuments*. New York: Abbeville Press.

Fischkin, Barbara. 1988. "Letter from Mexico City." *New Yorker*. June 20: 69–84.

Ford, Larry. 1994. *Cities and Buildings*. Baltimore: Johns Hopkins University Press.

Ford, Larry, and Ernst Griffin. 1981. "Chicano Park: Personalizing an Institutional Landscape." *Landscape* 25: 2–48.

Gallagher, Winifred. 1993. *The Power of Place*. New York: Poseidon Press.

Garcia, Mario. 1981. *Desert Immigrants: The Mexicans of El Paso*. New Haven: Yale University Press.

———. 1975. "The Californios of San Diego and the Politics of Accommodation, 1846–1860." *Aztlan* 6: 69–95.

Gardels, Nathan, and Marilyn Snell. 1989. "Breathing Fecal Dust in Mexico City." *Los Angeles Times Book Review*. April 23: 15.

Garreau, Joel. 1981. *The Nine Nations of North America*. New York: Avon.

Gasparini, Graziano. 1981. "The Present Significance of the Architecture of the Past." In *Latin America in Its Architecture*, ed. Robert Segre. New York: Holmes & Meier.

Gebhard, David, and Robert Winter. 1985. *Architecture in Los Angeles*. Los Angeles: Peregrine Smith.

Gleye, Paul. 1981. *The Architecture of Los Angeles*. Los Angeles: Rosebud Books.

Gómez Peña, Guillermo. 1996. "Excerpts from Warrior for Gringostroika." In *The Late Great Mexican Border,* eds. Bobby Byrd and Susannah M. Byrd. El Paso: Cinco Puntos Press.

González de León, Teodoro. 1990. "Arquitectura y Ciudad." *Vuelta* 158: 7–11.

Gordon, Ronald. 1968. *Complete Guide to Tijuana*. San Diego.

Goss, Jon. 1993. "The Magic of the Mall: An Analysis of Form, Function and Meaning in the Contemporary Retail Built Environment." *Annals of the Association of American Geographers* 83: 18–47.

Griffin, Ernst, and Larry Ford. 1980. "A Model of Latin American City Structure." *Geographical Review* 70: 397–422.

Griswold del Castillo, Richard. 1979. *The Los Angeles Barrio*. Berkeley: University of California Press.

Gritzner, Charles. 1983. "Cultural Landscapes." In *Borderlands Sourcebook,* ed. Richard Nostrand and Jonathan West. Norman: University of Oklahoma Press.

Hall, Edward. 1969. *The Hidden Dimension*. New York: Anchor Books.

Hall, Peter. 1988. *Cities of Tomorrow*. Oxford: Blackwell.

Hardoy, Jorge. 1968. *Urban Planning in Pre-Colombian America.* New York: George Braziller.

Hardy, E. L. 1929. "The New State College." *San Diego Magazine.* September 20: 3–4.

Harvey, David. 1989. *The Condition of Post-Modernity.* Cambridge: Blackwell.

Hayden, Dolores. 1995. *The Power of Place: Urban Landscapes as Public History.* Cambridge: MIT Press.

Henderson, Jeffrey, and Manuel Castells. 1987. *Global Restructuring and Territorial Development.* London: Sage.

Henkel, David. 1994. "Pre-European Regional Planning in the Border Region." *Mass.* Fall. 10: 18–27.

Henry, Jay. 1993. *Architecture in Texas, 1895–1945.* Austin: University of Texas Press.

Herrera Perez, Octavio. 1989. *Monografía de Reynosa.* Ciudad Victoria: Instituto Tamaulipeco de Cultura.

Herzog, Lawrence A. 1998. "Border Urbanism." In *Encyclopedia of Mexico: History, Society and Culture,* ed. Michael Werner. Chicago: Fitzroy Dearborn.

———. 1997. "The Transfrontier Metropolis." *Harvard Design Magazine.* Winter–Spring: 16–19.

———. 1993a. "Between Cultures: Public Space in Tijuana. *Places* 8: 54–61.

———. 1993b. "Is This the Way to Change Tijuana's Image?" *Buzz.* April: 28.

———. 1992. Unpublished telephone survey of real estate brokers in Tijuana and San Diego.

———. 1991a. "Cross-national Urban Structure in the Era of Global Cities: The U.S.-Mexico Transfrontier Metropolis." *Urban Studies* 28: 519–33.

———. 1991b. "Driven by Shame." *San Diego Reader.* June 13: 10–14.

———. 1990a. "Baja's Tourism Boom." *Hemisphere* 2: 32–34.

———. 1990b. *Where North Meets South.* Austin: University of Texas Press/CMAS.

Heyden, Doris, and Paul Gendrop. 1980. *Pre-Columbian Architecture of Mesoamerica.* New York: Rizzoli.

Hinojosa, Gilberto M. 1986. *A Borderlands Town in Transition.* College Station: Texas A&M University Press.

Hiss, Tony. 1991. *The Experience of Place.* New York: Vintage Books.

Hoctor, Fred. 1984. *Baja Haha.* San Diego.

Holston, James. 1989. *The Modernist City.* Chicago: University of Chicago Press.

Hornbeck, David. 1990. "Spanish Legacy in the Borderlands." In *The Making of the American Landscape,* ed. Michael Conzen. Boston: Unwin Hyman.

Hough, Michael. 1990. *Out of Place.* New Haven: Yale University Press.

House, John. 1982. *Frontier on the Rio Grande.* New York: Oxford University Press.

Hughes, Robert. 1991. *The Shock of the New.* New York: McGraw-Hill.

Iglesias, Norma. 1985. *La Visión de la Frontera A Través del Cine Mexicano.* Tijuana: Colegio de la Frontera Norte.

Jackson, J. B. 1992. "Cultures and Regionalism." *Mass.* Spring. 9: 12–13.

———. 1987. "The Popular Yard." *Places* 4: 26–31.

————. 1984. *Discovering the Vernacular Landscape.* New Haven: Yale University Press.

————. 1970. "Other Directed Houses." In *Landscapes: Selected Writings of J. B. Jackson,* ed. Ervin Zube. Amherst: University of Massachusetts Press.

Janson, Horst W. 1991. *History of Art.* New York: Harry N. Abrams.

Jenkins, C. L. 1982. "The Effect of Scale in Tourism Projects in Developing Countries." *Annals of Tourism Research* 9: 229-49.

Kaiser, Kay. 1986. "Commentary." *San Diego Union.* May 25: 1,8.

Kamerling, Bruce. 1979. *Irving Gill.* San Diego: San Diego Historical Society.

Kandell, Jonathan. 1990. *La Capital: The Biography of Mexico City.* New York: Henry Holt.

Kaplan, Samuel H. 1987. *L.A. Lost and Found.* New York: Crown.

Kearney, Milo. 1986. *Studies in Brownsville History.* Brownsville: Pan American University.

Kirker, Harold. 1986. *California's Architectural Frontier.* Salt Lake City: Gibbs M. Smith.

Knox, Paul. 1987. "The Social Production of the Built Environment: Architects, Architecture and the Post-Modern City." *Progress in Human Geography* 11: 354-77.

Krich, John. 1989. *El Beisbol.* New York: Prentice-Hall.

Krushelycky, Askold. 1991. "Europe Fumes at Tasteless Tourists." *Los Angeles Times.* August 25: L-5.

Krutch, Joseph Wood. 1961. *The Forgotten Peninsula.* New York: William Morrow.

Kubler, George. 1975. *The Art and Architecture of Ancient America.* London: Penguin.

Lazaroff, Leon. 1989. "Megadreams." *Mexico Journal.* September 25. 11: 16-22.

Lear, John. 1996. "Mexico City: Space and Class in the Porfirian Capital, 1884-1910." *Journal of Urban History* 22: 454-92.

Legorreta, Ricardo. 1990. *The Architecture of Ricardo Legorreta.* Austin: University of Texas Press.

————. 1989. Public lecture, School of Architecture inauguration, U.C. San Diego.

Lewis, Jack. 1992. "The U.S. Colonias: A Target for Aid." *EPA Journal* 18: 61-62.

Ley, David, and Roman Cybriwsky. 1974. "Urban Graffiti as Territorial Markers." *Annals of the Association of American Geographers* 64: 491-505.

Liggett, Helen, and David Perry. 1995. *Spatial Practices.* Beverly Hills: Sage.

Light, Ken. 1988. *To the Promised Land.* New York: Aperture.

Lofland, Lyn. 1989. "The Morality of Urban Public Life." *Places* 6: 18-23.

Logan, John, and Harvey Molotch. 1987. *Urban Fortunes.* Berkeley: University of California Press.

Lozano, Eduardo. 1990. *Community Design and the Culture of Cities.* Cambridge: Cambridge University Press.

Maciel, David. 1990. *El Norte: The U.S.-Mexican Border in Contemporary Cinema.* San Diego: Institute for Regional Studies of the Californias.

MacLachlan, Colin. 1991. *Anarchism and the Mexican Revolution.* Berkeley: University of California Press.

Mangin, William. 1967. "Latin American Squatter Settlements: A Problem and a Solution." *Latin American Research Review* 2: 65-98.

Maril, Robert. 1989. *Poorest of Americans.* Notre Dame: University of Notre Dame Press.

Markovich, Nicholas, Wolfgang Preiser, and Fred Sturm. 1990. *Pueblo Style and Regional Architecture*. New York: Van Nostrand.

Martinez, Oscar. 1978. *Border Boom Town*. Austin: University of Texas Press.

———. 1977. "Chicanos and the Border Cities." *Pacific Historical Review* 46: 85–106.

Mays, Buddy. 1982. *Ancient Cities of the Southwest*. San Francisco: Chronicle Books.

McWilliams, Carey. 1968. *North from Mexico*. New York: Greenwood Press.

———. 1964. *Southern California Country: An Island on the Land*. New York: Duell, Sloan and Pearce.

Meade, Adalberto W. 1983. *Origen de Mexicali*. Mexicali: UABC.

Meinig, Donald W. 1979. *The Interpretation of Ordinary Landscapes*. New York: Oxford University Press.

———. 1971. *Southwest*. New York: Oxford University Press.

———. 1969. *Imperial Texas*. Austin: University of Texas Press.

Metz, Leon. 1989, *Border: The U.S.-Mexico Line*. El Paso: Mangan Books.

Miller, Marjorie. 1992. "Anguish of Spanglish and Barbie." *Los Angeles Times*. June 24: A-1,8.

Miller, Tom. 1981. *On the Border*. New York: Ace Books.

Mills, James. 1986. *The Underground Empire*. New York: Dell.

Moore, Charles, Peter Becker, and Regula Campbell. 1984. *The City Observed: Los Angeles*. New York: Vintage Books.

Morales, Rebecca, and Jesus Tamayo. 1992. "Urbanization and Development of the United States-Mexico Border." In *Changing Boundaries in the Americas,* ed. Lawrence A. Herzog. La Jolla: Center for U.S.-Mexican Studies.

Morgan, Neil, and Tom Blair. 1976. *Yesterday's San Diego*. Miami: E. A. Seemann.

Moyers, Bill. 1986. "One River, One Country: The United States-Mexico Border." New York: CBS Broadcasting, television documentary.

Murray, William. 1989. "A Reporter at Large (To the Left of Zero)." *The New Yorker*. July 31: 57–66.

———. 1986. "A Reporter at Large (Twins)." *The New Yorker*. December 29: 63–75.

Mutlow, John, ed. 1997. *Ricardo Legorreta, Architect*. New York: Rizzoli.

Myerson, Allen. 1995. "This Is the House That Greed Built." *New York Times*. April 2: F-1,14.

Nolan, Mary Lee, and Sidney Nolan. 1988. "The Evolution of Tourism in Twentieth Century Mexico." *Journal of the West*. October 27: 14–25.

Padilla, Antonio. 1985. "Imagen Urbana de Tijuana, 1889–1920." In *Historia de Tijuana,* ed. David Piñera. Tijuana: UNAM-UABC.

Parachek, Ralph. 1967. *Desert Architecture*. Phoenix: Parr.

Paz, Octavio. 1990. "El Azar y La Memoria." *Vuelta*. January. 158: 12–14.

———. 1961. *The Labyrinth of Solitude*. New York: Grove Press.

Pereau, M. Jana. 1996a. "Defining Edges: Toward a Social Poetics of Housing." Unpublished manuscript.

———. 1996b. "Negotiated Settlements: Redefinition of the Court/Yard in the Borderland." Unpublished manuscript.

Piñera, David. 1991. *Los Orígenes de Ensenada.* Tijuana: UABC.

———. 1985. *Historia de Tijuana.* Tijuana: UNAM UABC.

Pitt, Leonard. 1966. *The Decline of the Californios.* Berkeley: University of California Press.

Portes, Alejandro, and John Walton. 1976. *Urban Latin America.* Austin: University of Texas Press.

Poster, Corky. 1993. "Sombra, Patio y Macetas: Modernism, Regionalism and the Elements of Southwestern Architecture." *Journal of the Southwest* 35: 461–500.

Predock, Antoine. 1992. "An Interview." *Mass.* Spring. 9: 22–26.

Price, John. 1973. *Tijuana: Urbanization in a Border Culture.* Notre Dame: University of Notre Dame Press.

Price, V. B. 1992. "A Regionalism for the Future in New Mexico: Four Levels of Meaning." *Mass.* Spring. 9: 27–29.

Ramírez Lopez, Jorge. 1983a. "Semblanza de Tecate." In *Panorama de Baja California,* ed. David Piñera. Tijuana: UNAM-UABC.

———. 1983b. "Tecate Contemporaneo." In *Panorama de Baja California,* ed. David Piñera. Tijuana: UNAM-UABC.

Ramírez Vázquez, Pedro. 1988. *Ramírez Vázquez.* Mexico, D.F.: Garcia Valades.

———. 1964. "Influence of the Maya on Contemporary Architecture." In *Living Architecture: Mayan,* ed. Henri Stierlin. New York: Grosset and Dunlap.

Rapoport, Amos. 1982. *The Meaning of the Built Environment.* Beverly Hills: Sage.

Reiniger, Clair. 1997. "Bioregional Planning and Ecosystem Protection." In *Ecological Design and Planning,* ed. George F. Thompson and Frederick R. Steiner. New York: John Wiley & Sons.

Relph, Edward. 1987. *The Modern Urban Landscape.* Baltimore: Johns Hopkins University Press.

———. 1976. *Place and Placelessness.* London: Pion.

Rendon Parra, Josefina. 1972. *Apuntes Historicos de Tijuana.* Tijuana.

Reynoso y Valle, Agustin, and Jancomina de Regt. 1979. "Growing Pains: Planned Tourism Development in Ixtapa-Zihuatenejo." In *Tourism: Passport to Development?* ed. Emanuel de Kadt. Oxford: Oxford University Press.

Ridgely, Roberta. 1966–68. "The Man Who Built Tijuana." *San Diego Magazine.* January, March, September.

Riding, Alan. 1986. *Distant Neighbors.* New York: Vintage Books.

Robinson, Willard B. 1981. *Gone from Texas.* College Station: Texas A&M University Press.

Rodriguez, Cecilia. 1991. "Latin Tourism: A High Price for Selling the Sun." *Los Angeles Times.* August 18: E-1.

Rodriguez, Richard. 1990. "Night and Day: Mexico-USA." In *Frontiers.* London: BBC Books.

———. 1987. "Across the Borders of History." *Harper's Magazine* 274, March: 42–53.

Rojas, James. 1991. "The Enacted Environment." Unpublished masters thesis. Cambridge: Massachusetts Institute of Technology, Department of Architecture.

Romero, Fernando. 1992. "Tijuana Bulldozing Landmarks and Its Heritage, Cries Historian." *San Diego Union Tribune*. March 1: B-2.

Romo, Ricardo. 1983. *East Los Angeles*. Austin: University of Texas Press.

Rotenberg, Robert, and Gary McDonogh. 1993. *The Cultural Meaning of Urban Space*. London: Bergin and Garvey.

R/UDAT (Regional Urban Design Assistance Team). 1988. *Corridor Design: The Lower Rio Grande Valley*. Washington, D.C.: American Institute of Architects.

Russel-Hitchcock, Henry. 1955. *Latin American Architecture Since 1945*. New York: Metropolitan Museum of Art.

Rybczynski, Witold. 1989. *The Most Beautiful House in the World*. New York: Penguin.

Sabloff, Jeremy. 1989. *The Cities of Ancient Mexico*. New York: Thames and Hudson.

Sale, Kirkpatrick. 1975. *Power Shift*. New York: Random House.

Sanford, Trent. 1968. *The Story of Architecture in Mexico*. New York: W.W. Norton.

———. 1950. *The Architecture of the Southwest*. New York: W.W. Norton.

Sassen, Saskia. 1994. *Cities in a World Economy*. Thousand Oaks, Calif.: Pine Forge Press.

Sawers, Larry, and Tabb, William. 1984. *Sunbelt/Snowbelt*. New York: Oxford University Press.

Schmidt, Robert, and William Lloyd. 1986. "Patterns of Urban Growth in Ciudad Juarez." In *The Social Ecology and Economic Development of Ciudad Juarez*, ed. Gay Young. Boulder: Westview Press.

Scully, Vincent. 1988. *American Architecture and Urbanism*. New York: Henry Holt.

Secretaria de Educacion Publica. 1989. *Catalogo Nacional: Monumentos Historicos Immuebles*. Tijuana: SEP-INAH.

Sennett, Richard. 1976. *The Fall of Public Man*. New York: Knopf.

Shacochis, Bob. 1989. "In Deepest Gringolandia." *Harper's Magazine* 279, July: 42–50.

Sklair, Leslie. 1991. *Sociology of the Global System*. Baltimore: Johns Hopkins University Press.

———. 1989. *Assembling for Development*. Boston: Unwin Hyman.

Smith, Jack. 1988. "Bullish on Baja." *Los Angeles Times Magazine*. April 17: 6.

Smith, Neil. 1984. *Uneven Development*. Oxford: Basil Blackwell.

Soja, Edward. 1989. *Postmodern Geographies*. London: Verso.

Sorkin, Michael, ed. 1992. *Variations on a Theme Park*. New York: Hill & Wang.

Spaulding, Richard. 1991. "Jack in the Box Chain Heads for the Border." *San Diego Tribune*. November 6: A-15,16.

Starr, Kevin. 1990. *Material Dreams*. New York: Oxford University Press.

Stevenson Olson, Martha. 1992. "In Baja's Lobster Village, Thirty Menus in Three Blocks." *New York Times*. December 13: V 6,19.

Stierlin, Henri. 1964. *Living Architecture: Mayan*. New York: Grosset and Dunlap.

Sudjic, Dejan. 1992. *The One Hundred Mile City*. New York: Harcourt, Brace and Co.

Suisman, Douglas, ed. 1993. "Plaza, Parque, Calle." *Places* 8: entire issue.

Suzuki, Makoto. 1983. "Purity and Development in Modern Mexican Architecture." *Process: Architecture* 39: 9–13.

Teaff, Julia. 1995. Unpublished manuscript. Ethnic Studies 189 course, University of California, San Diego, fall.

Toca, Antonio, and Anibal Figueroa. 1991. *Mexico: Nueva Arquitectura*. Mexico, D.F.: Ediciones Gili.

True, Philip. 1996. "Shantytown USA." *The Progressive* 60: 25–27.

Tuan, Yi-Fu. 1977. *Space and Place*. Minneapolis: University of Minnesota Press.

Ugalde, Antonio. 1970. *Power and Conflict in a Mexican Community*. Albuquerque: University of New Mexico Press.

Universidad Autonoma de Baja California (UABC). 1991. *Mexicali: Una Historia*. Mexicali: Instituto de Investigaciones Historicas-UABC.

Universidad Iberoamericana. 1991a. "Banco Internacional." Unpublished paper. Tijuana.

———. 1991b. "Bungalows de Agua Caliente." unpublished paper. Tijuana.

Urry, John. 1990. *The Tourist Gaze*. London: Sage.

Veregge, Nina. 1993. "Transformations of Spanish Urban Landscapes in the American Southwest, 1821–1900." *Journal of the Southwest* 35: 371–459.

Villa, Raul. 1998. *Barrio Stories/Heterotopias Chicanas*. Cambridge: Cambridge University Press.

Wambaugh, Joseph. 1984. *Lines and Shadows*. New York: Morrow.

Ward, Peter. 1990. *Mexico City*. Boston: G. K. Hall.

Weisman, Alan. 1986. *La Frontera*. New York: Harcourt Brace Jovanovich.

———. 1986. "Baja Boom." *Los Angeles Times Magazine*. November 30: 10–16, 44–46.

Wilson, Chris. 1994. "Spatial Mestizaje on the Pueblo-Hispanic-Anglo Frontier." *Mass* 10: 40–49.

Wilson, James R., and Cotton Mather. 1990. "Photo Essay: The Rio Grande Borderland." *Journal of Cultural Geography*. Spring/Summer 10: 66–98.

Wolf, Eric. 1959. *Sons of the Shaking Earth*. Chicago: University of Chicago Press.

Wood, Joseph Krutch. 1967. *Baja California and the Geography of Hope*. San Francisco: Sierra Club/Ballantine.

X. de Anda, Enrique. 1987. *Evolución de La Arquitectura en Mexico*. Mexico, D.F.: Editorial Panorama.

Yeates, Maurice, and Barry Garner. 1980. *The North American City*. New York: Harper and Row.

Young, Gay, ed. 1986. *The Social Ecology and Economic Development of Ciudad Juárez*. Boulder: Westview Press.

Zukin, Sharon. 1991. *Landscapes of Power*. Berkeley: University of California Press.

Field Interviews

TIJUANA, MEXICO

Argote, Rodolfo, 1992
Barrenechea, Guillermo, 1992
Esponda, Javier, 1992

Licéaga, Luis, 1992
Miramontes, Juan, 1991
Muñoz García, Armando, 1992
Ozorno, Jorge, 1992
Ramírez Vázquez, Pedro, 1992
Ravelo, Miguel, 1993
Souza, Julian, 1992
Velásquez, Eugenio, 1992
Venguer, Jaime, 1992

SAN DIEGO, CALIFORNIA

Kellogg, Kendrick, 1992
Larín, Alfredo, 1992
Martinez, Joseph, 1992
Quigley, Rob, 1992
Rosen, Manuel, 1992
Steele, Mark, 1992

INDEX

Numbers in *italics* denote illustrations.

About the Author

Lawrence A. Herzog was born in New York City and raised on Long Island, New York. He received a B.A. in Latin American studies at the State University of New York, Albany, and completed his M.A. and Ph.D. in geography at Syracuse University. Dr. Herzog is Professor of City Planning in the School of Public Administration and Urban Studies, San Diego State University. His previous books include *Changing Boundaries in the Americas, Where North Meets South,* and *Planning the International Border Metropolis.*

Related Books in the Series

The Library of Congress has cataloged the
hardcover edition of this book as follows:

Herzog, Lawrence A. (Lawrence Arthur)
  From Aztec to high tech : architecture and landscape across the
  Mexico–United States border / Lawrence A. Herzog.
       p.   cm. — (Creating the North American landscape)
  Includes bibliographical references and index.
       ISBN 0-8018-6009-1 (alk. paper)
       1. Architecture and society—Mexico, North. 2. Architecture—
  Mexico, North—Influence. 3. Architecture and society—Southwest,
  New. 4. Mexican American architecture—Southwest, New. 5. Mexico,
  North—Relations—Southwest, New. 6. Southwest, New—Relations—
  Mexico, North. I. Title. II. Series.
  NA2543.S6H48   1999
  720′.972′1—dc21   98-30340

  ISBN 0-8018-6643-X (pbk.)